Understanding the Development Jigsaw:

A User's Guide to Procedures

by

Wendy Le-Las

BUCCANEER BOOKS

© 1997 Dr. Wendy Le-Las
First published in 1997
by Buccaneer Books

**The moral right of the author
has been asserted**

*A catalogue record for this book is
available from the British Library*

ISBN 0–9529985–0–5

Artwork and Design by Gareth Jones

Typeset by Phoenix Photosetting, Chatham, Kent
Printed and bound in Great Britain by
Redwood Books, Trowbridge, Wiltshire

Contents

SECTION III: MOUNTING A CASE

SECTION IV: 'PUBLIC INQUIRIES'

SECTION V: REDRESS

SECTION VI

APPENDICES

Interface between Main-Stream Planning System and Other Regulatory Regimes

List of Figures

List of Maps

Abbreviations

BT	British Telecom
CPO	Compulsory Purchase Order
CPRE	Council for the Protection of Rural England
DG	Directorate General
DoE	Department of the Environment
DTp	Department of Transport
EA	Environmental Assessment
EC	European Commission
EHO	Environmental Health Officer
EIP	Examination in Public
ELF	Environmental Law Foundation
EMAS	Eco-Management & Audit Scheme
EPA	Environmental Protection Act
ES	Environmental Statement
EU	European Union
FoE	Friends of the Earth
GDPO	General Development Procedure Order
GPDO	General Permitted Development Order
HMIP	Her Majesty's Pollution Inspectorate
HSE	Health & Safety Executive
IPC	Integrated Pollution Control
LA21	Local Agenda 21
LAAPC	Local Authority Air Pollution Control
LEAPS	Local Environment Agency Plans
LGMB	Local Government Management Board
LPA	Local Planning Authority
LBCA	Planning (Listed Building & Conservation Areas) Act 1990
MAFF	Ministry of Agriculture, Fisheries & Food
MoD	Ministry of Defence
MPG	Minerals Policy Guidance Note
NALC	National Association of Local Councils
NGOs	Non-Governmental Organisations
NRA	National Rivers Authority
P&C Act	Planning & Compensation Act 1991
PPG	Planning Policy Guidance Note
P&R	Park & Ride
QC	Queen's Council

RPG	Regional Policy Guidance Note
RSNC	Royal Society for Nature Conservation
RTPI	Royal Town Planning Institute
SAC	Special Area for Conservation
SEA	Strategic Environmental Assessment
SI	Statutory Instrument
SRO	Side Roads Order
SSSI	Site of Special Specific Interest
TCP Act	Town & Country Planning Act 1990
UA	Unitary Authority
UCO	Use Classes Order
UDP	Unitary Development Plan
UKAS	United Kingdom Accreditation Service
WRA	Water Resources Act 1991

Acknowledgements

The author would like to thank the following colleagues for their comments, contributions and corrections: Mark Bacon, Dr. Malcolm Bates, Richard Buxton, Lee Coates, Erik Heijne C.B.E., Veronica Jones, Zana Juppenlatz, Peter Langley, Robert McCraken, Donald McGillivray, Denzil Millichap, Trina Paskell, Charles Pugh, Dr. John Raven, Peregrine Walker, Professor Lynda Warren, Dr. Walter Wehrmeyer. Also the cooperation of the following organisations, CPRE, LGMB, RSNC, SERPLAN. The author is appreciative of Lord Rogers and Miles Kington for allowing her to reproduce their writings in order to enliven her text. She is also much indebted to Mark Sullivan for his substantial contribution to the sections on road building procedures.

On a practical level she is grateful for the assistance of Mark Challis, Katherine Davis, Louise Duff, Dr. Dick Hughes Jones, Rosemary Lansdowne and Professor Ian Swingland. Last but not least, she would like to thank Gareth Jones for designing and illustrating the book, and his enthusiasm for the project.

Autobiographical Note

Dr. Wendy Le-Las became concerned about the environment in her undergraduate years at the University of Sussex, in the 'Swinging Sixties'. Thus she has watched with interest the development of the environmental consciousness, and the all too tardy response of government to the problems of creating a sustainable society for our children and grandchildren.

She was drawn into land-use planning, from academe, as a result of writing her best selling book, 'Playing the Public Inquiry Game': individuals and community groups asked her to conduct their cases, and she learnt on her feet! In 1990 she became Planning Consultant to the National Association of Local Councils, parent body to 7,400 parish, town and community councils in England and Wales.

She is still an academic, holding a Visiting Research Fellowship at the Durrell Institute for Conservation & Ecology, in the University of Kent. She is regularly invited to give lectures to academics, professional and lay people, in Britain and abroad, on environmental policy and procedures. Until recently she was a Council Member of UKELA and still convenes its Planning & EIA Working Party. She is a Member of the Royal Town Planning Institute and Fellow of the Royal Society of Arts.

Foreword

This book is intended to assist those who become involved in disputes over land use, whether they be lay people or professionals in this field. Any given conflict will have two characteristics: it will be pitched at a certain level in the planning system, which operates according to its own set of ground rules; and it is likely to be multi-faceted, involving various strands of law and policy, not all of which belong to the planning system.

Firstly, the issue in question may be at any level from from development planning to enforcement, taking in the odd public inquiry en route. Just to complicate matters there may also be subsidiary issues which are currently at a different stage in the system. For example the reader may wish to protect a greenfield site from housing development proposed in the deposited local plan, but meanwhile a developer has filed a planning application to build houses in that site. Both will have to be dealt with at the same time. This book sets out the the ground rules for winning the game at each level.

Those using the book as an instruction manual, are advised to start with Section III, Mounting a Case, because it sets out the general principles of how to present a case to best advantage. Then they should move to the stage reached by the issue(s) with which they are concerned: back to development planning and development control, or forward to inquiries, the Courts and Europe. If victory is achieved, then it is a matter of keeping a watching brief: it is no good winning a battle only to lose the war in the long term. Thus success at an appeal could be short lived unless the desired use for that land is incorporated into the development plan, and defended against all comers in the future.

Secondly, a given issue may bring together a whole range of subjects, each with its gamut of statute law and government policy e.g. minerals, nature conservation, common land, pollution, highways, listed buildings etc. Some of these fall within the Planning Acts, but others lie beyond in separate areas of law and policy. The regulation of land use in Britain defies rationality: different regimes were invented to deal with different problems. The book is an attempt to work out how this jigsaw of controls fit together – or doesn't! Thus within the planning system there are procedural oddities like Crown Land, local authority development, and statutory undertakers. Abutting the planning system are the separate regimes of pollution control, highways, Parliament, the Courts, and the various facets of 'Europe'. The relationship between these distinct systems is set out for each level of the planning system: insets with appropriate logos are to be found in the various Sections. Therefore, a reader concerned with pollution, for example, can follow the logo through the book from development planning to courts action.

The author is aware that the 'jigsaw' is even larger and more complex than the book would imply: the 'Useful References' logo denotes detailed reading for the subjects covered in the book; and there are many subjects beyond the 'edges' of what has been covered e.g. planning in Scotland, compulsory purchase, lawful use, and the various types of pollution. However, it is hoped that the areas most likely to to be of interest to lay people are covered in the text. If readers feel that a mainstream subject has been neglected in procedural terms, they should let her know.

The final Section looks at the regulation of land use within the context of the debate on sustainability. The author's interest in the subject began as an undergraduate at Sussex in the sixties. Although *'the Environment'* is now an issue, we seem to be no nearer to solving the myriad of problems involved, and time would appear to be getting short if we are to make a peaceful transition to a sustainable society. Readers may not agree either with her diagnosis or her radical proposals but the author would be interested to hear their views.

Dr. Wendy Le-Las
February 1997

To Hannah and William

Section I

The Planning Framework

The planning system regulates the spatial distribution of development instigated by either the private or the public sector. Most of this section will be concerned with the various denomination of development plans, which provide the framework within which decisions are made and development allocated. However, central government provides much of the policy input into these plans: those familiar with the Planning Policy Guidance notes (PPGs) produced by the Department of the Environment will see a family resemblance in the phraseology employed for a given topic in the development plan for their area. However, interposed between national policy and development plans is Regional Planning Guidance (RPG). Its primary task is to provide a wider frame of reference to the issues to be dealt with in greater detail by structure plans and unitary development plans.

REGIONAL PLANNING GUIDANCE

There is no formal tier of regional government in this country, although the idea surfaces from time to time when there is talk of wholesale re-organisation of local government: the counties have been an endangered species for some years. A number of people feel that there ought to be a democratic body between district councils and central government, and that a regional organisation might be more appropriate to modern needs because of their scale.

Nonetheless, there are regional groupings of planning authorities (see Map 1). The London and South East Regional Planning Conference (SERPLAN) has been established, in one form or another, for thirty years, but other regional groupings are more recent. Although PPG 12 refers to regional planning 'conferences', they rejoice in an assortment of names (see Fig.1). The reason for this is that some were set up to take an overall view of land use planning problems in their area e.g. SERPLAN for S.E. England, whilst others, like the N.W. Regional Association, were created primarily, for economic regeneration: they don't have "planning" in the title.

Map 1   The English Regional Planning Associations

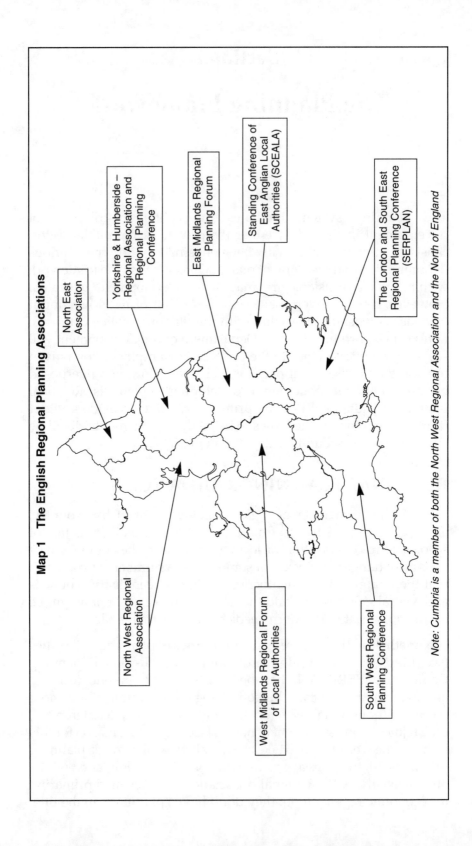

North East
Association

Yorkshire & Humberside –
Regional Association and
Regional Planning
Conference

East Midlands Regional
Planning Forum

Standing Conference of
East Anglian Local
Authorities (SCEALA)

The London and South East
Regional Planning Conference
(SERPLAN)

North West Regional
Association

West Midlands Regional Forum
of Local Authorities

South West Regional
Planning Conference

Note: Cumbria is a member of both the North West Regional Association and the North of England

Figure 1   English Regional Planning Associations

List of Addresses

East Midlands Regional Planning Forum
Department of Planning and Transportation
Leicestershire County Council   Telephone: 0116 232 3232
County Hall   Fax: 0116 265 7271
Glenfield
Leicestershire LE3 8RJ

North of England Assembly of Local Authorities (NEA)
Guildhall
Quayside   Telephone: 0191 261 7388
Newcastle upon Tyne NE1 3AF   Fax: 0191 232 4558

North-West Regional Association of Local Authorities
North-West Regional Association
New Town Hall   Telephone: 01942 8271511
261 Library   Fax: 01942 827502
Wigan WN1 1YN

The London and South-East Regional Planning Conference (SERPLAN)
SERPLAN
14 Buckingham Gate   Telephone: 0171 931 8777
London SW1E 6LB   Fax: 0171 828 9712

South-West Regional Planning Conference
South-West Regional Planning Conference
County Hall   Telephone: 01823 255017
Taunton   Fax: 01823 351359
Somerset TA1 4DY

Standing Conference of East Anglian Local Authorities (SCEALA)
SCEALA
4B St Marys Square   Telephone: 01284 722460
Bury St Edmunds   Fax: 01284 722464
Suffolk IP33 2AJ

West Midlands Regional Forum of Local Authorites
Principal Officer
West Midlands Regional Forum   Telephone: 01785 276240/1
PO Box 11   Fax: 01785 258243
Martin Street
Stafford ST16 2LH

Yorkshire and Humberside Regional Association (YAHRA)
Yorkshire and Humberside Regional Association
Barnsley Business and Innovation Centre   Telephone: 01226 733127
Innovation Way   Fax: 01226 244748
Barnsley S75 1JL

The recession of recent years means that all the conferences are very much concerned with economic regeneration. Certain planning conferences have actually been *born again* as economic development bodies with planning as a subsidiary responsibility: one only has to worry about where to put the fruits of economic growth, if it exists in the first place.

Members of these regional bodies are officers and elected members drawn from all the counties in a region plus representatives from the districts and metropolitan boroughs. Their purpose is to: achieve a better understanding of what is happening in the region; secure greater coordination of their planning policies

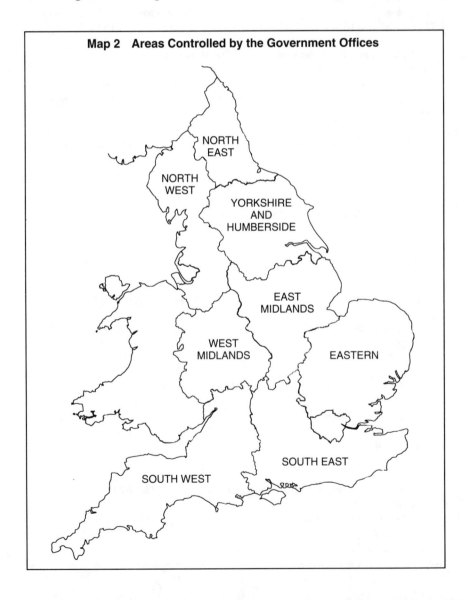

Map 2   Areas Controlled by the Government Offices

by study and discussion of regional planning issues; provide a channel for expressing a collective view of these issues to the various departments of central government; and a means of liaising with the European Commission (EC) over issues of importance in the region, such as agriculture, or attracting grants for economic regeneration. Local government does not suffer from the periodic bouts of xenophobia afflicting central government, and looks to Brussels as an ally in furthering the interests of their region.

It should be noted that the regional conferences are not coextensive with the territories of the new Government Offices – that would be too simple. (see Map 2 & Fig.2). These regional conferences play a lead role in the formulation of RPGs. They are expected to liaise with government departments and other government bodies about issues affecting their region. They are also expected to consult other major interest groups e.g. those representing agriculture, conservation, development, industry etc. Sometimes members of interest groups are co-opted onto working

---

Figure 2   Government Offices in the Regions

North West
2010 Sunley Tower, Picadilly Plaza, Manchester M1 4BA
Tel: 0161 838 5500/5505

Yorkshire and Humberside
City House, New Station Street, Leeds LS1 4JD Tel: 0113 283 5200

North East
Stanegate House, 2 Groat Market, Newcastle-upon-Tyne NE1 1YN
Tel: 0191 235 7201

West Midlands
77 Paradise Circus, Queensway, Birmingham B1 2DT Tel: 0121 212 5000

East Midlands
Cranbrook House, Cranbrook Street, Nottingham NG1 1EY
Tel: 0115 935 2419

Merseyside
Graeme House, Derby Square, Liverpool L2 7SU Tel: 0151 277 4111

Eastern
Heron House, 49–53 Goldington Road, Bedford MK40 3LL Tel: 01234 796238

South West
The Pithay, Bristol BS1 2NQ Tel: 0117 945 6770

South East
Bridge House, 1 Walnut Tree Close, Guildford GU1 4GA
Tel: 01483 882504/882499

parties. Topics covered are limited to those in the development plans, and to those which justify being considered over a wider geographical basis than a structure plan e.g. housing, transport, minerals, economic development, waste management. If you are interested, and have a regional perspective on a problem, contact the regional conference and get involved.

The regional conferences vary enormously in terms of size, population, terrain, and the resources they can muster to support a regional secretariat. However competent the staff, lack of funding inevitably affects the extent to which their recommendations on regional policy, for example, are underpinned by technical papers and research findings. RPGs are compiled by the DoE with reference to: European Union legislation (see Fig.13); national policy in the shape of PPGs, Minerals Planning Guidance (MPGs), and Circulars (see Appendix I): and the views of the regional groupings of planning authorities. The RPG is published in draft, and comments invited, so make an input before the Secretary of State finally issues the definitive version. Do not forget that RPGs, the policy advice offered by the standing conferences, and the research upon which it is based, constitute invaluable material for fielding in debates over structure plans, and major development issues. There is now complete coverage of England in terms of RPGs (see Appendix I). Although they are expected to suggest the development framework for at least 20 years ahead, they are expected to be reviewed and updated every four or five years.

The various regional conferences are charged with planning for sustainable development. To this end they are devising means by which regional planning guidance can be environmentally assessed. The European Union (EU) produced proposals in 1991 to extend Environmental Assessment (EA) to include programmes, policies and plans. As may be imagined, there is little enthusiasm amongst certain member states for subjecting national policy to such scrutiny, so the Directive has yet to appear. However the DoE has indicated to the regional conferences that they should formulate the methodology for the Strategic Environmental Assessment (SEA) of their proposals. This is proving quite a challenge because planning guidance is a different animal from plans and projects, being that much further removed from 'ground level'. Should central government either volunteer or assent to such an examination of national policies, they will find that much of the intellectual hard graft has already been done by local government.

It should be noted that regional planning in Wales is non-existent: the Strategic Planning exercise in Wales was abandoned. Meanwhile ad hoc sub-regional groupings of local authorities have set up a forum to further economic development e.g. the North Wales Economic Development Forum. Elsewhere the need for regional guidance is all too obvious e.g. the M4 Corridor in S.Wales.

 REGIONAL PLANNING: POLLUTION

The Environment Agency was created by the 1995 Environment Act. The Agency consists of an amalgamation of the National Rivers' Authority (NRA), Her Majesty's Inspectorate of Pollution (HMIP), the Waste Regulatory Authorities (formerly attached to the counties or associated with metropolitan boroughs) and the waste management divisions of the Department of the Environment (DoE). True to Britain's ad hoc approach to planning, not to mention local government, the Environment Agency divides England and Wales into yet a third set of regions (see Map 3 & Fig.3): the boundaries are modified versions of the river catchment areas used by the NRA, adjusted to follow local authority boundaries, with a goodwill gesture in the direction of Welsh patriotism.

Despite the mismatch in boundaries (compare Map 1 with Map 3), come the next round of regional policy formation, the Environment Agency regions will endeavour to make a coherent input into the deliberations of the regional planning conferences on the aspects of pollution, which the Environment Agency controls and areas where it has expertise of assistance to local authorities.

The Environment of England and Wales: a Snapshot, (The Environment Agency, 1996)

Map 3   Areas Controlled by Environment Agency Regional Offices

Figure 3   Environment Agency Regional Offices

Environment Agency Headquarters
Rivers House, Waterside Drive, Aztec West, Almondsbury, Bristol BS12 4UD
Tel: 01454 624 400   Fax: 01454 624 409

Anglian
Kingfisher House, Goldhay Way, Orton Goldhay, Peterborough PE2 5ZR
Tel: 01733 371 811   Fax: 01733 231 840

North East
Rivers House, 21 Park Square South, Leeds LS1 2QG
Tel: 0113 244 0191   Fax: 0113 246 1889

North West
Richard Fairclough House, Knutsford Road, Warrington WA4 1HG
Tel: 01925 653 999   Fax: 01925 415 961

Midlands
Sapphire East, 550 Streetsbrook Road, Solihull B91 1QT
Tel: 0121 711 2324   Fax: 0121 711 5824

Southern
Guildbourne House, Chatsworth Road, Worthing, West Sussex BN11 1LD
Tel: 01903 820 692   Fax: 01903 821 832

South West
Manley House, Kestrel Way, Exeter EX2 7LQ
Tel: 01392 444 000   Fax: 01392 444 238

Thames
Kings Meadow House, Kings Meadow Road, Reading RG1 8DQ
Tel: 01734 535 000   Fax: 01734 500 388

Welsh
Rivers House/Plays-yr-Afon, St Mellons Business Park, St Mellons, Cardiff
CF3 0LT   Tel: 01222 770 088   Fax: 01222 798 555

ROAD PLANNING: AN OVERVIEW

Since the Trunk Roads Act of 1936, trunk road and motorway planning and promotion by Central Government has been carried out under a system quite separate from general 'Town and Country Planning'. This is partly due to its earlier introduction and the failure of the 1947, and later, TCP Acts to bring trunk roads into the planning system.

In 1996 the Government proposed for the first time to alter this, if only in administrative terms. Trunk road and motorway planning would be done through the Regional Planning Guidance (RPG) process in England, at least in terms of principles. This is intended to give local planning authorities greater say in road planning and relate it better to land use planning. The proposals, in the 1996 Government 'Green Paper' *Transport: The Way Ahead*, have not been put into practice at the time of writing.

The Department of Transport (DTp) in 1994 'hived off' into the Highways Agency (HA) its road planning and building functions, by far its largest activity and one which previously dominated its thinking and ethos. Since then it has cut road building budgets drastically, and the HA is going through successive reorganisations and cut its administrative costs. The overall effect has been to respond, if indirectly, to the upsurge of opposition to further road building, at least in England. This has stretched from academic and expert critiques, notably the Royal Commission on Environmental Pollution 1994 Report *Transport and the Environment* through to the large number of local campaigns against roads to the publicised on-site demonstrations.

The DTp has been cutting down local authority road spending for some 20 years, and lack of funding constrains most local authority road planning. This is in principle (though not in all legal respects) related to town and country planning. The current financing methods, of the 'Package Bid' and 'Capital Challenge', make obtaining DTp 'Transport Supplementary Grant' (TASK) funding for new roads very difficult. Counties and Unitary Authorities have to show that needs cannot be met by non-road building solutions such as traffic management or calming. They must show how they are providing for the promotion of cycling and walking in their plans. It is all a great change from the attitudes of the 1980s when local authorities were discouraged from subsidising buses and encouraged to submit new road schemes for funding.

The Government has sought to bring private finance into road building. DTp schemes are increasingly being pursued on the 'Design, Build, Finance and Operate' (DBFO) principle. This means privately-financed construction with DTp paying the private firm back over many years. This is thought by many experts to put up the longer-term cost to the public purse. Local authorities are encouraged to try this too. But they have enough debt problems, and more realistically they are increasingly involving developers in paying for part or all of new road schemes. This runs the risk of roads being promoted, and land compulsorily purchased, to suit the needs of developers, not local residents or local councils.

In Wales, where the Welsh Office takes on the DTp role, one of the changes seen in England are taking place, but there is still significant road building for 'economic development' than is needed in traditional traffic terms. European money is frequently involved. The Welsh Office has not yet set up a Highways Agency.

DEVELOPMENT PLANS

The Plan-Led System

Individual planning applications are decided in the light of broad considerations:

> *regard must be had to the provisions of the development plan, so far as they are relevant to the application, and any other material considerations.*

> s.70 1990 TCP Act

As can be seen, one of the most important of these is the development plan, which sets out the local planning authority's intentions for the use of land in their area over the next 10 to 15 years. This has been the case since 1947, but in the early nineties there was a change of emphasis which elevated the status of the development plan to being a key factor when making decisions about development. Having consolidated much of the planning legislation, passed in the last two decades, into the 1990 Town & Country Planning Act, the Government proceeded to introduce important revisions in new legislation the following year. In the 1991 Planning and Compensation Act (P&C Act) there appeared this crucial sentence:

Where, in making any determination under the planning Acts, regard is to be had to the development plan, the determination shall be made in accordance with the plan *unless material considerations indicate otherwise.*

(1991 P&C Act,s.26, (alias s.54A 1990 TCP Act)

emphasis added)

Preceding this is the announcement that this oft quoted passage is to be grafted onto the 1990 Act as s.54A. You will look in vain for it in the cream bound volumes of the 1990 TCP Act: if you are lucky enough to have access to an encyclopaedia of planning law, then the amended text should be included. This inconvenience, and many others could have been avoided had the P&C Act preceded the consolidation of the principal Act, but such logic is too much to expect.

'Material considerations' will be discussed later, but for now we will focus on the development plan. Although purists will say that the wording of s.54A is little different from the equivalent section in the 1972 Act, the effect of s.54A and its interpretation by the courts, has been to shift the attention of would-be developers from the appeal system to the development plan process. It is therefore imperative that everyone else concerned about the future development of their area, should get involved at this stage:

Because of the role of the development plan in determining the future location of development, it is important that anyone with an interest in the future pattern of development in the plan area should participate in its preparation and help to influence its emerging policies. Anyone has the right to object to plan proposals prior to their adoption or approval.

PPG1 1997 para.41

Species of Development Plans

What is a development plan? As PPG12, para.3.2, ruefully explains 'the "development plan" is rarely a single document'. It is a generic term which covers the adopted versions of structure plans, local plans and unitary development plans (UDPs). For areas outside the big conurbations there are structure plans which supply the strategic framework and local plans which provide the detailed policies and proposals for an area. The metropolitan counties were rendered extinct in the mid eighties, and their powers balkanized between the metropolitan boroughs. With regard to land use planning, each metropolitan borough now produces a UDP which is comprised of a strategic element analogous to a structure plan (Part I), and a detailed element akin to a local plan (Part II).

To put it charitably, the recent review of local government has resulted in confusion with regard to development planning in the English shires: every conceivable, and some inconceivable, permutation and combination of structure and local plans, and UDPs is to be attempted by some group of hapless planning officers, as from April 1996 (see Appendix X). It is essential to check on the situation pertaining in the area you are concerned about, rather than making any assumptions. In the Principality the situation is simpler: the Local Government (Wales) Act 1994 requires each new unitary council to prepare a UDP in due course, but, in the interim, existing plans are to be used.

For the benefit of developers, many LPAs prepare Supplementary Planning Guidance (SPG) which is non statutory but closely related to the development plan: it is tailored to local conditions, such as design considerations in a conservation area. The Secretary of State encourages the productions of SPGs with the proviso that it is not misused to impose policies on the public without any public scrutiny. It will increase in weight if there has been some public participation in its formulation, and approval by the Members of the LPA. SPGs are rated as material considerations, and contribute to the determination of applications and the framing of conditions, or s.106 planning obligations.

Sometimes what starts out as SPG for the development of an area, becomes the groundwork for formulating a local plan for that area: clearly much depends on what stage has been reached in the local plan cycle. However, if the SPG pertains to an important redevelopment, which has implications for the rest of the LPA, and may be beyond its boundaries, and it is feasible to graft it into the local plan, then it is proper that the SPG should graduate in status, so that developers cannot lightly dismiss it.

Realpolitik

The decision to finally adopt any development plan rests with the local authority which drew it up in the first place. A question you must ask is 'What will be the attitude of the elected members towards my proposal or objection?' There is no point in putting forward a first rate case at an Examination in Public (EIP) or Local Plan Inquiry, and having it endorsed by the Panel or Inspector, if you neglect to cultivate the 'political gate-keepers' in the local authority. That said the Courts have limited their room for manoeuvre: they have to be seen to have weighed every word of the report with care.

A key issue to be addressed is whether, in reality, a given council is led by its councillors or by its officers?. If the former, you have to aim your persuasive powers in the direction of the Chairman, Leader and key members of relevant committees. If the council is dominated by its officers, then chief officers and senior staff are the parties to convert to your way of thinking. You do not want to find that you have won the game, only to lose the match. Influencing the shape of a development plan is essentially a political process, in terms of building alliances with other interested parties, and influencing the local authority: this has to be borne in mind right the way through from the consultation stage to final adoption.

Nonetheless, it should also be borne in mind that over 90% of inspectors' recommendations are accepted by LPAs: the Courts have taken to task elected members for not giving due weight to the inspector's recommendations. Therefore, if your position is endorsed in his report, either because you managed to persuade the LPA before the inquiry, or you convinced the inspector during the proceedings, you should be well on your way to achieving your objective.

Environmental Assessment of Development Plans

It is noticeable that the environment is not singled out as a specific topic in developments plans. Do not be alarmed. It has not been omitted. Rather it is considered to be an integral part of all the prescribed issues. To this end central government published, in 1991, 'Policy Appraisal and the Environment' which shows how, by the use of matrices and cost/benefit analysis, environmental impact can be assessed when formulating policies. This was followed by two documents which were regarded, by those preparing development plans, as being more user friendly: PPG12 (Feb.1992) and Environmental Appraisal of Development Plans: a Good Practice Guide (1993).

To date it is the counties which have taken the lead in undertaking environmental appraisal of their structure plans; no doubt UDPs and local plans will follow. Interpretations of the DoE's advice varies greatly. Some, like Hertfordshire and Humberside, have sounded out the views of the public, whilst others have not. Given the enhanced status of development plans, and the obstacles to effective input by the public during their formulation, it would be worth lobbying those preparing any sort of development plan to persuade them to involve those who live and work in the area, be it a county, a metropolitan borough or a district council. No doubt progress will be monitored. If public input can be shown to be effective the terms which the government understands i.e. speeding up the preparation and completion of the development plan process, rather than improving its contribution to sustainability, then public participation will be incorporated into future good practice guides.

The Coverage of Policy Areas

Development plans are land use plans, and, therefore economic, social and political factors manifest themselves in terms of the policies governing the allocation and development of land. Even if one accepts that planners see the world through this particular prism, there have been instances where development plans have been found wanting in terms of incorporating all the aspects of government policy relevant to a given area. If a subject is of interest to you, and to central government, but is not covered by the plan, then raise the matter with the LPA responsible. They should be amenable to inserting it into the plan: you may not agree with their vision but that can be challenged later.

Call-in by the Secretary of State

Should you fail, draw it to the attention of the Secretary of State at the earliest opportunity. This tactic can also be useful if an LPA owns land and is proposing to develop it in a way which is contrary to their own previously stated intentions and/or government policies. A last resort is to ask the Secretary of State to call-in the whole, or that part of the plan for his own decision. The only problem is that the Secretary of State cannot be relied upon to intervene, even when an LPA proposes to develop its own land in a way which will have a detrimental effect on the efficacy of that policy e.g. a business park, on a site owned by the county council in an area of low unemployment, could deflect firms from other business parks, elsewhere in the county, in areas designated as unemployment black-spots.

In these days when local authorities are forced to maximize the value of every asset, they may be tempted, on rare occasions, to bend the planning system to their own immediate advantage, even at the cost of the wider economic benefit of the area, and the Secretary of State may, quite legitimately, adopt a 'hands off' stance. In such a case only fierce lobbying at national level can hope to reverse the situation. Once the proposal is in the development plan it is too late: LPA's enjoy deemed planning consent for schemes in conformity with the development plan and they can even grant aid the road network to serve the development.

A Gleam in the Developer's Eye....

It is essential that all the proposals in a development plan be thoroughly examined. A seemingly innocuous proposal can foreshadow major development in years to come, and by the time people wake up to the implications the project is unstoppable: local plans have to conform to structure plans, and planning applications follow on. The only room for manoeuvre is over phasing, conditions, and s.106 planning obligations. Even then developers have ways of forcing the hand of the LPA (see Appendix IX). In order to avoid this situation, use your imagination as to the possible implications of a proposal or policy statement.

STRUCTURE PLANS

The Nature of Structure Plans

Structure plans are prepared by counties: usually there is only one for the whole county. They take their cue from national planning policy and the framework for the region set out in the RPGs. Structure plans ensure that local plans are consistent with those of neighbouring areas. A structure plan and Part 1 of a UDP is supposed to last for at least 15 years from the base date of the plan.

The point of a structure plan is that it should confine itself to a strategic approach to the issues. This is symbolized by the Key Diagrams illustrating the proposals, which are not Ordnance Survey based but merely serve to show the approximate location of a given feature e.g. Green Belt. Each feature is accompanied by a code denoting the policy in the accompanying text known as the *explanatory memorandum.* The latter has to cover the following topics: housing; transport; economic development; Green Belts and conservation of natural and built environment; minerals; waste treatment and disposal, and land reclamation; tourism, leisure and recreation; and energy. The interactions between these policies must be considered, and the plan be presented as a coherent whole.

The Consultation Draft

These issues of high policy are not considered to be suited to public participation because most people do not think in these terms. Thus there is no statutory consultation of the public prior to the deposited version of the structure plan. In practice however, most county planning departments go out of their way to consult with key groups. More surprisingly, however, although structure planning authorities consult each other, there is nothing in current legislation which obliges neighbouring structure plan areas to work together, so that authorities can declare UDI when the going gets hot. Any disputes are likely to get an airing at the EIP.

If you are concerned about a strategic issue e.g. the redevelopment of a major site in the county, the economic development of an area, transport or mineral extraction, you would be well advised to contact the country council and get your name on their list of interested parties. The county council may prepare a draft plan, or issue papers on subjects within that plan, and then hold a conference to discuss their ideas. Do attend any such events as you will discover who are the other parties to the debate, and the nature of your potential allies and opponents at a later date. Although they are not obliged to do so, most county councils hold a series of meetings for groups of town and parish councils to exchange views on the impact of strategic issues at ground level.

The Deposited Plan

How do you know when the deposited version of the structure plan has appeared? Devotees will scan the pages of the London Gazette for an official notice announcing the deposited version of the structure plan is available, where copies are to be found, the period during which objections can be registered, where objections should be sent etc. However, for more normal people the same information is to be found for two successive weeks in at least one local paper. If you are spoilt for choice with regard to local papers, and wonder which one will inherit the notice, enquire of your nearest LPA.

The Examination in Public

Mounting a Campaign

Unlike the local plan inquiry there is no *right* to be heard at an EIP if you object. Clearly, in such a situation, it does help if you have a recognizable 'constituency': you represent an environmental pressure group which operates at national level; a consortium of parish councils; or a group of amenity societies. The wider your geographical base, the better. National development interests are likely to be invited to the EIP. So if you can demonstrate the interests of the community, it is likely that you will be invited to secure a balanced debate at the EIP.

The purpose of the EIP is to provide the LPA with information to help them make decisions. Thus it is a matter of whether you raise an issue which ought to be discussed at the EIP. How are these chosen? According to PPG12:

> *Issues upon which further information and discussion may be required, and which may therefore need to be examined in public, include those which arise from conflicts between the deposited proposals and national or regional policies, or those of neighbouring planning authorities, or between the various general policies and proposals in the structure plan as proposed to be altered or replaced; or where there are issues involving substantial unresolved controversy.*
>
> Para.18

If you are afraid that your topic will be overlooked, deliberately or otherwise, you will have to rally key objectors to your cause. For example a proposal on a given site may adversely affect other areas of the county. Given the expense of purchasing a structure plan, and its conceptual approach to 'the environment', it may well be that considerable work will have to be done on, say, the housing or the employment figures, before the implications for a given area will become apparent. If the latter gives cause for concern, then public opinion will have to be aroused by supplying people with a simplified, accurate but apolitical version of the situation: you cannot expect everyone, whose support you need, to plough through the documentation. Bite-sized chunks are the order of the day.

Having debugged the figures, and distilled the general message, contact all the local authorities, including parish and town councils, and their relevant MPs. Do not forget to establish links with other environmental groups who could be potential allies (see Appendix IV). Where the issue is contrary to existing or emerging government policy, including Regional Planning Guidance for your area (see Appendix I), add the Secretary of State to your list. If the issue extends beyond the remit of DoE, involve the relevant Secretary of State e.g. the Minister of Defence over the disposal of defunct airbases. Notify the Government Office for your region (see Fig.2).

Comments on structure plans can be made only to the general policies and proposals, not the explanatory memorandum. The latter is not technically part of the plan, but its adequacy in terms of justifying the policies may be questioned. Make comments in plain English, but laced with references to RPGs, PPGs, and Development Plans, both within the county and across the boundary. Cite examples from elsewhere. In other words show off your fluency in Planning-Speak. You will thus be deemed to be 'One of Us', by the officers in receipt of your comments.

The penalty for not making an objection within the prescribed six week period, is that you forfeit the possibility of taking part in the EIP. An EIP must be held unless special dispensation is obtained from the Secretary of State, and this will be very rarely: only where it is obvious that no further investigation is necessary.

Topics for Discussion

Who selects the significant topics to be included? Since the advent of the 1991 P&C Act that responsibility has passed to the county councils instead of the old style DoE Regional Offices. If you view this with suspicion, you should be reassured to some extent by the fact that the Secretary of State still appoints an independent Panel to preside over the EIP: *de facto* they keep their eye on the county council and see fair play. Although formally they do not select the issues to be discussed, their involvement prior to the EIP should ensure nothing which should be discussed gets swept under the carpet. On the other hand, it is an unsatisfactory situation and potentially open to abuse, once the county councils have got used to the new system and know just how far they can work it to their own advantage. As for the choosing of the participants and the balancing of the different interests, this is done jointly by the Panel and the county.

A Seat at the Table

Having got the issue on the agenda, are you willing to appear at the EIP? If yes, say so when you submit your formal objection. Please note that you may be able to claim their expenses. These could include travel, subsistence and an amount for loss of salary or wages. Not everyone who has objected on a given issue will be invited: it will be question of the Panel getting a balanced discussion with all the different interests represented. If you really wish to participate, you will have to demonstrate by the *quality* of your objection that you deserve a place at the EIP. This can be a tall order if you are trying to put together a major case in six weeks. Don't panic. Send in a comprehensive outline objection, and through both covering letter and personal contact with the Secretary to the Panel, indicate that more detailed information will follow. There is nothing in either the 1990 Act or the 1991 P&C Act which says you cannot augment your case. Especially if you wish to appear at the EIP, you would be well advised to make a friend of the Secretary.

In due course the Secretary will make a list of issues and participants and circulate them to all who have sent in objections. Any comments you may have on either will be considered by the county council, after consultation with the Chairman of the EIP. Alterations may be made at this stage, but it is unlikely, certainly on any substantial scale. If you are bidden to the EIP, there is likely to be a preliminary meeting to sort out procedure and timetables, and deal with any queries you may have. It is vital to attend this meeting to 'get the feel' of the forthcoming forum and make your own assessment of the characters involved.

EIP Personnel

The Secretary to the Panel is appointed by the county council, but not from the planning department: this individual will undertake an analysis of the original objections, be responsible for commissioning additional information for the Panel, deal with correspondence on behalf of the Chairman, and assist with the writing of the report. Who are the Panel? The Chairman of the Panel will be someone experienced in the ways of central and local government, or from the land use professions, or in the conduct of investigations of this kind, such as a lawyer. Normally the Panel will have just one other member, or although sometimes there is a third. One member of the Panel will always be from the Planning Inspectorate. Where there are technical matters to be investigated, which are beyond the expertise of the Panel, an assessor will be appointed to advise them.

At the Examination in Public

Although an EIP is classed as an inquiry under s.1(1)c of the Tribunals & Inquiries Act 1971, it is conducted as a structured discussion with all the parties interested in a given topic sitting round a table. Each party has a spokes-person either appearing alone, or with advisors alongside, or behind them. If you are unable to be present, someone you choose can take your place, but have the courtesy to discuss the matter with the Chairman first. There is no reason why your representative should not be a lawyer but he or she must not expect to expect to make speeches or cross examine opponents: avoid barristers who are congenitally unable to speak unless standing up. An EIP is not a lawyer's love-in like so many large inquiries, including those into objections to local plans and UDPs. At an EIP the Panel set the tone by dispensing with the services of our learned friends.

So how are matters progressed? The Chairman will announce the topics to be covered during that session. It is likely that the county council will be asked to state their position, followed maybe by those who support it, be they part of central or local government, the private sector or voluntary groups. The Chairman will then switch his attention to the opposition and they will state their case. As the discussion continues, the batting order changes under the Chairman's direction: he is endeavouring to ascertain the truth of the matter and will call upon whoever can make the most useful contribution at that point. All documents submitted to the EIP are taken as read, and although people may have notes to hand, they speak to them or consult with their advisors, rather than reading out pre-prepared statements. In terms of presentation, you will put your case across more clearly if you use short sentences, interspersed with the odd rhetorical question to keep your listeners on their toes.

Although taking part in an EIP appears to be easier than giving evidence at a public inquiry, do not be lulled into a false sense of security, and, after your initial statement, lapse into a dull silence or embark on noisy repetition. To be effective you will need to be widely read on your subject: current government policy [see Appendix I]; recent research findings, not forgetting those produced by regional planning bodies; and verdicts of other EIP Panels etc. After a well thought out initial statement, you may well be called upon to make supplementary remarks as the debate unfolds on a given issue, and to neatly summarize your position at the end of the session: the ability to think on your feet is essential. If this is laced with humour and a generosity towards opponents, you will make an impressive showing. As we shall see, all these skills are useful at a public inquiry. There is, however, another parallel, which is perhaps more important: in both fora you are there to help those adjudicating to make up their minds. Put yourself in their position, perhaps by setting out the options open to them, the form of words which would reconcile opposites, or build in safeguards. The Panel may be grateful for your constructive suggestion.

Site Visits & Reports

The session at the EIP will be the end of your involvement at this stage. Visits to various locations are made, but unlike those connected with an inquiry, they are unaccompanied. In terms of the presentation of your evidence, you should bear in mind the fact that the Panel are looking at the general suitability of a given area for a given policy designation, rather than allocating specific sites, as is done in a local plan. After the completion of the EIP and site visits, the Panel begin their report writing. The report will be an assessment of the issues selected, and the discussion at the EIP. It will conclude with recommendations to the county council as to how the structure plan should be modified in the light of their findings.

Modifications

If the report accepts the plan as it stands, and does not recommend any changes, the local authority will proceed to adopt it, that is make it the statutory plan, after an interval of 28 days. However, *if alterations are proposed, a local authority is not obliged to accept any of the Modifications suggested.* If your objection or proposal has been endorsed in the report, then you will have to lobby officers and councillors to ensure that they accept it. If they chose not to, they are required to prepare a detailed statement as to why not, and give good reasons for each negative verdict. However, it is open to you to object to the absence of a Modification, provided you do it within six weeks of the intention to adopt or when objections to other Modifications are being filed.

Where the local authority do propose Modifications to the plan, they must publish a list in at least one local newspaper for two successive weeks, give their reasons for doing so, and invite comment in terms of representations of support, or objections *to the proposed Modifications* during the six weeks following the publication of the notice. Please note that objections at this stage may only relate to the issues dealt with at the EIP: either the Modification proposed by the Panel has been ignored, or the one proposed by the local authority, is unacceptable. Guidance notes are supplied with the Modification form, and they explain the situation.

Intervention by the Secretary of State

Another safeguard against the pig-headed refusal to alter a plan by a local authority, is the power of the Secretary of State to direct that a plan be modified to adequately reflect national or regional policies, or harmonize with other development plans. If he does intervene the authority must consider the DoE's modifications, and implement the above procedure for dealing with them. If the authority do not intend to comply with the direction of the Secretary of State, they must give reasons for not doing so. If there are objections from the public, another EIP must be held. This causes delay and expense which most sensible local authorities would wish to avoid. On the other hand, it is an option if the fault lies with an overbearing Secretary of State.

A more drastic alternative for the Secretary of State is to call-in all or part of the plan. Calling-in is done but rarely, and not always when you would expect it. However, the power allows such intervention in special circumstances, such as if the plan raises issues of national or international importance, or has given rise to substantial controversy, perhaps beyond the boundary of the local authority. The Secretary of State will then propose modifications, but there is no obligation to hold an EIP if one has occurred already.

Adoption

When all these matters have been resolved, a local authority may move towards the adoption of its plan. This is followed by announcements in the London Gazette and local newspapers, together with personally contacting anyone who has said that they require to be informed. It can be seen that the convoluted nature of procedures after the EIP are designed to provide a fail-safe system. This is particularly necessary since the 1991 P&C Act empowered local authorities to adopt their own plans instead of going through the Secretary of State, as hitherto had been the case.

DEVELOPMENT PLANNING: POLLUTION

Development plans in general play an important part in separating people and sensitive environments from pollution and making realistic provision for these necessary but unneighbourly activities. The Environment Agency will be making an input on matters which are their responsibility: the heavy industrial processes to which integrated pollution control is applied; the management of the water environment, marine or terrestrial; the hazards of radiation; and waste management. They also intend assisting local government with the task of tackling contaminated land and local air pollution control.

With regard to structure plans and UDP Part I, amongst the key topics they have to address are major industrial developments, and waste treatment and disposal facilities. These strategic plans must provide enough space for these activities within the plan period, by showing areas of search, and setting out the criteria by which planning applications will be judged. Where there is a shortage of sites, counties may give those that do exist priority. They may also identify constraints on development where there is the danger from the cumulative impact of polluting activities.

Local plans dealing with pollution fall into four categories: UDP Part IIs; district local plans; waste local plans; and minerals local plans. UDPs deal with both industrial development and waste. District local plans confine themselves to industrial development, whilst the county councils and National Park authorities prepare waste local plans* or, where appropriate, combined waste and minerals local plans.

LPAs have to consider the overall need for such developments in their area. With notable exceptions like petro-chemicals, pharmaceuticals and power stations, most polluting activities used to fall within the Special Industrial Use Classes Order, but in 1995 these were eradicated and most became part of the General Industrial category [B2], or *sui generis*. From then on, polluting industries were defined as those subject to the beady eye of the Environment Agency (see Section II).

Suitable sites, and their surroundings, have to be found for such industries which conform to the ever stricter statutory requirements, many of them originating in the EU (see Fig.13). Consideration has to be given to the past history of the land e.g. contamination, and the possibility of restoration to something useful in the future. The objective of the plan, in the final analysis, is to safeguard human health, natural resources and the environment in general.

District local plans are not supposed to trespass on the issues dealt with by the county's waste local plans. Waste policies, too, owe much to European legislation. The amended EC Framework Directive on Waste (75/442/EEC, 91/156/EEC & 91/692/EEC) is contained in the Waste Management Licensing Regulations 1994 (S.I.1994/1056). Most of its provisions are the concern of the Environment Agency but some fall within the bailiwick of the local planning authorities.
Waste local plans have to take account of:

1. policies to minimize and recycle waste;
2. the aim of self sufficiency in waste management facilities and the need to minimize the adverse impact of transporting waste;
3. land use and transport requirements;
4. opportunities for power generation;
5. the potential to return mineral waste to former mineral workings, and the possibility that these could be used for general land fill.

These local plans have to identify future sites for all types of waste treatment and disposal, including chemical and clinical waste, and broad areas of search set in the context of the criteria against which any planning application would be judged. The distinction between the development plan system and development control can become something of a fiction at waste local plan inquiries when certain issues are under discussion e.g. the proposed allocation of a site for an incinerator, when those who will lodge the eventual application are waiting in the wings with the very details which cannot be discussed at the local plan inquiry. Unlike other site allocations e.g. housing or retail, the devil is in detail: the pollution effects determine the suitability of a given site.

The other problem is that local people, at a waste local plan inquiry, are supposed to concern themselves with planning issues, not pollution issues (see PPG23, Pollution). This is arrant nonsense. Very often the whole reason for appearing at a waste local plan inquiry is to voice concern on pollution issues, yet people find themselves having to skew their arguments into discussions about topography, meteorology, transport and the juxtaposition of the built environment. Hopefully this absurd situation will be rectified when PPG23 is revised. Meanwhile anyone with anxieties, or indeed expertise to offer, should discuss the issue with the officer responsible in their LPA, and area office Environment Agency (see Map 3 & Fig. 3).

In years to come the scarcity of landfill sites, the levy on every tonne of rubbish, and increased controls will make landfill expensive. This, together with the Government's long overdue commitment to end the dumping of sewerage sludge at sea, will make incineration combined with power generation appear more 'attractive', at least financially. Such issues will no doubt be argued at future local plan inquiries.

Noise is also an issue dealt with in local plans and Part II of UDPs, although, in exceptional cases, it may be relevant to include them in strategic plans (structure plans and Part I of UDPs). If noise policies apply to the whole of the plan area, then they should be presented like any other policy. If they are area-specific, then the relevant bound-aries should appear on the proposals map, but noise contours are thought to be too detailed for development plans: nonetheless, PPG24 does not specify anything useful, like how else you can define the boundaries. However, the idea is that noise sensitive developments such as houses, schools and hospitals, should be sites away from actual or potential uses which generate noise.

*The Waste Local Plan should not be confused with the Waste Management Plan which used to be prepared by the counties and other waste regulation bodies. The advent of the Environment Agency has changed all that. It is obliged to produce a National Waste Strategy, but not regional or local waste management plans. It is pos-sible that it may be producing some form of regional waste strategy in the future. More certain is the fact that it will be Local Environment Agency Plans (LEAPs) which will deal with the integrated manage-ment of the environment at the local scale, covering all the interests and and responsibilities of the Environment Agency.

Development Plans & Regional Guidance (PPG 12)
Planning & Pollution Control (PPG23), Chapter 2 & Annex 6
Planning & Noise (PPG24) paras. 3–7

CROWN LAND

What is Crown Land? It is defined as land belonging to the Queen, in the right of the Crown, or to a Government Department, or to the Duchies of Lancaster or Cornwall. (1990 TCP Act, s.293) As Her Majesty and central government are above local government in the hierarchy, it follows that superior authorities do not have to consult authorities beneath them when deciding what should be done with their own property. This may sound positively feudal, but one has to admit it is logical. What's more the Crown still governs its own devel-opment on its own property. Thus it does not need planning permis-sion, or listed building consent, and is beyond enforcement action.

Until the 1980s it was assumed that, once acquired, land would remain under the control of the Crown forever, but changes in Government policy ranging from 'Community Care' to the 'Peace Dividend', have meant that, since the early eighties, Departments of central government have been anxious to dispose of their assets for the best possible price. They found themselves hoist by their own petard. The downside of not having to apply for planning permission is that the land had no value on the open market: planning permission for a given type of development is a large component in determining the value of a site. If the land is to be sold on from Crown control, then it necessary to ascertain its value in the big wide world of the property market.

The relevant Circular says that:

> *Disposing Departments will endeavour... to ensure that future use of land...will be be in accordance with the current planning and environmental policies for the area. Where the land to be disposed of and its existing use conflicts with those policies, the disposing Department will draw this fact to the attention of the planning local authority, and be prepared to discuss the situation with them.....*
>
> DoE 18/84, Part II, para.2

The Circular piously points out that the LPA might draw the attention to the disposing Department that the facilities might be of use to the wider population, given that public money has been invested in them. That might be the case in certain instances, but is anyone queuing up to take over, for example, 56 defunct F111, bomb proof aircraft hangars costing half a million pounds apiece to blow up?

What follows can be an interesting bargaining process between the Government Department, under a statutory obligation to maximize the value of its assets, less the cost of cleaning up the site, and the LPAs endeavouring to integrate, sometimes very large sites into their respective development plans without throwing the surrounding area completely out of gear. Under such circumstances the local community, which perhaps has had a long association in employment and social terms with the relevant Department, can find that its interests are completely sidelined whilst talks proceed between the major players. They would be well advised to retain professionals who can represent their interests at the negotiating table, rather than relying on the rights of public participation accorded under the development plan process.

LOCAL PLANS

The Character of Development Plans

Outside the metropolitan areas, local plans complement the structure plan: they set out the detailed policies and proposals which will govern the day to day decisions on development of an area. Local plans come in three varieties: those dealing with minerals, those dealing with waste, and those focusing on planning policies. With regard to the former two, the re-organisation of local government in 1996 (see Appendix X), has meant that the counties are not the only minerals and waste authorities in the shires: the new unitary authorities (UAs), not granted UDP status, are also minerals and waste authorities. These UAs may: produce minerals and waste local plans, conforming to the structure plan; produce a joint local plan with the county, if they are dependent on their neighbours for waste disposal; or, if granted the appropriate Change Orders by the Local Government Commission, devise a comprehensive local plan, combining minerals and waste policies with the district wide planning policies.

District wide local plans contain detailed policies on the whole range of policies contained in the structure plan i.e. nature conservation, housing, contaminated land, Green Belt, rural economy, urban economy, transport, air pollution, tourism and energy, with cross references to the separate minerals and waste local plans prepared by the county and UAs.

Local plans, of all denominations, comply with the relevant policies of EU, national, regional and structure plans. Local plans are expected to last for ten years, with revisions every five years. However, some policies such as those pertaining to minerals or conservation may have a longer or indefinite timescale.

The Need for Participation

Whereas the structure plan deals with general policy issues expressed in diagrams, an ordinance survey map is used to delineate the exact extent of the policies and proposals in the local plan. These are backed up by text known as the *reasoned justification*. Therefore they are much more accessible for most people, and the DoE envisages the formulation of the local plan to be the main means by which people participate in the development plan system in the shire counties:

> *The preparation of local plans gives local communities the opportunity to participate in planning choices about where development should be accommodated in their area. Particularly in areas of development pressure, **it is not sufficient for local planning authorities to seek to rely only on national and regional guidance and the provisions of the structure plan.***
>
> PPG12, Para.3.7 (emphasis added)

So this is your opportunity to have your say about your area. It is also the opportunity to make secure any previous victories you may have won. For example, if you have prevented the destruction of woodland by development, or the change of use from something valuable to the community to a 'quick-buck' scheme, then make sure that the land retains its character under the local plan.

The plan consists of general policies and specific proposals. Basically if you wish something to remain as it is, then it should be protected by appropriately worded policies, and if you wish a site to be redeveloped in a given manner, then check to see that there is a proposal for the area *and* that it conforms with the views of your community. Particularly if the site has been the subject of controversy before, it is essential to be vigilant: even if the consultation draft and the deposited version of the local plan echo your views, the likelihood is that the would-be developers will be seeking to change the mind of the local authority, and will appear in force at the local plan inquiry. So be warned!

Developers know that if a given piece of land can be scheduled for, say, housing under the local plan, then they apply for planning permission from the LPA they are likely to get it: they will not have the expense and time wasted in going to appeal. Sometimes developers with a common interest, in say offices or retail development, form a consortium. Thus they can afford to retain barristers and expert witnesses to put their case to best advantage during the development plan process. Neither has the shift in emphasis from development control to the wider field of the development plan, gone unnoticed by objectors. The local plan inquiry has supplanted the planning appeal as the chief battlefield between conservation and development.

The Consultation

In the good cause of reducing the time needed to deliver an acceptable local plan, local authorities are no longer *required* to produce a document called a consultation draft of a local plan:

nonetheless, many LPAs still do. However they are advised to consult widely and are obliged to contact the bodies listed in Annex E of PPG12. The nearest that this part of the exercise comes to public participation is the inclusion of parish, town and community councils. So they will be the first to become acquainted with the local authority's ideas for the local plan, and be in a position to speak for the community. Apart from the statutory consultees, the amount of publicity and the number of additional consultees depends on the discretion of the local authority. Thus if the plan is fundamentally different from its predecessor, it will be have the word 'Replacement' in the title, and be subject to great publicity and a much wider round of consultees than if it was just being updated in certain aspects: in the latter case the words 'Revised' or 'Review' will appear in the title. If you know that a local plan is being incubated, and want to have an input, take the initiative and contact the planners responsible: they will listen to those with legitimate concerns, and constructive ideas.

The Deposited Local Plan

The deposited version of the local plan appears after submissions and views, mooted at the consultation stage, have been considered. The publicity for the period of objection to the local plan follows the same pattern as that for structure plans. You have six weeks in which to submit your objection and it is important that this be done within the allocated time because then you have the statutory right to appear at the local plan inquiry. If you are late, then you may only appear at the discretion of the inspector, and he is only likely to be sympathetic if there is good reason for your tardiness e.g. a dramatic change of circumstances with regard to a proposed site, such as an unexpected application for some horrific development.

This also applies if one is objecting to a policy in the existing local plan which is being carried forward into the emerging plan. Obviously this provision is to stop endless arguments about policies established when the previous local plan was adopted. On the other hand, if circumstances have changed substantially since that time, then the inspector can use his discretion as to whether this topic warrants the use of valuable inquiry time.

All submissions should be made in writing to the appropriate address on the notice. It must relate to a specific policy or proposal in the plan, or the reasoned justification, and state the reason for the objection, and whether they are content with a written objection or whether they wish to appear at the inquiry and call witnesses.

Objections may relate to omissions in the local plan, such as in a certain policy area, and an additional proposal be put forward. Sometimes an objector will put forward alternative proposals to those proffered by the local authority as the solution to a problem. Whatever your stance on the local plan, make it clear what exactly you would like to see in the local plan: too often objections are less than transparent. Keep a record of what you say at this stage because this will be the basis of your case at the local plan inquiry: it can be a little embarrassing when counsel for the local authority points out that you took a rather different line at an earlier stage. It is essential to appear, at least, to be consistent....

If there are no objections then the local authority may proceed to adopt the plan. However, this is highly unlikely: the length and complexity of local plan inquiries is causing increasing concern for government: the local plan inquiry takes an average of seven weeks, but the preparations for it and its repercussions mean that it absorbs the energies of the LPA's planners for many months, if not years!

Equating speed with efficacy means that objectors are encouraged to submit written objections rather than appear at the inquiry. Certainly you should only take up valuable inquiry time if you wish to contest something which is in the plan, rather than just comment on it. The way to minimize stress amongst inexperienced objectors and maximise their impact on the inquiry is for them to join a group, which takes professional advice, and selects individuals to put the case on behalf of the rest. Until developers decide *en masse* to use written representations to put their case at local plan inquiries, and it is they who take up the bulk of the time, then local people should continue to appear, otherwise they could be disadvantaged by losing the right to comment on points put by allies and opponents at the inquiry as it has progressed to date, and answering the inspector's questions.

Supporters of the local authority can also be put in a difficult situation. Maybe they have persuaded the LPA to change its mind on an issue during the consultation period and are anxious not to lose ground to articulate developers during the inquiry. It is unlikely that an inspector will wish to use inquiry time to hear supporters: technically the inquiry is *into objections* to the deposited version of the local plan. If you feel the LPA's case would be strengthened by your arguments e.g. by supplying the inspector with local knowledge, then suggest to the planning officers that you supply a witness to be called by the LPA when this issue is being heard.

Amendments to the Plan

In the interval before the local plan inquiry, the local authority should be approached to ascertain their reaction to your objection or proposal: get your ward councillor on your side, plus senior members of the planning committee. Request a meeting with senior officers: press them on the point if their response has been just to reiterate their original position without further explanation, because the latter may help you to sharpen up your arguments for the inquiry. Even if you do not reach agreement you may learn things to your advantage. In any case you should state in your evidence to the inquiry that you *tried*: for this you should accrue Brownie points, from the inspector.

A local authority may amend the plan as a result of negotiation with objectors, but the problem is that by the time the public is consulted to any degree, it is so often too late for the professionals to change their minds; egos and promotion prospects are firmly nailed to the mast and bright ideas, or even commonsense suggestions can suffer from the *'not invented here'* syndrome. If so, the arteries of the plan, if not the planners, are clearly hardening. Moving the local authority in the direction of an amendment can be difficult. If they do put forward an amendment, check that your proposal is not watered down to such an extent that it is unrecognisable as your suggestion.

Officers should try to reach an agreement with you over your objection, before the inquiry, in order to save inquiry time. If you do reach a satisfactory conclusion, try to ameliorate possible opposition to the amendment. *Should an amendment be agreed, do not withdraw your objection:* there are local authorities which suggest that you should, but this is wrong because the inquiry is into the *objections* to the deposited version of the local plan, and the proposed amendment has no official status, being a suggestion to the inspector alongside all the other material relating to the local plan. Only if there has been some misunderstanding with the LPA over the true nature of the local plan, should you make an unconditional withdrawal from the inquiry. If you have agreed an amendment with the LPA, leave your objection on the table, but write to the inspector and tell him that you wish the amendment to be put forward as a proposed Modification to the plan. If the proposed amendment provokes opposition, then you can always appear at the inquiry to defend your position.

Any amendments to the local plan should be advertised if at all possible, before the inquiry and six weeks allowed for objections: an early sign of such an agreement might be the withdrawal of an objection to be heard at the inquiry. So be alert to possible deals, and, if you are unhappy, lodge what is known in the trade as a *counter-objection*: you can do so at any stage, including during the local plan inquiry. If you wish to be heard, it will be at the inspector's discretion, so don't count on it: put in a well argued written objection in case there is no time for an oral presentation. If the proposal, to which you take exception, emerges as a proposed Modification to the plan, then you have the opportunity to object later. However, the matter may be urgent because of an impending planning application, so it is important to have made angry noises in the direction of the inquiry, so that you can field the correspondence when commenting on the planning application.

There are moves afoot to formalise this pre-inquiry stage, so that amendments agreed have some statutory status, and the inquiry is confined to the remaining objections. It is hoped that this would shorten the inquiry and obviate the need for the modifications stage. However, this would require legislation and even if that were to come to pass, it would not affect plans currently in the pipeline.

Rogue Applications

There is often a considerable delay before a local plan inquiry, and developers, with an eye to the main chance, may well put in a planning application on a site proposed for a that type of development. Planning applications are not allowed to be held up for the local plan, and a favourable decision by an inspector, allowing an appeal, is likely to appear long before the results of the local plan inquiry are known, let alone the plan adopted. By using the appeal system, developers endeavour to steal a march on their competitors. However, if the application is likely to jeopardise key provisions in the development plan, the Secretary of State will serve an Article 14 Direction on prematurity grounds.

If such an application does appear you will have to fight it (see Section II) lest the local plan be overtaken by events, and your efforts prove worthless. You can find yourselves in one of two situations. If you are in opposition to the LPA over the local plan, there is no point in winning the battle at the local plan inquiry if, meanwhile, you lose the war over the development on the site. Alternatively, it might be that you are supporting the local authority in their proposal in the deposit version of the plan: then it is essential that you write in to support them by filing an objection to the application.

Assuming that the local authority refuses the application, and the developer goes to appeal, an option open to the appellant and the local authority is to run the appeal concurrently with the local plan inquiry, in order to save all concerned, including third parties, from having to rerun the same arguments at another inquiry. If this does happen, then the appeal will be recovered by the Secretary of State for his own decision so that the inspector will not find himself making the judgement on the appeal but merely a recommendation to the local authority on the local plan. Although they appear to accord with commonsense, concurrent inquiries are not popular because inquiries into Local Plans and those relating to appeals are different animals: the former are largely concerned with broad issues of principle, whilst the latter are site specific and tend to focus on details.

The Pre-Inquiry Meeting

Some weeks before a local plan inquiry there will be a pre-inquiry meeting for all participants. This is your first chance to meet the inspector and find out how he/she intends to conduct the inquiry. They will introduce themselves, and state their qualifications: note these as they might indicate the way in which his mind will work. If you feel that there is an issue which they are not professionally equipped to deal with, request an assessor to assist the inspector with the technical detail: on the other hand, it is likely that they have experience in this area, which is why there were selected for the job in the first place.

The inspector will give the date for the commencement of the inquiry, and whether there will be an adjournment in the middle: this is quite usual if there are no public holidays to recharge the batteries of the inspector and other key participants. There are two key questions for all objectors:

a) how many sets of evidence do we have to produce? (A 'set' may comprise a proof, appendices, a photograph album, and a series of maps)

b) when is the submission date for their proofs of evidence? (Usually it is four weeks before your actual appearance at the inquiry.)

The pre-inquiry meeting is also the occasion to discuss venues for inquiry: if your local authority inhabits a recycled RAF station miles from anywhere and devoid of public transport, now is the time to suggest the inquiry be held in a suitable venue in a local town.

Requests for evening sessions are also heard at the pre-inquiry meeting. If extracting background information from the local authority is akin to pulling teeth, then explain the problem to the inspector he/she may bring pressure to bear on the local authority, which will benefit you and others. For ease of future reference, Minutes of the pre-inquiry meeting are circulated to all participants.

Another key player at any local plan inquiry is counsel for the local authority: the latter usually retain a middle ranking barrister, who is not as expensive as a Queen's Counsel (QC), because of the inconvenience of tying up local authority solicitors for weeks on end. Given that developers have shifted their focus towards the local plan process, and retaining counsel and expert witnesses in an effort to influence the local plan in their direction, local authorities now feel that they need someone skilled in advocacy to defend the plan. The pre-inquiry meeting is also an opportunity to see the range of interested parties who wish to participate in the local plan inquiry, and who is representing them in terms of counsel and consultancies. PPG12 (para.51) stresses that it is not necessary to be professionally represented at a local plan inquiry. On the other hand the pre-inquiry meeting will show you that you will be up against the professionals. If you feel nervous and/or the issue is very important to you, retain some professional help to put the policy side of the case, whilst you appear as their witnesses supplying the inspector with local knowledge and opinion.

Proof Writing

From the pre-inquiry meeting until the date of submission of proofs is usually a very busy time. Advice on mounting a case and compiling a proof of evidence is to be found in Section III. However, there are points which should be borne in mind when writing your proof for the local plan inquiry. On the cover there should be the objection number which you have been given by the Programme Officer, as well as the exact title of the Local Plan and your name, or that of your group. Unlike an inquiry into an appeal or a called-in application, you are not obliged to produce a summary of your proof if it is longer than 1500 words. However, the inspector may well ask for summaries of longer proofs, and you would be ill advised to ignore his request.

The main body of your proof should commence with a reference to the offending policy or proposal, using its official designation. It may be that you do not disapprove of the whole of that policy or proposal, but just a subsection of it. Be careful to object only to that, otherwise you may unwittingly undermine your whole case. For example, Policy S2 may reflect government guidance on out of town shopping to be found in PPG6. The proposal that Site W should be allocated for supermarket development in Boggleswick is contained in subsection (b), and so it is S2(b) which you oppose, not S2 as a whole. If you do you will be summarily dismissed by the local authority for suggesting they contravene government policy on the issue. You are supposed to suggest a form of words which will express what you would like the policy to say instead. It may be as simple as 'Delete S2(b)', but if it needs rewriting and you have problems with *policy-speak*, get advice from a tame lawyer, surveyor or planner. Otherwise express the gist of what you want and ask the local authority and inspector to formulate it into appropriate phraseology.

If you are not to incur the wrath of the inspector at a local plan inquiry, it is essential that you confine your objection to the principles which lie behind the allocation of a given site for a given use. Voluminous, detailed evidence and hypothetical examples are frowned upon by the inspectorate, and may induce acid comment from your opponents. The place for the examining the minute particulars, is when the application comes in. Rest assured that an elegant attack on LPA's underlying rationale, can be quite as deadly, and much more satisfying than getting everyone bogged down in minutia.

The Run-up to the Local Plan Inquiry

When your evidence arrives in the office of the Programme Officer it will be open for inspection by all concerned, and it will also be copied and circulated to all interested parties, including those likely to oppose you. Do not baulk at this arrangement. You will upset the inspector if you do not comply with his requirement to submit your proof early. In return for your cooperation, you will receive proofs of all other parties, including your opponents. You will receive an official response from the local authority. Do not wait in nervous anticipation, for all too often these are just a reiteration of their known position rather than evincing considered argument, let alone original thought. If on the other hand the local authority do produce a detailed response, but, in so doing delay it, so that you have no time to consider your position before the hearing, then ask for the inquiry to be adjourned to give you enough time to do so.

Keep in touch with the Programme Officer to find out the date of your hearing. A local plan inquiry is likely to go on for a couple of months, and issues are dealt with on a topic by topic basis e.g. housing, transport, retailing etc. In between times there will be days set aside for site visits, administration etc. Programme Officers do endeavour to keep to the dates given to participants because otherwise it would cause havoc with the diaries of counsel and other busy professionals. That said, it is almost inevitable that there will be changes in the timetable. For example Landowner A may suddenly decide to retain counsel to press his case because events have enhanced the chances of his being allowed to develop his field for housing. Thus landowner A's hearing may expand from half a day to two days or more. Landowner B, on the other hand, withdraws his objection and Action Group Q decide to combine their objection with that of Nether Boggleswick Parish Council. These examples result in bringing forward of the programme in your section.

The job of the Programme Office can be very trying: keeping the inspector happy, the inquiry moving, dovetailing hearings so that everyone can have their say, and making sure that all the documents are available. Thus be prepared to be flexible, if you can, about the exact timing of your hearing: a sympathetic attitude towards the Programme Officer will reap dividends, from cups of tea to tit-bits of information, and special requests to the inspector.

At the Local Plan Inquiry

Right from its inception, the Local Plan Inquiry has been conceived of as a more informal affair than other types of inquiry because of the need to involve all parties, including the general public, in discussions about their area. There are no statutory Inquiry Rules, but merely a Code of Conduct, based on best practice. Given the importance of the development plan in determining the future of an area, there has been a certain amount of experimentation. At the macro level. 'Round Tables' have been found to be the best way to thrash out area wide issues like the distribution of housing. At the other end of the scale, there is the option of Hearings, which are informal sessions with the inspector and the LPA officers: this procedure has been adapted from its namesake used for small appeals for lay objectors. That said, in the hands of a sensible inspector, and a sensitive LPA barrister, conventional inquiry procedure seems to adjust to the needs of local people.

The niceties of optimizing inquiry procedure is discussed in Section IV, but it should be noted that the batting order for a given hearing at the local plan inquiry is different from, say, an appeal (compare Fig.4 with Fig.19). At a local plan inquiry the local authority states its case right at the beginning of the inquiry, so if you want to hear their view on a given topic you must attend on that day, but generally what they have to say will be contained in the deposited version of the local plan plus, any amendments which they are tabling for the consideration of the inspector. Some months could elapse before you appear, but when the hearings begin into the topic of interest to you, you would be well advised to attend. Not only will it give you the opportunity to add to your case by citing the evidence of your allies, and undercutting that of the opposition, but also you will get the 'feel' of the inquiry: the daily rituals, the characteristics, attitudes and quirks of the inspector and

---

Figure 4   Batting Order at Local Plan Inquiry

Inquiry Opening

Opening Statement by LPA outlining their case plus any intended alterations. [If inquiry long and complex this may be done on a topic basis]

Points of clarification put by objectors to LPA.

TIME INTERVAL BEFORE YOUR HEARING

Your Hearing

Outline of case by Objector's Team Leader

Witness Statements

Cross-Questioning of witnesses by LPA

Re-examination of Objector's Witnesses by their Team Leader

Inspector's Questions of Witnesses

LPA Witness Statement

Cross questioning of LPA Witness by Objector's Team Leader

Re-examination of LPA witnesses by their Counsel.

Inspector's questions of LPA Witness

Closing Statement by LPA

Closing Statement by Objectors.

key players, the 'in-jokes' etc. All this helps you to relax, and you will need this familiarity to enable you to cope with the speed of events at your own hearing.

When your turn comes, events move very fast. All documents are taken as read, so there is no settling in period, as at an appeal when the appellant sets out his case. Your team leader will briefly introduce your case. Then each witness will read out their proof or its summary, if any, plus verbal amendments. They will then be cross-examined on the *whole* of their evidence evidence. This can be a rude shock if they have not familiarized themselves with the details of the case, compiled months ago. Techniques for optimizing your performance during the different moves in the inquiry game are set out in Section IV.

At the end of your hearing, the Team Leader may be asked to sum up, or the inspector may choose to hear all the closing statements, for a given topic, together at the end: this session will consist of the cast of objectors in order of appearance, rounded off by the closing statement on that topic by counsel for the local authority. If you cannot attend this closing session, tell the inspector and submit your closing speech in writing, or ask a colleague to read it on your behalf at the session on closing statements.

The Site Visit

With regard to site visits, the inspector will have made unaccompanied visits before, and maybe during the inquiry. However, there will be accompanied site visits either during or after the inquiry. These will be arranged so that representatives of the local authority and objectors can attend. Normal rules of engagement for all site visit will prevail. Site visits pertaining to the Local Plan Inquiry, may be quite divorced in time from your hearing, and this can pose problems. If you, or your representative, cannot attend the site visit, then send the inspector a list of items which you would like him to look at on his rounds. Given the ground-rules, this can be just as effective.

The Inspector's Recommendations

Unlike the report compiled by the Panel after an EIP, that prepared on objections to a local plan includes the written objections, not just the evidence and proceedings of the actual inquiry. More important, however, is the similarity to the Panel's Report: it contains only *recommendations* to the local authority, not a verdict such as inspectors issue after an appeal in which they take the decision in lieu of the Secretary of State. (see Fig.11) That said, the LPA has to consider carefully any recommendations made, and have good planning grounds for not accepting each of them.

The report will be submitted direct to the local authority, and is likely to be published within two months of its arrival. It is important to keep track of the final stages of the local plan procedure, as much may change after the inquiry, and you could lose any ground you gained in the inspector's report. If the LPA does not publish the report immediately, the contents of the inspector's report may get leaked to the local press before the council has had time to deliberate the findings. If you have persuaded the inspector to your way of thinking, keep up the pressure on the elected members to make sure they take the same line. You could find yourself up against a developer who has decided to take advantage of the local authority's original proposal for a given type of development in the Local Plan, and they will be powerful opponents during the ensuing battle over Modifications.

Modifications

The same procedure is followed as that pertaining to the Modification of the structure plan i.e. you have six weeks in which to make objection, but this time lobbying has to be directed at the relevant committees and key elected members of the LPA. Make sure that the LPA has informed all the statutory consultees (see Appendix V) about the proposed modifications e.g. if the housing has been moved from Site A to Site B, it may be necessary to involve English Nature because there is an SSSI in the vicinity of Site B, whereas there was no SSSI near Site A. Enlist the support of other organisations and elected bodies in the vicinity if their interests are affected. If the Modifications are substantially different from the deposited plan, you should campaign for a modifications inquiry to review the new evidence: put your case to the Chief Planner of the Government Office for your region (see Map 2 & Fig.2).

Involving the Secretary of State

If you are still unsuccessful, try to involve the Secretary of State, particularly if the issue is an infringement of national policy e.g. Green Belt or the urban regeneration of a large area. The first step is to inform the Government Office, and hopefully they will prevent the LPA proceeding to adoption by making a Direction under Regulation 23 of S.I.1991 No.2794: this is similar in effect to an Article 14 Direction in development control. The Secretary of State may 'sit on' the plan for some time, perhaps awaiting the outcome of relevant appeals, and then either take the brakes off, or direct that the plan be modified, or call in the plan for his/her own approval under s.44 of the 1990 TCP Act.

If agricultural land is involved it might be possible to persuade the Secretary of State for Agriculture, via your local MAFF office, to request that the Secretary of State for the Environment calls in the proposal.

Adoption

As with the structure plan, the final stage in the procedure is the adoption of the plan. If there is a dramatic change of government policy or a major event during these late stages it is probably better that the plan be adopted and then consider possible alterations to accommodate the changes. Either way, in order to adopt a plan the authority gives 28 days notice of its 'disposition to adopt' the plan. This is your last chance to get the Secretary of State to call in the plan. The plan comes into force on the date specified in the notice.

DEVELOPMENT PLANS: ROADS

The classification of roads is confusing. Motorways can be local-authority built and run, but are nearly always DTp roads (in England), the responsibility of its Highways Agency.

All motorways (blue signs) and primary routes (green signs) together form the 'National Motorway and Primary Route Network', for traffic routing purposes. Primary Routes include all trunk roads and the more important local authority-run 'A' roads. 'A' roads with white signs are a lesser breed, called 'principal roads'. All lesser roads, 'B' numbered or smaller 'C' and 'D' (numbered for official use but unnumbered on signs and yellow on OS maps), are a local authority's. These make up 96% of total road length. If in doubt about the lineage of a road, your local authority highways department will be able to tell you.

The Structure Plan Key Diagram shows its area's road system in rather diagrammatic form, whereas Part 1 of UDPs do not usually have similar maps. This, or another plan in the document, may show a 'county strategic road network'. This concept must be treated warily. *Strategic* is a term used to enhance importance, often misleadingly:

it has no status in national, or DTp road planning. There was a time when the DTp used to use the phrase 'strategic road network' for its own major schemes, but their use of the term had no connection with counties' use, but this confusing practice appears to have ceased.

A 'County Primary Network' may alternatively be defined. Again this can mislead; it is rarely the same as the 'primary routes' defined by DTp. By defining other roads in this way the local authority may be seeking to qualify them for DTp funds. Clearly it is a matter of keeping one's wits about one! A road's designation can be opposed in structure plan procedures.

The DTp has until now imposed its road schemes on a local authority area from Olympian heights and it has been impossible to contest their existence through the development plan process. But for local authority roads there is a role for planning.

> *'The plan should set out any major improvements to the network proposed by the local highway authority and its broad policy on priorities for minor improvements. In this way the* need *for strategic local road schemes can be* investigated *as the structure plan is prepared.'*
>
> PPG 12, para. 5.28

> *'In the case of local authority road schemes of a strategic nature, shown in the structure plan, consideration in the local plan process should normally be limited to detailed alignment* because the need will already have been examined.
>
> PPG 12, para. 5.31

On the other hand, PPG 12 adds:

> *'If detailed consideration of the scheme were to reveal that* it would cause unacceptable damage to the environment, *consideration could be given to its deletion or relocation, together with associated changes in development. In the case of local authority road schemes of a non-strategic nature (ie. not in the structure plan) the local plan procedures provide the means to examine* both *the need in relation to the development proposed* and *the line the road is to take.'*
>
> PPG 12, para. 5.31 *(emphases added)*

This guidance, PPG 12, makes the best of a confusing relationship between roads and structure and local plans. The use of the future perfect passive tense in para. 5.31, *the need will already have been examined*, which is curious, not to say rare, in official planning documents, highlights the difficulty inherent in the system PPG 12 envisages. In practice, structure plan procedures do not examine the need for individual road schemes; they tend to include schemes already proposed. As locations of housing and employment within districts are no longer specified in most structure plans, these being left to district-wide local plans, a structure plan cannot easily assess the need for a road. Moreover, discussion of transport at EIPs is normally discursive and individual road schemes are not usually able to be debated at this level.

Nor are local road schemes fully covered in Local Plan or UDP procedures. These define routes for new roads in most cases, but often only in general terms, such as on a 1:50,000 scale map in rural areas. Only where the road is directly related to other proposed land-uses, for example as boundary of new housing, is its actual route going to be fixed by the Local Plan. The Local Plan does not define width, standard or junction type. But a road scheme involving new alignment would not be proposed without appearing in the Local Plan.

Local Plan Inquiries are moreover long and complex enough without taking detailed evidence on a new road's alignment. In strict terms they are designating the land shown in the plan as suitable for use as a road. Recent District-wide Local Plan Inspector's Reports have invariably passed general comments on the route of a road shown in the Plan, but stated that the right place to settle this and other details is the deemed planning application, and compulsory purchase order and side roads order (CPO/SRO) procedures. This is despite the principle of primacy of the Plan, established by s.54A of the 1990 TCP Act.

The revised *Notes for Guidance for Inspectors holding Inquiries under the Highways Act* (Planning Inspectorate 1994) at para. 39 covers these relationships in some detail. It shows that unless the new road has been debated in full detail at the Local Plan inquiry, all relevant arguments can be deployed in objections at a later CPO/SRO Inquiry, even if a deemed planning application has also been granted.

Nevertheless, it is always desirable to voice opinions on road schemes as early as you can, and before official minds are set on a particular scheme or route. It is best to think of the road planning process as continuous, with the public keeping and eye on what officials are doing at all stages. Ward councillors can be invaluable if involved, notably for their right of access to chief officers.

Also look out for Motorway Service Area (MSA) proposals. The procedure for these is summarised in Annex A of PPG 13. These are now private-sector developments, and the Government has told local authorities that they should have policies to handle such proposals in Local Plans. Recent experience shows that designations such as National Parks, AONBs, Areas of High Landscape Value, Special Landscape Areas and Green Belt are powerful controls on MSAs.

Campaigner's Guide to Road Proposals, CPRE 1993
PPG 12, Development Plans and Regional Planning Guidance
PPG 13, Transport
PPG 9 Nature Conservation
Notes for Guidance of Independent Inspectors holding Inquiries under the Highways Act (available only from DoE Planning Inspectorate Agency)

UNITARY DEVELOPMENT PLANS

UDPs have been prepared by the metropolitan boroughs since the demise of the metropolitan counties in the wake of the feud between Mrs Thatcher and Ken Livingstone in the mid eighties. Now although the number of UAs has increased in the more urbanized parts of the shire counties, there are in fact only five more actually producing UDPs (see Appendix X). Nonetheless, west of Offa's Dyke, UAs have taken over local government and each will be producing a UDP.

UDPs are comprehensive, with policies on minerals and waste, as well as land use planning. UDPs are comprised of both the strategic and detailed aspects of planning, in Parts I & II respectively. The former is a written statement of the authorities general policies for the development and use of land in their area. The latter also contains a written statement, a map on an Ordnance survey base showing the location of the proposals, and a reasoned justification relating Part II to Part I. It should be noted that the two stages proceed simultaneously, rather than Part I occurring before Part II in the way that a structure plan is supposed to preface a local plan. The examination of Part I issues does, however, precede the detailed proposals of Part II.

The Procedure for a UDP is analogous to a Local Plan. With regard to the inquiry, therefore, anyone who objects has a right to appear, and this includes those whose objection is to Part I: there is a contrast between having to lobby for a place at the table in an EIP, and having it as a right in a UDP. In practice it does tend to be the national interest groups ranging from the house-builders to the Friends of the Earth which pitch their objection at a strategic level, but it is open to anyone with the imagination to see the issue at a borough wide level, to partake in the proceedings.

The Inspectorate are introducing round table sessions to deal with key issues during Part I e.g. the housing allocation. All those with views on the subject can attend. They prepare position paper beforehand which are read by all parties, and the inspector prepares an agenda for discussion. Only one speaker is allowed from each group, but they may well be flanked by other members of their team: legal eagles are to be seen hovering but strangely silent. Such sessions have been found to aid the clarification and understanding of the issues for all concerned. The residual areas of dispute are then subjected to the inquiry procedure where cross-examination can be used to test the evidence. So here again there is a difference from the EIP. Part II tends to attract the most attention from third parties, and advances from topic to topic like a local plan inquiry, with the inspector making cross references between the two Parts of the UDP.

If there are found to be problems with that which is proposed in either Part, then the inspector can integrate the two by making the necessary adjustments in his recommendations e.g. problems with a major housing site which come to light during Part 2, mean that the housing allocation in Part I has to be met by other means. The inspector's report will set out the problem and suggest Modifications to the UDP, but it will be up to the unitary authority to choose a site either from amongst those put forward during the UDP process, or sites which have come on stream since it started. Their choice will then feature in their Modifications to the UDP: these are then advertised, and objections to the Modifications considered. The UDP inquiry may have to be re-opened for the examination of new evidence relating to a site not considered at the original inquiry. In the case of problems with Part I of a UDP, the Secretary of State may decide to hold an EIP, as the usual local plan inquiry is not deemed appropriate.

The UDP then progresses through the stages to final adoption, set out on pages 40, 41 above.

Policy Appraisal & the Environment, (London, HMSO, 1991)
Environmental Appraisal of Development Plans: a Good Practice
Guide, (London,HMSO, 1993)
Planning Policy Guidance Note No 12 (PPG12)
Development Plans: what you need to know (DoE)
Planning Charter Standards, (London, DoE) Part One
A Campaigner's Guide to Local Plans, (London, CPRE, 1992)
A Campaigner's Guide to Minerals, (London, CPRE 1996)

REDRESS

If anyone wishes to challenge the validly of a structure plan, the various denominations of local plans, or a unitary development plan, then there is provision for doing it under the 1990 TCP Act, s.287. For more information see Section V on Redress.

Section II

Control of Development

GROUNDWORK

Before discussing what happens when an application arrives, it is useful to understand the foundations of the system. Since 1947 it has been necessary to apply for permission to develop land. It is noteworthy that certain activities are not considered to involve 'development' at all (s.55 1990 Act). For example: minor alterations and maintenance of buildings; road maintenance; inspecting, repairing, and renewing sewers, pipes, cables etc.; the enjoyment of your own home and its grounds; and the use of land and associated buildings, for agriculture or forestry. Beyond these special cases, lies 'development': this is divided into two distinct categories: 'operations', and 'change of use' of premises or land. If anyone is in doubt as to whether their proposal involves either category of 'development' they are advised to ask their local LPA, sending in full particulars, and if their proposal does indeed constitute 'development', they will be issued with a Certificate of Lawful Use. (see P&C Act 1991, s.10, alias 1990 TCP Act, s.192,193,194).

Operations

So called 'Operations' encompass such diverse activities as building, engineering and mining, or other operations in, on, over or under land (s.55 1990 TCP Act). How do you decide what is a building? This apparently naive question has exercised some of the best minds in the land, and been found to include any artificial structure or erection which is intended to be a permanent addition to the scene, even if it is mobile. Thus everyman's understanding of a building has been augmented by mobile cranes, radio masts, flag-poles, and hoardings. The point is illustrated by shelters for livestock: those anchored to the ground by foundations, and furnished with such mod cons as piped water, have been held by the Courts to qualify as buildings, whilst pig arks and movable poultry houses have failed to make the grade.

Until 1991 demolition was not controlled, with the honourable exception of listed buildings and buildings in conservation areas. Clearly a hole in the townscape could have as adverse an effect on visual amenity as erecting an eyesore, so under the 1991 P&C Act (s.13), 'building operations' were augmented to include demolition, rebuilding, structural alterations and rebuilding, and other operations normally undertaken by a person carrying on business as a builder. Needless to say, fun could be had in Court defining what is a normal operation for a builder, and, indeed, 'Who is the builder?'

As if regretting the rash move made under the 1991 P&C Act, subsequent Directions have been made by the Secretary of State to limit the infringement on our liberty to demolish buildings by having to apply for planning permission. The results would do credit to the Medieval Schoolmen. If you are concerned about the possible demolition of a building, you would be well advised to consult a planning lawyer because there are so many pitfalls: amongst them are the provisions not only of the 1991 P&C Act, but also permitted development rights and Article 4 Directions, and the provision of the Town & Country Planning (Demolition – Description of Buildings) Direction 1995, not to mention those demolitions classified as engineering rather than building operations.

Owing to the idiosyncratic definition of building operations, it includes many activities which could fall into the category of engineering operations e.g. bridge construction. However, engineering is an equally wide term, limited in this case to civil engineering by the phrase 'In, on, over or under land'. In practice it means making a physical alteration to land, and can include such diverse operations as constructing an access road, excavating for a swimming pool, removing earthworks, and laying out a golf course.

Mining operations remain undefined but 'mineral' includes virtually anything except that which is 'animal' or 'vegetable'. The removal of any substance from the land is treated as mining: thus, in addition to extracting minerals from the earth, it includes reworking spoil heaps, and even the proceeds of a wild urge to dig up the railway embankment. There is also a commercial dimension to this: cutting peat for domestic use is excluded from control, whereas cutting it for sale is treated as a mining operation. The winning and working of minerals is a subject in itself, within the planning system, and controlled by a distinct body of policy in the form of the MPGs (see Appendix I).

DEVELOPMENT BY
LOCAL AUTHORITIES

Local authorities have never been absolved from the need to obtain planning permission for their own development. However, prior to the Regulations introduced in 1992 (S.I.1992/1492), they were only required to adhere to a simplified procedure: basically they had to first resolve to seek planning permission of themselves, then publicize and consult on the application, and finally, pass a second resolution if they wished to carry out the development. This brought deemed consents into disrepute, so in July 1992 the system changed: the reader will judge whether, in practice, any material improvement will have been achieved.

Before discussing the new Regulations, a few preliminaries need to be considered. If the LPA is also a highway authority, certain maintenance and improvement works are not deemed to be 'development'. The benefits of the planning system also accrue to LPAs i.e. they have the same rights as the rest of us in terms of the Use Classes Order (see Appendix II) and Permitted Development (Fig.5): with regard to the latter, Part 12 allows all manner of small scale development on LPA property. If in doubt about whether a planning application is necessary, the LPA, like the rest of us, can apply for a Certificate of Lawful Use, except that their application has to be made to the Secretary of State, rather than themselves. If an LPA erroneously proceeds with a development without an application, then the Secretary of State can issue an Enforcement and/or Stop Notice: it may be that he was goaded into this by enraged third parties. Their only other course of action is via judicial review (see Section V).

Now for developments which actually require a planning application. The scope of the 1992 Regulations is set out in Regulation 2. It applies to Parts III, VII and VIII of the 1990 TCP Act i.e. development control, enforcement and various amenity provisions. There are exceptions if the land lies within the territory of national parks or Urban Development Corporations.

Regulation 4 applies in situations where the local authority does not intend to carry out the development itself, or with another party, or where the application would normally be determined by another LPA e.g. a county council receiving an application from a district council. All other applications are treated in the normal way. Regulation 4 enables local authorities to dispose of land with the benefit of planning permission.

Regulation 3 of the 1992 regime applies to cases where the local authority wishes to develop land in its ownership, or in that owned jointly with another party. With regard to the latter the local authority involvement has to be *significant*: otherwise Regulation 4 applies. The resulting planning permission is 'personal' to the local authority, and its partner (if any). Application is made in the same way as for any other person, even down to the application fee, ES (if any), consultation, publicity and imposing conditions!

Thus constructive or adverse comment is given an airing, but the local authority appears to remain judge and jury in its own cause: a safety precaution is supposed to be provided by the fact that the planning application comes from another department, outside of planning, so that those responsible for the development are not taking the decision. Of course, the application may be called in by the Secretary of State – but that has its own problems. (see p. 77)

Town & Country Planning, General Regulations 1992, S.I.1992/1492
DoE Circular 19/92, Annex 1

Material Change of Use

The second aspect of development is 'material change of use'. Two examples are given in the 1990 TCP Act, in respect of the sub-division of houses and the vexed issue of 'land raising'. If a house, hitherto used as a family dwelling, is converted into separate units for multi-occupation, there is a 'material change' because the inherent character of a house is transformed. Similarly obliging landowners, willing to accept waste, minerals or refuse on payment of a tidy sum, can no longer claim that raising the level of land is just an agricultural practice designed to promote drainage: it is material change requiring planning permission.

The concept of material change of use has given rise to much litigation: each word has been weighed carefully. Let us begin by looking at 'Material': it must mean substantial rather than just trivial; there must be physical implications; and it must be relevant in planning terms i.e. the amenity of the neighbourhood or placing an additional strain on public services. Secondly, there must be an identifiable 'Change' – therein lies the act of development: each change requires a separate permission even if it is from A to B and back again to A. Thirdly, it includes an intensification of the same use.

In 1987 the Use Classes Order (UCO) needed radical reform in order to bring it into line with the realities of life in the latter part of the twentieth century e.g. premises for financial services, fast food outlets, and premises for hi-tech industries. As can be seen from Appendix II, the 1987 UCO is divided into four parts:

Part A   shops and other 'high street' businesses;

Part B   offices, research laboratories, and industrial processes;

Part C   housing, hotel and hostels;

Part D   premises providing public services, and leisure facilities.

 GENERAL DEVELOPMENT ORDERS

The concept of a General Development Order was first introduced in the 1919 Housing and Town Planning etc. Act. Until that point planning was confined to what we would now call the development plan process: the orderly expansion of towns through the laying out of new estates. There was no means of dealing with individual cases except by demolition by the LPA of development contrary to the scheme. The General Development Order (GDO) was introduced as a means of providing a framework for interim development control. As with so much legislation affecting the environment, measures devised by local government set the pattern for national legislation in due course. The 1932 TCP Act gave Ministers the power to make an General Interim Development Order, but it was still confined to new development. In 1943 interim development control was extended throughout the country.

However, it was not until the seminal 1947 TCP Act that this system of interim development control was converted into the mechanism for controlling day to day development and bestowing permitted development rights. By 1995 the GDO had become so complex that it was was split in two: the General Permitted Development Order (GPDO), which focuses on the ever expanding catalogue of Permitted Development; and the General Development Procedure Order (GDPO) which deals with the process of development control from application through to enforcement and appeals. These two statutory instruments are the key to much of the development control process, even through their abbreviations are a recipe for confusion. Tip – Keep your eye on the position of the 'D'.

Not all uses are catered for in the UCO. Those falling outside, in what is known as a *sui generis,* are a motley collection, all of which require special consideration but for widely different reasons: from theatres, which are to be safeguarded from closing, to Formula 1 race-tracks, amusement arcades and scrap-metal merchants, not to mention users of radioactive and hazardous substances, any of which may not be considered to be an ideal neighbour. On the other hand, one's beautiful launderette, in 1987, was accepted as a normal part of life, and made it back from *sui generis* to the high street in Part A of the UCO. Now there are proposals to create a special use class for Rural Business.

Whereas planning permission for operations will include change of use, the same courtesy does not apply in reverse: a grant of planning permission for a change of use does not entitle the owner to alter his property in any significant fashion.

Permitted Development

Given that everything is caught within the net of 'development' which is not beyond the Pale of s.55 1990 TCP Act, the burden laid on the planning system would be excessive were it not for a class of development which is allowed without having to apply for planning permission. This is known in the trade as Permitted Development, and defined in detail by 1995 GPDO, Article 3, Schedule 2: this is divided into a number of Parts (see Fig. 5). Anyone who is uncertain as to whether their proposed activity constitutes development which is permitted under Sch.2 would be well advised to research the subject, and take professional advice, because it is of immense intricacy.

Of interest is to see how the 1988 GDO has been updated in the 1995 version in terms of categories of Permitted Development: satellite dishes have appeared in Part 1; the dangers of surreptitious housing development, and the existence of industrial agriculture have been recognised in Part 6, and safeguards introduced; the privatised utilities have made their debut in Part 17; the possible existence of toll roads and driver information systems, have been acknowledged in Parts 29 and 30; the purveyors of virtual reality and other telecommunications equipment are catered for in Parts 24 and 25; and, post 1991 P&C Act, demolition is allowed under strict controls in Part 31.

Another underlying trend of the last fifteen years has been to place as few burdens as possible on development. Thus as much development as possible is 'permitted'. Of particular note, in this

Figure 5 Permitted Development

S.I. 1995 No. 418

**TOWN AND COUNTRY PLANNING, ENGLAND
AND WALES**

The Town and Country Planning (General Permitted
Development) Order 1995

SCHEDULE 2

PERMITTED DEVELOPMENT

PART

regard, are the Use Classes, which make another appearance as Part 3 of 1995 GPDO. We have already seen that a 'material change of use' constitutes 'development', but within the classes set out in detail in the Use Classes Order (S.I.1987 No.764), mobility is permitted (see Appendix II). Thus one can change a shop from one type of retail outlet to another (Part A1), an office into a laboratory (Part B1), or a concert hall into a dance hall (Part D2), without having to apply for permission to change the Use. The 1988 GDO introduced flexibility between classes, but only in certain directions, thus creating a ratchet effect: this trend has been continued in the 1995 GPDO. In practice this means that when a given use class is applied for, one has to have half an eye on how the development could metamorphose in years to come, without an application for a change of use. On the other hand the system is designed so that uses change from the more contentious to the less contentious, so that there should be an improvement in amenity, should it happen.

Permitted development rights can be withdrawn or limited by four things: the need for an environmental assessment of the project, Article 4 Directions; conditions attached to planning consents (see Appendix IX); and SACs and SPAs.

Town & Country Planning (General Permitted Development) Order S.I.1995, No.418
Town & Country Planning (General Development Procedure) Order S.I.1995, No.419
DoE Circular 9/95, General Development Order Consolidation 1995
DoE Circular 3/95, Permitted Development & Environmental Assessment

DEVELOPMENT CONTROL:
POLLUTION

Use Classes Order:

An updated version of the 1987 UCO is to be found in Appendix II. However, industrial works dealing with dangerous pollutants are beyond the UCO, amongst the other unusual or unneighbourly uses of *sui generis*. These polluting works fall into three groups: hazardous substances, radio-active substances, and works under the Alkali Act.

Hazardous substances are defined in the Planning (Hazardous Substances) Regulations 1990 (S.I. 1992 656), include such well know household products as arsenic, ammonia, formaldehyde, and lead, but also many others whose names require private rehearsal before public utterance. This use class is concerned with works storing and processing substances which could, in quantities and above specified limits, present the hapless public with risks of a major fire, explosion or toxic hazard.

Apart from uranium, other radio-active substances are defined in the Radio-active substances Act 1993, Sch.1, include actinium, lead, polonium, protactinium, radium, radon, and thorium. Those storing, using and disposing of radio-active material are subject to strict control through an inspectorate of the Environment Agency which supervises a system of registration.

Works under Alkali Act 1906, which appear still to be around.

Permitted Development:

As has been said on p. 54, development is 'permitted' within the respective categories of the UCO: this appears, in another guise, as Article 3 of the GPDO (see Fig.5). Nineteen ninety five saw the end of the special use classes, B4–B7: in our de-industrialized country. As can be seen from Appendix II, classes B4–B6 are reminiscent of the nineteenth century, and one requires a strong stomach to peruse the list under B7. In 1995 all these works were transferred into class B2 (see S.I.1995 No.297). The idea was to streamline the system and leave pollution control agencies free to get on with it.

The problem is that although these uses are declining nationally, there are serious amenity problems for those concerned with the remainder: just as the unemployment rate feels like 100% if it affects YOU, so it is worrying and unpleasant for those likely to find themselves neighbours of such plants. The wider problems of public amenity are not really taken on board by the pollution control authorities, and they will not come before the planning officers and elected members unless there is development requiring permission. It might have been preferable to create one special industrial category for all, polluting industries, which would include those not included at all such as petroleum and pharmaceuticals. On the other hand the worst offenders are still under wing of the Alkali Acts in the *sui generis* category: these include industrial processes under the regime of Integrated Pollution Control (IPC) imposed by the Environment Agency, and those under the watchful eye of Local Authority Air Pollution Control (LAAPC).

Under the 'ratchet' provision whereby users can progress from B2 'general industrial' to B1 'business' without having to apply for a change of use (see DoE Circular 13/87), industries can only migrate to the B1 class, provided they are thoroughly house-trained: (B1) being a use which can be carried out in any residential area without detriment to the amenity of that area by reason of noise, vibration, smell, fumes, smoke, soot, ash, dust or grit.

Looking at the list of the erstwhile special industrial uses, rapid absorption into the business class seems unlikely.

The 1987 Use Classes Order ranged:

'in ascending order of environmental impact, from the mildly offensive (for example pickling metal in acid) to the downright disgusting (for example the breeding of maggots from putrescible animal matter).

Professor Malcolm Grant,
Planning & Environmental Law Bulletin, March 1995

As can be seen from Fig.5, Part 6, agriculture is largely exempt from planning control under permitted development rights. In recent years this has been curtailed somewhat by bringing the more industrial aspects of agri-business within the planning system by requiring Environmental Assessment for some of the more intensive methods of food production (see Appendix III, Sch.2). However, for much of its activities, agriculture still enjoys a certain amount of leeway, but that does not mean that it is totally off the hook: MAFF has a code of good agricultural practice relevant to such operations as the spreading of slurry from livestock units etc.

Article 4 Directions

An Article 4 Direction can be made which withdraws some or all permitted development rights: nevertheless it should be stressed that an Article 4 direction does not rule out certain actions, but merely has the effect that property owners have to apply for planning permission instead of enjoying an automatic right to do that which is permitted. LPAs are warned that applications which are approved, without a condition covering the subject matter of the Article 4 Direction, could give rise to a claim for compensation for loss or damage incurred by having to comply with it.

Article 4 Directions can be made by the relevant planning authority e.g. one pertaining to conservation areas or temporary uses by the district council, or one concerned with waste disposal by county council. Alternatively, they can be imposed by the Secretary of State. With regard to restricting development rights over minerals, Article 7 directions are more likely to be used by the relevant LPA.

LPAs are not obliged to consult owners before making an Article 4 Direction. Having done it, they should notify owners, or, if this is impractical, because, say, of the size of the area, they should publish a notice in the local paper. Article 4 Directions apply to potential or incomplete development, not to permissions once given, so it is not a way of rescinding planning permission. It may only be used where there is a real and specific threat to 'an interest of acknowledged importance' e.g. a Listed Building or a nature conservation site of international importance. With regard to certain types of Permitted Development e.g. agriculture and forestry, LPAs have rights of *prior approval*, so should make full use of these before embarking on an Article 4 direction.

In the following instances LPAs may act swiftly, without prior notification of the Secretary of State:

a) Article 4 Directions are used most often to withdraw Permitted Development rights with regard to Parts 1 – 4: development within the curtilage of a dwelling house, minor operations, changes of use and temporary buildings and uses. The LPA may make such a move if it considers that there is a threat to the general amenity of an area or action is being taken by owners which is prejudicial to proper planning. Although the Article 4 Direction comes into effect immediately, it has to be confirmed by the Secretary of State within six months, or it lapses.

b) With regard to listed buildings or development within their curtilage, or a building deemed by the Secretary of State to be of architectural or historic interest, provided that it does not affect the Permitted Development rights of Statutory Undertakers.

Under the 1995 GPDO (Article 4(2)), LPAs have been given discretionary powers to withdraw permitted development rights with regard to houses, in conservation areas, where the permitted development would front onto a highway, motorway or open space. Home improvements which could be affected include satellite dishes, changes to the roof, the demolition of a wall, or the erection of a gate. No approval by the Secretary of State is necessary but the LPA is required to take on board responses to the notices served on individual properties, or to the legal notice in the local newspaper, before confirming the Article 4 Direction. Twenty eight days have to elapse before the Direction can be confirmed by the LPA, by means of either letter or another advertisement in the local paper.

You may be relieved to know that the existence of an Article 4 Direction does not prevent action in an emergency: there are all manner of 'get out' clauses lurking in Article (4) or amongst the Parts in Schedule 2 on Permitted Development.

If all this sounds fiendishly complicated, it is, so you are advised to consult both the literature and a lawyer!

The Town & Country Planning (General Permitted Development) Order 1995, S.I.418
DoE Circular 9/95, General Development Order Consolidation 1995 paras.24–27, and Appendix D.

STATUTORY UNDERTAKERS

Who are the ominously named 'statutory undertakers'? Once many of these services were run by the State but during the eighties they were privatised. However, they are deemed to remain statutory undertakers by virtue of the legislation which released them from State control. Whatever their history, the statutory undertakers are a motley crew. The 1990 TCP Act defined them, in s.262, as persons authorized to run transport services by land, sea and air. The GPDO 1995 added a few more services, like the Post Office, NRA (now Environment Agency), the Civil Aviation Authority, and the purveyors of water, gas and electricity. Much of their day to day activity, which may be allowable under the Planning Acts, is, in fact, controlled by their licences. However, that such privatised services are still deemed to be statutory undertakings, is, to say the least, food for thought.

Nevertheless, the statutory undertakers occupy a privileged position in the planning hierarchy. Connoisseurs of road works will not be surprised to learn that the street can be excavated in the good cause of inspecting, repairing and renewing sewers, mains, pipes, cables etc. without it even being categorised as 'development' (TCP Act 1990 s.55 (2c)). Then there are the occasions when statutory undertakers benefit from the immunity enjoyed by Government Departments (TCP Act 1990 s.268). For those activities which do qualify, many of them are exempt under Permitted Development rights. A glance at Fig.5 shows that many Parts are personal to a given statutory undertaker, and, they enjoy the general rights such as Parts 1,2, and 3. In addition, their Permitted Development rights may be augmented by local or private Acts of Parliament.

In sensitive locations, the rights under of these Parts can be withdrawn under an Article 4 direction. If you feel their privileged position is being abused, check with a lawyer before asking the local authority to impose an Article 4 Direction: as can be seen from the above, the Permitted Development rights of statutory undertakers are a complex business.

Types of Planning Permissions

Occasionally there is an instance of a condition restricting occupancy: to a given individual, that is a personal permission; a type of incumbent, such as an agricultural worker; or else the granting of a temporary permission, perhaps to see whether a new farm is really viable (see DoE Circular 11/95 paras. 93, & 108–112). Usually, however, planning permission runs with the land, regardless of who owns it at a given time. If the land is sold, therefore, the permission goes with it. Indeed the planning permission given to a property will be a major determinant in assessing its value when being sold. During the recession of the last few years it has not been unknown for planning applications to be lodged, and appeals fought in order to raise the value of a piece of land owned by a company which is in the hands of the receivers: there is no intention of actually laying a brick in the near future, but it would improve the book price of the company's assets if the value of a given property were to be enhanced by obtaining a permission which means that someone could make more money from it in due course e.g. permission for an industrial estate on a disused airfield.

Planning applications come in two varieties: outline and full. Outline applications leave certain details to be resolved at a later date. These are known as *reserve matters* and are strictly specified on the application form. Reserve matters are restricted to siting, design, external appearance, access and landscaping. An outline application may omit one or more of these issues at this stage, but it is open to the LPA to insist that details be supplied on all or any of these matters within a month of the receipt of the application. There can be a third type of application: that for approval of reserve matters subsequent to an outline approval.

From the point of view of the applicant, an outline application enables him to 'take the temperature of the water' without the expense of preparing detailed plans, the payment of the full fee, and the time spent arguing over details with planning officers and others. Thus a quick result over the principle of development can be achieved which may be important in terms of landing the contract in the first place. In a big scheme it may well be that the detailed requirements of the prospective client is unknown during the initial stages. Nonetheless, it may be that the local authority will be unwilling to determine the application unless enough detail is provided for them to make a proper judgement. If the applicant is unwilling or unable to provide it, then he is at liberty to go to appeal on grounds of non-determination (1990 TCP Act s.78 (2)(a)).

A moment's thought will make one realise that completing an individual permission using this 'drip-feed' method can take years, especially if the outline permission and also certain reserve matters go to appeal en route (see Fig.15, Example 1.). Whilst it is accurate to say that one cannot dispute the principle of the original outline permission once it is granted, there are instances where one can argue that this interpretation of the reserve matters goes against the spirit of the original permission, and therefore effectively prevent development for the duration of the permission. Although wording outline permissions so that they are difficult to fulfil, is frowned on by DoE, quick witted objectors can make it very difficult.

Portia:	*"A pound of that same merchant's flesh is thine:*
	The court awards it and the law doth give it:
	Tarry a little: there is something else.
	This bond doth give thee no jot of blood...
	Merchant of Venice Act IV, Scene I

The LPA have the power to impose conditions in the granting of planning permission. With an outline approval all conditions, which relate to the proposed development, must be imposed at that stage. General conditions may not be added at the stage of approving reserved matters, although conditions may be imposed where it relates to the carrying out of that specific matter. Having achieved an outline permission, reserve matters can be submitted singly or in groups, provided all reserve matters are dealt within three years of the outline approval. The actual development to which the permission relates must start within five years of the outline approval or two years of the last reserve matter (1990 TCP Act s.92 (2)a,b.). Furthermore it is possible to have more than one set of reserve matters, and therefore more than one approval. You could be spoilt for choice. It is, therefore, essential to check up which set is being discussed, or implemented when the time comes.

Twin-Tracking

Another complication is twin-tracking. These do not exist just to trip up the unwary at planning appeals, although there are times when one could be forgiven for thinking so. The difficulty is that once a developer has gone to appeal over non-determination, that particular planning application passes on to the 'Secretary of State' i.e. the appropriate Government Office (see Fig.2). This means that the LPA and developer cannot continue to negotiate over that application. Therefore an identical application is submitted at the same time, or a few weeks after the first, so that they can continue negotiating. The theory is that if they reach a satisfactory conclusion on the second application, the appeal is withdrawn on the first, but, if not, battle commences.

Local people are liable to feel aggrieved if negotiations reach a 'satisfactory' conclusion after the appeal has been heard, and the Inspector refuses the appeal shortly after the LPA has granted permission. The key as to whether this is deemed to be 'unreasonable', in a judicial sense, depends on whether the two applications are still identical: if the second one has been amended, with maybe certain conditions attached, then it is deemed to be sufficiently different from the original application which the inspector refused. If not there could be a case for judicial review, but you will need an opinion from a lawyer, well versed in the subject, before embarking on such a course.

Repeated Applications

It was not unknown for developers to abuse the planning system by submitting very similar planning applications in the hope of 'wearing down' LPAs and third party objectors. This practice was curtailed, in the most genteel fashion, by the 1991 P&C Act, s.17: it gives a LPA power to 'decline to determine an application for development' if:

a) within the period of two years, the Secretary of State has refused a similar application which he has already refused, having called it in for his own determination under s.77 1990 TCP Act;

b) within two years, the Secretary of State has refused a similar application on appeal (s.78(2) 1990 Act).

c) if this application has not yet gone to inquiry, but, in the opinion of the LPA, there has been no *significant* change, in the relevant part of the development plan, or pertinent material considerations, since the last refusal or dismissal (see (a) & (b) above).

Clearly argument is liable to hinge on the similarity of past and current applications, and the significance of any changes in circumstances.

With regard to inexperienced would-be developers, it means that they should take good advice from those with professional knowledge and *experience* in the field of planning law and policy. Otherwise they could find that, if their application is refused because its substantive justification was inadequate and/or the procedures were mismanaged, a perfectly good scheme may languish for a couple of years, which may cause hardship to those involved, especially if it is a retrospective application. On the other hand, from the point of view of the LPA and third parties, the two year interval gives some breathing space, but it is not long for all concerned to accumulate the funds to fight yet another battle.

MONITORING AN APPLICATION

From what was said in the last chapter you may have the impression that participation in the local plan obviates the need for input into the development plan process. Unfortunately, this is not so. Firstly, the development plan process takes time, and decisions on individual applications cannot be held up until the relevant plan is adopted. Thus the likelihood is that whenever an application arrives, there is a plan grinding its way through the system: the rule is that the nearer it is to adoption, the greater the weight it has (PPG 1 1992 para.33) but until formal adoption the old plan is still the extant plan.

The plan, therefore, may not be up to date, and all manner of factors, known in the trade as 'material considerations', may now have greater weight. Secondly, DoE discourages rigid plans so there is usually some room for manoeuvre on the part of developers, the LPA and objectors. Thirdly, there is scope for discretion in interpreting policies and according weight to material considerations – otherwise how would lawyers and land use professionals make a living? Thus, although getting your views incorporated into the development plan is a great advantage in the long term, it should not be seen as the end of your involvement.

Publicity

How do you know if **that** application has arrived? Basically the bigger the scheme the more notice one has of its coming. It is likely to be greeted by banner headlines in the the local press, and really big developments make it into the regional and national media. You may get early warning of a development for which an Environmental Assessment (EA) is required: amongst the matters covered by the Environmental Statement (ES) could be the impact on the affected population (See Appendix III). Sometimes developers will embark on their own public participation exercises, but not infrequently these descend into pubic relations junkets, which can totally alienate the local community. For smaller scale proposals, you may be informed about them by a tame officer or conscientious councillor, or, indeed, the tenant of a landowner who is proposing development. Whatever the scale of the project, you cannot make formal representations before the application is registered, and its fees paid.

STATUTORY UNDERTAKERS

It is government policy that both normal planning applications and certain developments to be undertaken under Permitted Development rights, should be subject to publicity. Whether or not the latter type of proposal is advertised depends on whether it will have a substantial effect on the public. Developments which in one location might pass unnoticed, could have a significant effect on another, more sensitive, area e.g. a conservation area. A site notice might not be sufficient: neighbour notification might be more appropriate (see DoE Circular 15/92, para.33). Comments by the public are fed into discussion between the LPA and statutory undertaker when discussing how a proposal should be amended to overcome objections. With regard to planning applications, the normal procedures are followed.

June 17th 1992 was the end of an era. Until then there was a special category of applications called Bad Neighbour Developments which had to be widely advertised at the developer's expense. The list of such projects had their roots in nineteenth century public health hazards to which twentieth century nuisances had been added e.g. bingo halls and skyscrapers. In 1992 the terminology was sanitized into 'major' and 'minor' applications, although closer reading of the relevant circular (DoE Circular 15/92) shows the old public nuisances lurking beneath the surface. In addition, the LPA became largely responsible for publicity to the usual refrain that the increase in costs would be small, so there would be no extra funding from central government to help defray the additional expense: the novel twist was that any increases could be taken into account when application fees were raised. However amongst LPAs, the requirement to advertise in the press is considered both costly and ineffective: letters are cheaper and elicit more response. Unfortunately that is not what the GDPO requires, and fear of the Ombudsman keeps LPAs on the straight and narrow. Fig.6 sets out the statutory publicity for applications plus some explanation .

As has been said, many applicants indulge in twin-tracking but there is no duty laid upon the local authority to advertise both applications although any publicity should make it clear that twin tracking is occurring. More problematic is the fact that there is no

---

Figure 6   Statutory Publicity for Planning Applications

According to Article 8 of the GDPO 1995, the LPA must publicise an application for planning permission for the following types of development:

  a) that which is subject to Environmental Assessment, be it mandatory or discretionary;

  b) a departure from the development plan for the area;

  c) that which would affect the implementation of Part III of the Wildlife and countryside Act 1981.

The above are colloquially known as 'paragraph 2 applications', referring to Article 8 of the General Procedure Development Order 1995, alias S.I.419. The LPA is required to post a notice on site for 21 days and place a notice in a local newspaper.

  If the application does not fall into the 'paragraph 2' camp, it may still qualify as a 'major development'. Major developments are defined as follows: 10 or more dwellings; a housing site area in excess of 0.5 ha.; floorspace in excess of 1000 sq. m.; a building site greater than 1 ha.; activities relating to mineral extraction; and all developments concerning waste.

  In addition there is the grey area of applications which do not fall into the 'major' category, but nevertheless can give rise to public anxiety and therefore might just be worthy of advertising in the newspaper in addition to site notices or letters to neighbours. In terms of the Table, they could be denoted as *significant* minor development'. They are those: afflicting nearby property with noise, smell, vibration, dust etc.; attracting crowds etc. into a quiet area; keeping unsocial hours; introducing significant change e.g. tall buildings; reducing light, or privacy beyond nearby properties; affecting the setting of an ancient monument or archaeological site; affecting trees protected by preservation orders. The list is not meant to be exhaustive but indicative of this problematic area.

  With regard to proposals to develop mines, the applicants have to notify all those with land on top of the site, and post notices in every parish and community with land included in the application, whilst the LPA is obliged to notify the owners of other minerals on the site: the Coal Authority, the DTI for oil and gas; and the Crown Estate Commissioners for silver and gold (GDPO 1995, Article 16).

---

obligation to advertise changes to applications, or the submission of reserved matters following a grant of outline planning permission. Given that such information can be of great public interest, it is up to the LPA to decide whether further publicity is desirable on the grounds of:

  a) were previous objections substantial;

  b) are the changes significant;

  c) have the matters being considered changed;

  d) and/or are new people affected?

Thus deciding on the appropriate level of publicity is an art rather than a science, and you would be well advised to find out the interpretation of your LPA.

What Information is Available?

Full & Outline Applications

An application for *full* planning permission can contain details of the site, its area, parking provision, any proposed demolition, current use of land and buildings, the number of residential 'units', drainage, access to highways, trees, materials, together with plans and drawings.

Outline applications are allowed to omit details about the exact siting of the buildings, design, external appearance, access and landscaping. These can be left until a later date and filed under reserved matters. There does have to be a site plan, edged in red, with any adjoining land, owned by the applicant edged, in blue. Any illustrations must indicate whether they are to be taken as part of the application, otherwise developers can be hoist by their own petard and be expected to produce that glamorous structure when the time comes. If you are unhappy with an outline application because it is difficult to judge the impact of the proposed development, lobby your LPA and they may request the developer to lodge a full application. If the applicant does not agree he may go to appeal for non determination (1990 Act s.78).

If you have been alerted to a proposal by an outline application, it is up to you to watch the planning register for reserved matters, as

CROWN LAND

In the latter part of the twentieth century, it has been considered courteous to develop a 'shadow' planning regime for Crown Land. Now the Crown does consult the LPA, usually a district council or unitary authority, of its intentions, before proceeding with development or material changes of use. Where the development would be an issue of public concern, these courtesies even extend to advertising the proposal in order to elicit public opinion. Notices, like planning applications, come in two denominations, outline and full, and are entered in the planning register alongside applications from lesser mortals. The onus is on the LPA to publicise Crown proposals in the normal way unless there are security considerations which make it difficult. If there is a disagreement as to whether genuine security issues are involved, the dispute is referred to the DoE. Requests for information flow in the opposite direction from usual: the LPA has to form fill for the Ministry, and, needless to say, no fees are payable.

no notices will appear. The reserved matters may be dealt with in a single application or by drip feed through the system. It is even possible to file more than one set of reserved matters, in the hope of obtaining several permissions. So be vigilant.

Environmental Assessment

In the USA, during the sixties, people began to realise that investment decisions were taken on purely short term economic and technical grounds with no thought as to their environmental consequences. In 1969 Congress passed an Act which made impact assessments obligatory for all projects undertaken by the Federal Government, or requiring its blessing in the form of funds or licenses. In 1974 the Australian Federal Government passed a similar Act for the vetting of its projects. In this country we had no legislation on environmental assessment until the mid eighties, although large and controversial projects such as the Sullom Voe Oil Terminal in Scotland, and the proposal to develop the Vale of Belvoir coalfield, did have impact studies.

Having outlined, at the beginning of this Section, the areas which do not fall within 'planning', it is necessary to explain the somewhat confusing situation with regard to environmental assessment. As a result of Directive No.85/337/EEC, the Town & Country Planning (Assessment of Environmental Effects) Regulations were introduced in 1988. Amongst both the mandatory and discretionary subjects, in Schedule 1 and 2 respectively, there are those which are not controlled by LPAs, and no planning application has to be lodged, most notably in relation to: agriculture; forestry; salmon farming; power stations and land drainage etc. Instead, an application has to be made to the bodies which control these activities, and in some instances e.g. agriculture and forestry, it is triggered by the need for a grant rather than the need for permission, per se. In instances where bodies, such as the Crown Estate Commissioners, MAFF or the Forestry Commission, decide an EA is required, they consult the public, take the decision, and any appeals are made under the legislation pertaining to that activity.

An Environmental Assessment consists of three entities: the Environmental Statement produced by the applicant, the views of the statutory consultees, and the views of third parties. It is on the basis of these three components that the actual assessment (EA) is made by the appropriate decision-making body: the LPA, or the Secretary of State for the Environment, if the application is called-in or goes to appeal.

So, what sort of planning projects are subject to EA? The majority are to be found in the 1988 Regulations (S.I.1988 No.1199) but provision has now been made for the Government to add to the list as the need arises. Thus, in 1994, private toll roads, wind farms, coastal protection works and motorway service areas (MSAs) made their debut. In order to prevent accidental destruction under Permitted Development rights, these were withdrawn in 1995, in instances where the project as a whole is to be subject to EA (see DoE Circular 3/95, Permitted Development & Environmental Assessment). For Schedule 1 proposals, EA is mandatory but for those listed under Schedule 2 it is discretionary: a factor which could tip the balance would be the possible impact on an Site of Special Scientific Interest (SSSI), and International nature conservation sites such as SACs and SPAs. Basically Sch.2 projects,deemed worthy of EA, should be:

a) major projects of more than local importance;

b) occasionally for projects of a smaller scale which are proposed for particularly sensitive or vulnerable locations;

c) in a small number of cases for projects with unusually complex and potentially adverse environmental effects.

DoE Circular 15/88 Para.20

DoE Circulars 15/88 and 7/94 go on to detail the circumstances under which a Schedule 2 project would graduate to requiring an EA. The philosophy underlying all this advice is the minimization of costs for business. If the LPA ask for an EA, and the applicant is unhappy, they may apply to the Secretary of State for a ruling. If you feel strongly that an EA should be applied to a project, and the LPA will not ask for one, third parties can petition the Secretary of State and ask him to require one of the applicant. However, they will have to couch their arguments in terms of Circular 15/88. For borderline cases it has to be said that it helps if your MP is both sympathetic, and a senior member of the same political party as the Secretary of State and/or someone with political influence takes up your cause. Finally, there is also provision for the Secretary of State to require an EA at any stage before the application is determined, whether it is by the LPA or himself because the application has been called in or is the subject of an appeal.

If you are having a problem persuading your LPA or the Secretary of State of the significant environmental impact of a given proposal, and the need for an EA, you could cite the *Dutch Dykes* case, which came before the European Court of Justice (ECJ) in 1996.

The Court found that all projects which significantly affect the environment should have an EA. This is a 'catch all' provision which means that damaging proposals falling below the thresholds set by Member States, or outside the grant system could still be liable for EA. You can now challenge your LPA or the Secretary of State to state, in full, their reasons for not considering the impact to be significant. This means they will have to investigate the matter: they cannot just fob you off with a one line dismissal. If they do, then you can threaten them with judicial review (see Section V).

> *'However, although the second paragraph of Article 4(2) of the directive confers on Member States a measure of discretion to specify certain types of projects which will be subject to an assessment or establish the criteria or thresholds applicable, the limits of that discretion are to be found in the obligation set out in Article 2(1) that projects likely by virtue,* inter alia *of their nature, size or location, to have significant effects on the environment are to be subject to impact assessment.'*
> *Dutch Dykes*, Case C-72/95, heard on 24th Oct.1996 at the European Court of Justice (ECJ) in Luxembourg

If the developer recognises that his proposal is of the 'significance', which requires the EA process, *before* they register their application, they are rewarded by the local authority paying for their publicity (DoE Circular 15/92 para. 15), but if they have been forced into submitting an environmental statement later in the day, they have to pay for the statutory publicity themselves, as set out in DoE Circular 15/88.

How do you know that an ES accompanies an application? The community should have been consulted during the formulation of the ES if the project is likely to have any sizable effect on people in the locality: on the other hand socio-economic impact assessments are of variable quality, and people may not actually have been *asked* about the impact of the proposed development. Failing that, the site notices and advertisements will say where and when the ES is available for inspection, and its price. Applicants have been exhorted, by government, to make copies available at cost or at a 'reasonable' charge. Whilst one may not need to re-mortgage the house, some of them are not exactly cheap because they run to many volumes and are viewed by the applicants as finished reports rather than working documents. Their glossy production is an important part of a public relations exercise to sell the idea to the decision makers. On the other hand, it does provide details of a scheme at an earlier stage than might be the case, and thus give more time for critical appraisal, to those opposing a scheme: if they don't have the expertise themselves, then they must acquire it fast in order to make any useful contribution to the debate.

Whether an ES is volunteered or extracted under duress, what information does it contain when you get it? The subjects are outlined in the 1988 Regulations, Schedule 3. Briefly it is the effect of the proposal on humans, other living creatures, vegetation, the Platonic elements, climate, landscape, the cultural heritage, and material assets. The interaction between these factors may be important. The ES should propose actions to avoid or minimize any adverse effects which it identifies.

The problem for all those involved, be they developers, local government or third parties, has been the interpretation of Schedule 3. Over the years, concern has been expressed about the quality of ESs. Training people to produce ESs to an adequate standard has become a major industry of international dimensions. It has also been necessary to educate officers in LPAs on what they should expect of a good ES, and when to ask for more information. The Environmental Assessment Unit in the University of Manchester, the Planning Dept. of Oxford Brookes University, and the Institute of Environmental Assessment are central to this effort in Britain (see Appendix IV).

Just to add to life's rich pattern, the EC has just revised the Directive in the light of a Commission Report which highlighted the weaknesses in the original directive and the disparity in interpretation between Member States. The new Directive will tighten up on screening requirements (determining which projects require assessment) and scoping requirements (deciding what should be included in a given assessment). In addition it brings the Directive into line with new international obligations e.g. transboundary effects covered by the Espoo Convention signed by the EC in 1991.

Appendix III includes the list of projects, the selection criteria for discretionary projects, and the subjects to be included in an ES. On the subject of scoping, the Directive says that this should be done at an early stage by means of consultation between developer and LPA, although, it should be noted that this is usual practice in the UK. There is also provision for Member States to create a new procedure whereby EA requirements are aligned carefully to supply information for both planning and licensing functions with regard to Integrated Pollution Control.

The Town & Country Planning (Assessment of Environmental Effects) Regulations 1988, S.I. No.1199
DoE Circular 15/88, Environmental Assessment
DoE Circular 7/94, Environment Assessment: Amendment of Regulations
There is a plethora of literature on EA. You are advised to contact the DoE Public Enquiry Office (see Appendix IV) for the latest list.

Consultation

In addition to notifying the public, by whatever means are prescribed for that type of development, the LPA consults other bodies which might have a view about the desirability of the development. These are divided into *statutory* and *non-statutory* consultees (see Appendix V).

Statutory Consultees

The 1995 GDPO Articles 10–13, lists a veritable stage army of statutory consultees. The term is a recipe for confusion because, although many of them are organs of government, the LPA is not obliged by law to consult them over *all* applications but only with regard to those in which that body has a professional interest, defined by statute but also mentioned in all the Circulars and PPGs relevant to that issue. In addition, there is scope for the Secretary of State to direct that a given body be consulted.

> *When is a Statutory Consultee not a Statutory Consultee?*
> *When it is a official body which does not always have to be consulted.*

Just to add to the confusion, there is a motley collection of *non-statutory* consultees, most of which are also official bodies: they are cited in various PPGs and Circulars on given subjects, but the seeking of their opinion is discretionary. A given LPA may also be in regular contact with local branches of national environmental organisations, amenity groups, civic societies and residents associations. In a situation where there is a legitimate expectation of consultation, if a decision is taken without having consulted a relevant non-statutory consultee, there could be grounds for having the decision quashed in the High Court. Statutory and non-statutory consultees are given 14 days in which to respond, but true to the Government's philosophy of 'yesterday if not sooner', the LPAs and the statutory consultees have been exhorted to create efficient communication links to save time.

In the shires most applications are dealt with by district councils but they are obliged to notify the county in respect of applications involving: land owned by the county, or in which they have a strong interest; development which would conflict or have a major impact on structure plan policy; potential development sites which would affect the winning and working of minerals, other than coal; land which the county wishes to develop itself; and land which the county has earmarked for waste disposal. Twenty-eight days is allowed for the county's response. (Article 11 GDPO 1995)

However, counties do take the decision themselves on a restricted range of applications: highways; minerals; and waste disposal. These are known in the lingo as 'county matters'. (see Article 12, GDPO 1995) For their part, counties do have to consult district councils over reserved matters because the latter will have to live at close quarters with them, but for just that reason it does not apply the other way round. With regard to the unitary authorities the consultation process takes place in-house, with the relevant departments sending in their views to the planning department.

Parish, Town and Community Councils (alias *Local Councils*) are also statutory consultees, but they have to contact the LPA in writing to say that they want to be put on the mailing list to be informed of some, or all, planning applications in their area: the applications may pertain to full, outline or reserved matters, listed building consent, conservation area consent, advertisement consent and consent to lop, top or fell trees protected by Tree Preservation Orders. It has to be said that whilst most LPAs have good relationships with their local councils and send them the information, some make them fetch it: unfortunately the statutory provision only goes as far as saying that the LPA have to inform the local council of its existence, not that they have to post them! (see 1990 TCP Act, Sch.1, para.8 & GDPO 1995, Article 13)

Local councils have to inform the LPA whether they have a view on the matter, and, if so, what it is. On paper they are supposed to respond within 14 days, but with a little cooperation on both sides, this can be extended. The important thing is to have a system observed by both parties. LPAs have to take on board the views of local councils but are not obliged to agree with them. Whatever the eventual decision, the local council has to be informed. From the point of view of people living in the rural areas or urban fringe, this systematic consultation of the local councils is an important source of information, especially in cases not blessed with other publicity.

An applicant producing an ES has to provide copies for all the statutory consultees which were obliged to provide him with information when compiling his ES, namely: GDPO Article 10 consultees; any principal council in the area if not the LPA; the Environment Agency; the Countryside Commission; and English Nature. Once the application has been submitted, the LPA must obtain the opinions of these bodies and allow 14 days for their reply.

Public Participation

LPAs are given eight weeks in which to process a planning application. For those undergoing the EA process, this has been extended to 16 weeks in recognition of the extra time taken to digest an ES. However, whether or not an application is accompanied by an ES, the public are only given 21 days in which to comment on it. Time, therefore, is of the essence. It is a very steep learning curve if you find yourself confronted with a proposal you do not like, when you know nothing of the structure of local government in your area. As the Irish might say 'You shouldn't start from here'. You need to build a long-term relationship with the LPA(s) in your area. The anatomy of local government in the nineties is changing fast (see Appendix X), so acquaint yourself with the situation in your area: if you are to become an effective participant in environmental decision making in your local area you need to put in the ground-work. Begin by finding out:

a) which authority is responsible for what services;

b) who are the key players amongst the councillors and officers;

c) and how the procedures work in practice

Then plug yourself into the system. (see Fig.7)

It can happen that you have only 21 days to make an objection to an application about which you knew nothing until it appeared on the planning register, but if you have established links with your LPA and local council you may well have been alerted to it some weeks beforehand.

The major problem for third parties is that there is no right of appeal against a grant of planning permission: the British system has always been biased in favour of development. Therefore it is

Figure 7   Plugging into Planning at Local Government Level

Your Representatives

Who is your MP?
Who is your county councillor (if any)?
Who is your ward councillor?

The Planning Authority

The Planning Committee

Do they sit on the Planning Committee?
Who are the Members of the Planning Committee?
Who Chairs the Planning Committee?
Which political party controls the Planning Committee?

The Main Council

Which councillors Chair other Committees concerned with the environment:
Transport; Housing; Environmental Health etc.?
Who is the Leader of the council?
Who Chairs the Council?
What is its political complexion?
When is the next election?

Officers

Who is the Chief Planner?
Is the planning office divided into sections e.g. forward planning, development
control, conservation etc.?
Who are the senior officers in these divisions?
Are you on their mailing list if an interesting development hoves into view?
Who are the Chief officers in other departments concerned with the
environment?
Who are the key 'environmental' officers in these departments e.g. country-
side officer, the noise expert, the officer implementing 'park & ride'?

Procedures

Are some decisions on planning applications delegated to officers and, if so,
which?
When is the officers report available before each Planning Committee
meeting?
What is their pre-meeting routine of the Planning Committee?
Under what circumstances are decisions referred to the full Council?
How often to do you attend meetings of the planning committee and full
council?
Are members of the public ever allowed to speak at these meetings?

Your Local Council*

Key Facts

Who is the Clerk?
Who Chairs the council?
Who are the Members
When do they meet?

Procedures

Do they receive planning applications regularly?
What is the routine regarding planning applications?
When and where do they meet?
Do members of the public ever speak at these meetings?
When is the next election?

Have they ever invited an officer to speak to them about a forthcoming development plan or proposal?
Do they attend meetings for local councils staged by the LPA?
How good is their relationship with the LPA?

Receiving Information

Having acquainted yourself with the system, plug into it by getting to know the dramatis personae, and supplying them with your particulars:

>   Your name, address, phone and fax no;
>   The name of your group, its address, phone & fax no.
>   The issues you are interested in.

Make sure you update the LPA if you move, or the Secretary to your group changes: they cannot keep in touch if they lose track of you.

Meanwhile, in your office, develop a filing system. For example:

>   correspondence to and from the LPA;
>   documents pertaining to a given case
>   documents pertaining to a given site
>   documents pertaining to a given developer.

Information on how to run an effective pressure group is available from the National Council for Voluntary Organisations (see Appendix IV)

*Local Councils are Parish or Town Councils in England, and Community or Town Councils in Wales.

imperative that if you wish to stop something altogether, or support it, but subject to certain conditions, that you lobby your LPA, its officers and members, and also your local council, if you have one.

Your success will rest on three inter-related factors:

a) the quality of your case (see Section III)

b) the reputation of your group based on past cases

c) the alliance between your group and other groups, on this issue.

d) the amount of time before the decision is taken.

With regard to (c), if there have been meetings or exhibitions, courtesy of the developer or LPA, you may have met up with kindred spirits, and therefore know who are your potential allies. If you are an assortment of community groups and/or local councils, and are united in the views you wish to put forward, then it is a good idea to form a consortium, and perhaps you can afford to retain professional advice, if you need it. Such an umbrella group gives you both geographical identity, and political clout as more than one elected member is involved.

However, often a looser alliance is appropriate because there are differences of emphasis between the respective members. National pressure groups usually prefer to retain their identity so that they can be seen to be taking action by their supporters. It is essential, however, for you to find out what exactly is the stance of a certain group: you do not want to waste your resources, or alienate the LPA by duplicating the evidence. Sort out who is doing what at an early stage, but, later on, check up that X has actually done what X promised to do, or you could be put at a grave disadvantage at a later stage.

Once a planning application has formally made its debut in terms of the planning register, the question to ask is 'When will it come to planning committee?'. If you are very short of time to mount an effective campaign, it might just be worth checking the applicant's paperwork: if there are errors or inconsistencies in the application form or the amount of fee paid, then you must point it out to senior officers and members, and this will delay the start of the 21 days consultation period until all is in order, postpone the date of the council's decision, and therefore give you valuable time in which to marshal your allies and your arguments.

Whose Decision?

Which authority takes which planning decisions? As would be expected unitary authorities take all planning decisions in their area. In two tier authorities district councils take all the decisions apart from those deemed to be 'County matters' i.e. minerals, waste disposal, and highways. (for details see 1990 TCP Act Sch.1). The National Parks Boards and Urban Development Corporations (with the exception of Cardiff Bay, which has yet to come of age) take decisions on all applications within their boundaries. On rare occasions, however, the Secretary of State is moved to intervene.

The Call-In

There is provision for the Secretary of State to call-in a given application for his own decision, rather than leaving it to the LPA, but this power is used sparingly: the applications need to be of more than local importance. For many years governments of all political persuasions have been reluctant to interfere with local decision-making over planning applications. Indeed a House of Commons Select Committee on the Environment, in the mid eighties, advocated giving third parties the right to have an application called-in under certain circumstances: departure from the development plan; areas of designated importance would be affected; the over-ruling of Chief Planning Officer; and/or where the LPA had a financial interest. They felt that 45 call-ins a year almost amounted to a dereliction of duty on the part of central government, especially given that the chosen few did not appear to be of 'more than local importance'. They cited the example of the Isle of Man where 3rd party rights to appeal exist, as they do in Eire. The Government asserted that the right to petition the Secretary of State was sufficient. By 1995/96 there was an 'improvement' – there had been no less than 76 inquiry decisions from called-in applications! This amounts to 1 in 5,000 applications per year. Now clearly it would be inappropriate for every house extension to be sent to the Secretary of State, but there are likely to be more than 100 applications in a given year, which are 'of more than local importance'.

There are ways of increasing the chances of a call-in. A controversy between a bevy of LPAs is helpful because Big Brother in Whitehall feels he has to keep the peace. Sometimes a major application, if implemented, would derail the development plan (see Fig. 8), or sink town centres in the vicinity (see Fig.9): in such instances the Secretary of State has 21 days in which to call-in the application, or at least impose an Article 14 Direction whilst he thinks about it: basically it means that an LPA may say "No", but it cannot say "Yes" to an application (see 1995 GDPO, Article 14). If

Figure 8   'Departures' from Development Plans

Applications for large scale developments, not featuring in the Development Plans for an area, are known in the lingo as 'Departures'. Since July 1992, LPAs have been directed to inform the Secretary of State about certain categories of development which:

1. do not accord with the provisions of the development plan in force in the area where the application site is situated;

2. and which the LPA *do not intend to refuse.*

3. and which fall into the following categories:

    a)   development which consists of, or includes

       (i)   more than 150 residential units;

       (ii)   or more than 10,000 m. of retail floorspace;

    b)   development of land of an interested planning authority, or for the development of any land by such an authority, whether alone or jointly with another person; or

    c)   or any other development which would prejudice development plan proposals.

DoE has advised that the latter category might include proposals:

   i)   for development of major importance, having more than local significance;

   ii)   proposals which raise important or novel issues of development control; or

   iii)   involving major proposals involving the winning and working of minerals, or major waste disposal, storage, treatment and processing facilities;

   iv)   any proposal which whilst it is not significant in itself, may significantly prejudice the implementation of the policies and proposals in the development plan became of their likely impact on their setting or location. This particularly applies to proposals in national parks, AONBs, conservation areas, and SSSIs.

Departures are notified to the Secretary of State who has 21 days in which to call-in the application for his own decision, or at least impose an Article 14 Direction.

DoE Circular 19/92, Development Plans and Consultation Directions, Annexes 2 & 3

CROWN LAND

In the event of a departure from the development plan, the Secretary of State at the DoE has the option of setting up a non-statutory public inquiry, especially if the LPA side with a dissident community. Even if there is no actual departure, but a major local controversy ensues, the Crown has to notify the DoE itself.

Figure 9   Shopping Development Direction 1993

Since September 1993 the Secretary of State has required LPAs, before they make a decision, to inform him of applications for large amounts of retail floorspace:

a)   gross shopping floorspace of more than 20,000 sq.m.;

b)   gross shopping floorspace of less than 20,000 sq.m., but which will exceed it when added to another application of not less than 2,500 sq.m., where an application for the latter:

   (i)   has yet to be determined;

   (ii)   has been approved within the last five years;

   (iii)   has been substantially completed within the last five years.

   (iv)   is within 10 miles of the former.

The LPA are required to send the Secretary of State, at the Government Office: a copy of the application, plus plans and drawings; copies of any objections or representations made to the LPA; and the views of other LPAs and government departments.

The relevant LPA must not grant permission until 21 days after the above bumf was sent to the Secretary of State: this gives him the opportunity to call-in the application for his own decision, or at least issue an Article 14 Direction.

Reference: PPG6, Town Centres and Retail Developments, Annex D.

---

the application is called-in for the Secretary of State's decision, a public inquiry is highly likely: according to s.77(5) 1990 Act, if the applicant or LPA want the opportunity to argue their case before an inspector, it will be granted them.

As can be seen from Fig.8, the catchment area for Departures to be notified to the Secretary of State has been widely drawn. Nevertheless there could be doubt as to whether a given proposal falls within it. If you are concerned that you LPA might 'forget' to tell the Secretary of State, write to him yourself, and lobby your local councillors. With regard to the 1993 Shopping Development Direction (Fig.9), there is less room for doubt about what should be referred. However, even if an application is referred to the Secretary of State, there is no guarantee that it will be called in. One has to demonstrate that the matter is of more than local importance, and significant at the regional or national level.

Given that there is no appeal for third parties against a grant of planning permission in this country, call-ins are important to ordinary people who do not trust their local authority to be objective, and feel that the full facts will not emerge unless there is a public inquiry. However, there can be prodigious obstacles to be overcome, if it is not immediately apparent that this is a regional issue. Anyone in this position will need to marshal as much evidence as possible to prove that the application in question would have a widespread impact on a number of counts e.g. traffic generation, tourism,

Your case will then have to communicated to those with power and those with influence. Lobby your MP by post and at his surgery, and write to the Secretary of State. Contact the person in charge of planning at your DoE Government Office in your region (see Fig.2) and keep him abreast of developments by phone and fax. Persuade pillars of society to write to the national press and specialist journals. Invite the national media to take up the cause: having a public relations specialist or news agency working for you can be a great help but much can be achieved by faxing the bare bones of the case, written in a punchy style, to named environmental journalists in national newspapers. Try for a slot on regional television, if your case does not figure as national news.

It is likely to be a race against time because you could have as little as 21 days to get it called in: otherwise the LPA will pre-empt the decision. If you are in this unenviable situation, you will need *simultaneously,* to take preventative action by doing all you can to get the LPA to turn down the application in case the Secretary of State does not oblige you by calling it in. (See next subject)

The first sign that you might be having the desired effect is that the Secretary of State imposes an Article 14 Direction (1995 GDPO) on the LPA. This state of limbo can be for a specified period or indefinitely i.e. until the Secretary of State has decided what to do. In practice, decisions tend to be made just before major public holidays, so that the office is empty when the aggrieved parties wish to vent their spleens. Unfortunately for those campaigning for a call-in, the brakes can be released as quickly as they were imposed. From a political point of view it does, at least, look as though the Secretary of State at least considered the possibility, but decided to let the LPA go ahead after all.

Given that so few applications are called-in, the exercise of ministerial discretion is bound to be a political lottery, in every sense. However, it would be naive to ignore the fact that party politics are not a key issue: it does help if your MP is a cabinet minister, it is an election year, and/or you have some political heavyweight, or donor of party funds, residing in the district. If you do embark on trying to get a call-in, stamina, black coffee and ginseng are the order of the day!

DEVELOPMENT CONTROL:
DECISIONS INVOLVING
POLLUTION CONTROL

Which authority will be taking the decision? In two tier systems, county councils will take those on the disposal of rubbish by means of landfill or land raising. However, other applications, which have a pollution component, may fall within the ambit of 'county matters': the extraction of minerals may give rise to noise and dust, and national parks seem to act as a magnet for extractive industries. All other decisions will be taken by the district councils e.g. those involving air pollution under the LAAPC regime, and non-minerals applications involving noise. Whether the decision is being taken by the county or the district council, the other council will have an important input into the proceedings, so it is worth lobbying their planners and members. It should be noted that applications involving a significant risk of pollution, are usually *full* rather than outline applications.

Who gives expert advice to the planners on pollution? The Environmental Health Officer (EHO) of the district council is a key player. If the decision is being taken by the county council, then the EHO of the District Council will be consulted by the county planners, as well as the having an input into the recommendation to Members made by planners of the district council. If the latter is taking the decision, then it is a straight forward input into the district planners report to Members. Therefore, it is worth lobbying not only your local planners, but also the EHO: if you are retaining some sort of pollution expert, send them to see him.

The opinion of the district council, officers and members, will be an important element in the decision-making process, therefore lobby the officers so that they recommend to their members whatever it is that you wish to see happen, and lobby the members, just in case the officers don't comply with your wishes or would not succeed without your assistance!

The other key player, in certain cases, is the Environment Agency. Those employed by them are the Government's pollution control watchdogs, before, during and after the cessation of a polluting activity. With regard to development control, their statutory input into the system is to advise the applicant on their Environmental Statement, and as a statutory consultee on applications involving water pollution, flood defence, wildlife conservation, fisheries, IPC and waste regulation. If you are anxious about a development in any of these spheres, or indeed, have expertise to offer, contact the relevant officers at the local office of the Environment Agency: to track them down, begin with Map 3 & Fig.3.

Applications for plants operating processes which fall within the category of Integrated Pollution Control, and also for waste disposal sites, will require licences, having first obtained planning permission. Clearly this demarcation between planning and pollution is unsatisfactory, but we have to live with it for the moment. What it means in practice is that the Environment Agency will liaise with the planning authority on on the planning aspects of the case. Granting a licence is a separate matter: that the Agency has taken a benign view on planning matters, in no way guarantees that they will do the same with the licence application.

The Environment Agency will also be consulted by the LPA over past pollution i.e. applications to be sited on land which is either known to be contaminated or is likely to be contaminated. It may also need to be consulted on applications within the vicinity of a polluting activity e.g. schools, hospitals, residential units, retail, commercial or leisure facilities: 500m of a plant operating under the regime of integrated pollution control (IPC), 250m of plant emitting pollutants into the air, or 250m of site used for landfill within the last 30 years.

In PPG23, Planning & Pollution Control, Local authorities are constantly reminded not to duplicate the controls of the Environment Agency. Therefore, in lobbying the LPA, you need to focus your objection on the *planning issues* e.g. the topography of the land, traffic, nature conservation, the effect on people working, living or playing nearby. PPG23 accepts that there may be circumstances where a development is likely to get its licence or consent from the Environment Agency, but still could be refused planning permission because of its possible impact on social, economic or environmental factors.

If the application is to be granted planning permission, then conditions will need to concentrate on purely planning issues e.g. limiting hours of use or protecting amenity. PPG23 warns that lack of confidence in the pollution control system is no reason for refusing planning permission! One can only hope that the new Environment Agency will command more respect than the erstwhile Her Majesty's Inspectorate of Pollution (HMIP).

As with any other planning application, if it is refused by the LPA, the applicant may go to appeal, and third parties have another opportunity to put their case on *planning* grounds (see Sections III & IV). The EPA Act 1990, however, has also built in public participation into the granting of licences: these are not advertised in local newspapers but keep your eye on the Public Register kept in your local office of the Environment Agency for licence applications. Objections may be lodged on *pollution* grounds. If the application is refused, or granted subject to conditions which the applicant finds unacceptable, then he has the opportunity to go to appeal. Should that happen, then third parties are allowed to appear at the hearing.

* Much pollution legislation originates in Brussels in order to provide a level playing field for industry. See Fig.13 and Section V.

Stephen Tromans, The Environmental Protection Act, 1990, (London, Sweet & Maxwell)
Environmental Protection (Applications, Appeals & Registers) Regulations, SI 1991 No.507
PPG 23, Planning & Pollution Control
PPG 24, Planning and Noise
MPG 11, The Control of Noise at Surface Mineral Workings, 1993
DoE Circular 11/92 Planning Control for Hazardous Substances
DoE Circular 6/96 Environmental Protection Act 1990: Part II, Special Waste Regulations

The LPA Decision

(i)   Compiling Your Response

Over the years LPAs have grown larger, after each re-organisation of local government. In order to counteract the likelihood of 'remote control', many LPAs have delegated planning powers to sub-committees in that area. In one London Borough, a unitary authority, local forums have been created, consisting of residents and businesses in the area working alongside councillors: they take the majority of the planning decisions for the area. A rural district council in the south west has delegated the majority of planning decisions to parish councils. These LPAs are exceptions, but do not be surprised if the Committee taking the decision in which you are interested, is not **the** Planning Committee for the entire LPA, but a more localized version.

Nonetheless, if the application is not called-in, you probably need not worry that any major controversy will be delegated to an officer. Every LPA decides for itself precisely which applications are dealt with in this way, but they do tend to be of the smaller, uncontroversial variety. If an application, in which you are interested, appears on the Register but somehow vanishes from the agenda of the Planning Committee, make enquiries. If you feel it should be dealt with by them, lobby your ward councillor and the Chair of Planning to that effect. In terms of influencing the decision, discuss the matter with the case officer.

With regard to having an input into the LPA's decision, a basic question to ask is whether the LPA is *de facto* officer or councillor led? Do councillors rely heavily on their officer's advice, or does it just guide their decision? You will need to have witnessed the machinations of the LPA, preferably at first hand, as recommended above, before you can arrive at a view on this. The answer to this question will determine the weight and direction of your lobbying.

Even if the elected members are very much 'top dog', you should aim to have your point of view put forward as a recommendation in the Officer's Report. Find out who is the Case Officer assigned to this application and telephone for an appointment: planning officers have a predilection for site visits on fine days, so they may not be there if you just drop in. If you are having any difficulty interpreting the application, your initial meeting is the time to ask: the officer may have advised the applicant at an earlier stage, and therefore be more familiar with the drawings, for example.

Enquire as to the views submitted by the relevant statutory consultees and ask to see the correspondence: suffice to say that there are times when your interpretation of a letter may differ from that of an officer. You do have the right to see all the background papers to an application, and to make copies for a reasonable charge, thanks to the 1985 Local Government Access to Information Act. If an item is 'missing', ask if you can accompany your ward councillor to look at the full file. The view of the statutory consultees on an ES might be particularly instructive. Quiz the officer on his understanding of both this correspondence and the ES in general: there can be a problem with officers suspending their professional judgement, not to mention commonsense, in the light of statements put forward by a prestigious consultancy.

The likelihood is that the planning officer will be well versed in the development plan and government policy on the various planning issues in the area, but will not have your detailed local knowledge, and would welcome comments along these lines. Ask whether the officer thinks the application will be acceptable to the LPA, and carefully note the response: it will influence the stance you take when lobbying the LPA.

Blackburn Borough Council has received the planning application described on the accompanying Notice. Government Regulations require the council to serve this Notice on you. ... Please bring this letter if you wish to inspect the application. ... If you wish to make any observations on it, I shall be pleased to receive your comments within 21 days of the date of this letter. Please note that under the terms of the Local Government (Access to Information) Act, 1985, any comments which you may make can be examined by any member of the public. You should not therefore make any comments which could be construed as libellous or offensive.

March 1996
Emphasis added.

It is very important to write a formal letter to the LPA, within the time allowed i.e. 21 days from the appearance of a site notice or 14 days from the date the advertisement appeared in the newspaper. If necessary, send in a short letter, indicating that more details will follow. In complex cases, or where there has been a very recent change in government policy, you may find yourselves compiling a lengthy submission, more akin to a proof of evidence. If so, it is advisable to produce an Executive Summary to make an impact on officers and members, and provide you with a list of points for lobbying Councillors. Such correspondence should be headed with the number of the planning application, and addressed to the case officer. In terms of style, avoid references to personalities or party politics, however tempting it might be! Be clear and concise, itemizing your points. Finally, but most important of all, couch your arguments in good planning grounds: this is the subject of Section III.

(ii)   Traps for Councillors

There are three traps for councillors: being dazzled by an ES, bamboozled over costs and tempted by 'Planning Gain'. With regard to the first, the process of producing an ES may involve the community, and eradicate or mitigate problems at an early stage. However, there is the real danger that LPAs, hungry for economic development, will take one look at a glossy ES, complete with seductive pictures, graphs and endless statistical detail, and promptly switch off their critical faculties. In many cases there is no time before the meeting to absorb the documentation, and only one copy provided for all the committee members. Under such circumstances there is a tendency to assume that any problems must have been dealt with by the developer's sophisticated consultants, and to say 'That looks attractive. We'll have one of those.' It is up to the officers, the LPA's consultants auditing the ES [if any], statutory consultees and third parties to point out the downside of the scheme, and whether or not the ES has been 'economical with the truth'.

More frequently councillors are coerced into giving permission for a development because either the developer, the officers or an influential councillor raises the issues of costs i.e. that the developer would go to appeal, win and claim his expenses against the council (see Fig.10). Even worse, there are occasions when members are threatened with being personally surcharged with the amount awarded against the LPA (see Fig.11). Given the shortage of funding to local government, this threat is not one which any responsible local authority would willingly incur. On the other hand it is nothing short of BLACKMAIL if they have observed the proper procedures and there are good planning ground for refusal. Go through the small print of DoE Circular 8/93 with councillors, if they need reassurance.

The third problem is the seduction of LPAs by a juicy s.106 planning obligation, other wise known as 'planning gain' (see Appendix IX). In these days when an LPA may be eager to re-develop a run down area, and desperately short of funds, they may be all too willing to listen to the siren songs of anyone prepared to make an investment. Usually, s.106 planning obligations are tied to the provision of necessary infrastructure e.g. access roads and drainage, but sometimes they are more imaginative and generous. Clearly there is the potential for planning permissions to be effectively 'bought' and 'sold. The important thing to remember is that:

a) applications must be acceptable, in principle, in terms of the development plan and other material considerations;

b) there should be a *direct relationship* between the proposal and any community benefit on offer, and that developers should not be expected to remedy existing deficiencies.

DoE Circular 1/97 advises LPAs not to take into account benefits which exceed that set out in (a) & (b) above: this might be considered unrealistic in the current climate. On the other hand, if you are concerned that your LPA has been won over against its better judgement, you can point out, to the Secretary of State and the appropriate Government Office (see Fig.2), that the LPA's conduct is contrary to the guidance given in the Circular, and hope to have the matter called-in for his own determination: the Secretary of State promises that he will not be impressed by excessive benefits. Alternatively, you may threaten to judicially review the LPA's action. This can have dramatic effects, but be sure of your facts and take legal advice (see Section V).

The Circular also warns LPAs that developers have the right of appeal to the Secretary of State if they consider that the LPAs are too greedy, or the Secretary of State may intervene of his own volition, or at least prompted by a *mole*. In addition, there is an oblique reference to the possibility of landing in the Courts, which 'have held that that Government policies are themselves material considerations to be taken into account when planning decisions are made'.

Figure 10   Costs

The threat of 'costs' is used by all sides to bring pressure to bear on elected members, opponents, and recalcitrant public bodies. What situations can generate claims for costs?

Awards Against Appellants:

Procedure:

(i)   Failure to notify the DoE in writing that an appeal is to be withdrawn, with a failure to turn up on the day, thus compounding the felony;

(ii)   If an appeal is withdrawn, without any change in the substance of the LPA's case, and three working days have elapsed since the DoE formally notified everyone of the date of the hearing, the LPA and third parties may be eligible for reimbursement of their wasted expenses;

(iii)   If the appellant does have successful discussion with the LPA, which lead to a withdrawal of an appeal, this should be done as soon as possible, if possible before the formal arrangements have been made, or an award of costs may be in order;

(iv)   If an appeal is withdrawn too late for an inquiry or hearing to be cancelled (lead time three working days), then it is highly likely that the appellant will be liable for everyone' costs: the DoE, LPA and third parties can put in for expenses incurred in both preparation and attendance at the abortive appeal.

Substance

An appeal is considered unreasonable if:

(i)   there has been a recent refusal by the Secretary of State of a very similar proposal on the same site, especially if it is within two years of a previous refusal;

(ii)   there are no relevant material considerations, and an up to date development plan, in accordance with national policies, which rules out such a proposal;

(iii)   the LPA has demonstrated that the proposal would indeed prejudice the development plan process because the appeal is premature;

(iv)   relevant Planning Guidance and or judicial authority, show that the appeal had no reasonable chance of success.

Awards Against LPAs

Procedure:

(i)   Late cancellation of an inquiry resulting in wasted expenses for the appellant and other parties (see 1.(ii) above);

(ii)   Unless it is done immediately, the withdrawal of one, or more, of the reasons for refusal after a change in circumstances, may result in an award of costs for the wasted expense incurred by the appellant.

Substance

The appellant my be justified in asking for costs if:

(i) the proposal accords with the development plan, and there are no other material considerations, then the appellant is justified in asking for costs;

(ii) each of the reasons for refusal cannot be substantiated by reference to the development plan and planning policy guidance, DoE Circulars, judicial authority etc.;

(iii) they misunderstand, and therefore go against, the professional advice of officers and statutory consultees, with having good planning grounds to back up their decision;

(iv) 'prematurity' cannot be justified (see 2.(iii) above);

(v) the degree of design control exceeds that allowable for development in that location, even if it is in a conservation area, national park etc.;

(vi) a local furore against the proposal has influenced the LPA, yet it should be allowable in terms of the development plan and material considerations;

(vii) it is evident from a previous appeal decision that the Secretary of State or Planning Inspector would have no objection to a revised application which was allowed the first time around;

(viii) the LPA is being greedy with regard to asking for unnecessary benefits in the form of s s.106 planning obligation (see Appendix IX);

(ix) it cannot show good reason for failing to renew an extant or recently expired planning permission.

> *'It is a well-established principle that an award of costs does not "follow the event" of an appeal decision (as in litigation in the court). Therefore I see no reason for authorities to feel intimidated by developers in the way you suggest. Provided each of an authority's reasons for refusing planning permission is objective, clear cut and sustainable on its planning merits, and they can show, in any appeal proceedings that they properly considered the merits of the application, by reference to stated national and local planning policies, they need not fear an award of costs against them. The great majority of planning appeals do not result in a costs application, let alone an award.'*
>
> Viscount Ullswater, Minister for Construction & Planning,
> House of Lords Hansard, 22 June 1995

Strictly speaking Viscount Ullswater was right, but only because costs cannot be applied for if an appeal is heard by Written Representations (see p.143), as 80% of appeals are heard using this method. On the other hand it is standard form for one or even both sides to an appeal, heard at an inquiry, to go for costs, although awards are made in only 27% of cases: of those nearly 80% went to the appellant in cases decided by inspectors. Although the Secretary of State made only 89 awards, 46% were made to LPAs (1995/6 figures). Perhaps the key issue is for LPAs to guess whether or not the developer will go to inquiry and who will take the decision?

Figure 11   Surcharging Councillors

What is the truth about councillors being personally surcharged with the costs of a developer who has had an application refused, or a condition imposed, and has taken the matter to appeal? The root of the issue is to be found in the 1982 Local Government Finance Act, s.20:

(1)   Where it appears to the auditor carrying out the audit of the accounts under this Part of this Act –

   (b) that a loss has been incurred or deficiency caused by the **wilful misconduct** of any person,he shall certify that the sum . .... is due from that person and. .... that he and the body in question may recover that sum or amount for the benefit of that body; and if the auditor certifies ... that any sum ... is due from two or more persons, they shall be jointly and severally liable for that amount.

(3)   Any person who is aggrieved by such a decision may appeal against the decision to the court and -

   (a) the court may confirm, vary or quash the decision.

(5)   Any sum or other amount shall be payable within fourteen days. ...

It all hinges on the definition of *wilful misconduct*. Not accepting the recommendations of an inspector who has presided over a local plan inquiry, or refusing planning permission or imposing conditions, is the prerogative of councillors provided they have **good planning grounds**. Members should not allowed themselves to be blackmailed into accepting recommendations, giving permission or lifting conditions, if they have sound planning reasons for doing otherwise. If in doubt, Members should take advice from the LPA Solicitor or Auditor. If they would prefer an outside opinion, they should contact the Local Government Ombudsman.

MONEY by Dana Gioia, published by Peterloo Poets

Money breeds money,
Gathering interest, compounding daily,
Always in circulation.

It greases the palm, feathers a nest,
Holds heads above water,
makes both ends meet.

Money. You don't know where its been,
but you put it where your mouth is,
And it talks.

Abridged

(iii)   Lobbying

A few days after the arrival of your letter of objection, telephone the officer to find out how well it was received. Your objective at this stage is to influence the report the officer will make to the members, which will recommend the acceptance or refusal of the application in question. Your submission will then be appended to the officer's report. The applicant will have the right to see your submission, so keep an eye open for any rebuttal he may make. You may have to make further representations which will be circulated to the members before the meeting. Of course a canny applicant may wait until the last minute before responding, but that's democracy!

People enter local politics for all manner of reasons, and bring with them a range of experience and expertise. Most of them have full-time day jobs. It is, therefore, not surprising if they find themselves on the Planning Committee without a detailed knowledge of the planning system, and/or an intimate acquaintance of the facts behind a given case. Hence, do not assume that the elected members:

a) are well informed on planning law and policy;

b) are acquainted with your locality;

c) have done a mental critique of the ES, if any;

d) have read all the background papers before the meeting of the Planning Committee.

A campaign, using the local media, is appropriate at this stage: letters to the press, interviews on local radio etc. Persuade other groups to support you publicly, to demonstrate widespread support for your views. Utilising the media is an art in itself: take advice form seasoned campaigners in the area. Helpful literature is available from the National Council for Voluntary Organisations (NCVO). (see Appendix IV)

In the limited time available you will have to lobby the elected members, certainly on the Planning Committee, and the full Council, if the matter is likely to be referred to them for a decision. Obtain a list of their names and addresses from the council offices and send them individual letters, appending extracts from Circulars, PPGs etc., as necessary. A well reasoned letter putting your point of view in the context of good planning grounds and widespread political support, is essential, particularly if your views do not accord with those of the officers. Then follow up your letter with a phone call to Members: use the Executive Summary of any lengthy submission as a 'shopping list' of points you wish to get across to them. Many Planning Committees are non Party Political, but those which are, need to be lobbied until majorities are obtained in each Party. This must be done before their Party decides how it will vote at the Planning Committee meeting.

Having sent the letter, outlining the main points of your objection, request meetings with the main parties on the Planning Committee, or the Council as a whole. A key question is whether planning matters are decided along party lines, with the application of the party whip over controversial issues. You will have to judge how best to achieve majority support for your point of view, but clearly all lobbying will have to be completed before the public meeting of the planning committee: if the planning committee operates along party lines, then you will have to complete your lobbying before the parties meet, prior to the main planning committee meeting, to decide how they will vote.

Notwithstanding, if it would be helpful, you can request your ward councillor to address the meeting of the Planning Committee if they are not already a member: that may be usual practice , but it may be at their discretion. If the LPA allows members of the public to address the planning committee, contact the council offices before the meeting to make arrangements for you to speak. You will usually be able to speak for a few minutes, but obviously this will depend on the complexity of the issue, and the discretion of the Chairman. To make the maximum impact, keep it short and to the point, citing that your views are supported by both government policy and significant number of electors in the area. However aggrieved you feel, do not insult the officers or elected members, as it is a sure way of alienating the sympathies of the entire council: sworn political rivals will embrace, and make common cause against an outsider who questions the honour of the LPA.

If councillors feel that insufficient information is available, and/or they would prefer to defer the issue until they have had a site visit, then they may postpone the issue to the next meeting of the Planning Committee, and risk the developer going to appeal for non determination. Site visits are attended by several councillors from the planning committee plus officers from development control and any other departments relevant to the case e.g. highways, environmental health. Interested parties may attend and speak at the discretion of the Chairman.

In exceptional cases the Planning Committee may prefer to duck the issue, because of the controversy or complexity, and refer it to the next meeting of the full Council. If you feel that this issue really should be decided by the full council, lobby key people on the Planning Committee and your ward councillor to this effect.

(iv) The Resolution

Whoever takes the decision within the LPA, it must have regard to all the documents filed with the application, the views of the statutory consultees, and those received from the public. The decision has to be taken in the light of:

> the provisions of the development plan, so far as material to the application, and any other material considerations.
>
> 1990 TCP Act, s.70(2)

At what stage in LPA proceedings is planning permission actually granted? Should anyone think this is rather an arcane question, they should be assured that it is not. The problem can arise when the Planning Committee pass a Resolution that they are minded to accept an application, but then send away the planning officers to sort out the s.106 planning obligation. If negotiations are delayed or get bogged down, this can take time – seven years has been recorded! The problem can then arise as to whether it is legitimate for the LPA to reappraise the application in the light of changes in circumstances, or whether they are bound by their original Resolution. The Courts have, in successive cases, ruled that planning permission is not actually granted until the applicant receives notification. This means that the Planning Committee is free to revisit the application in the light of the extant development plan and contemporary material considerations. In order to prevent these complications, it might be a good idea if outstanding planning applications were reviewed by Committee, after a decent interval for negotiations, and formally refused if no progress were being made. This prevents the applicant pressurizing the LPA into believing, no matter what length of time has elapsed, and how much has changed, that the LPA is only allowed to discuss a submission on the s.106 planning obligation, otherwise the LPA will be charged costs should the applicant go to appeal (see Fig.10). Here again, this is BLACKMAIL, if the LPA has good planning grounds for refusal.

(v) The Decision

Elected members are expected to take into account the views of the whole community when they take planning decisions:

'... they must take into account any relevant views on planning matters expressed by neighbouring occupiers, local residents, and any other third parties along with all other material considerations.'

It is important that elected members receive open and impartial advice from their Planning Officers. Elected members should make planning decisions on the basis of a written officer's report. Councillors should have good reasons, based on land-use planning grounds, if they choose to resist such advice.

PPG1 1997 paras.60 & 61

It goes on to warn members about the dastardly deeds in North Cornwall DC, and the dangers of offending against the National Code of Local Government Conduct where national policy advice is ignored. However it would be a pity if para.61 were used to manipulate councillors into following the officer's report regardless of whether there were good planning grounds to the contrary: there are times when an officer has been over impressed by the developers consultants, or frightened by the threat of an appeal and a successful application for costs; and there are other times when there is legitimate scope for a difference of interpretation or opinion. So councillors may need the courage of their convictions, boosted perhaps by sound planning advice from other quarters, in order to exercise their legitimate right of discretion.

If granted, planning permission may be granted outright or subject to conditions. Although, according to s.70 1990 TCP Act, LPAs may grant planning permission 'subject to such conditions as they see fit', the courts have seen to it that LPAs do not behave unreasonably. Conditions have been limited to:

a) strictly planning purposes rather than, say, a social objective;

b) matters relating to the site, or land under the control of the applicant.

c) securing the provision of X off site before the development can go ahead. (The legendary Grampian condition was named after a dispute between Grampian District Council and Aberdeen District Council over road access to a proposed industrial estate. This was settled, in a creative fashion by the House of Lords in 1983)

The courts have precluded as unreasonable any payment of money, infringements of property rights and removal of statutory rights. Thus the scope for conditions is limited, and they can be appealed against (DoE Circular 11/95, para.12). As has been mentioned, the granting of planning permission, by an LPA, may also contain a legal agreement under s.106 1990 TCP Act: details of the agreement are available for public inspection amongst the background papers to a given permission. However, government policy still favours conditions because it allows the applicant to appeal against all or any of the conditions, in less than the five years required before the review of a s.106 planning obligation. (See Appendix IX)

In the mid nineties almost 90% of planning applications were approved by LPAs. If permission is granted, the actual development must start within five years – unlike line orders for roads which can haunt communities for decades to come. Where reserved matters are involved, application for approval must be made within three years of the granting of the outline permission, and the actual development must start within five years of the latter, or two years from the final approval of the last of the reserved matters. (1990 TCP Act.s.91,92). But *beware*, the LPA is allowed to vary the times at its discretion (1990 TCP Act s.91(1b) & s.92(4)). Look at the small print of a given permission, and you might just know what to expect.

It should be noted that if a planning permission is liable to lapse because action on site has failed to materialize, but the developer wishes to renew the permission, it is difficult for the LPA to refuse unless there has been a significant policy change. Otherwise they would be liable to pay compensation to the potential developer, or costs if he challenged the decision on appeal (see Fig.10).

(vi) Refuseniks

If a permission is actually refused, reasons have to be given. It is important to have as comprehensive a list as possible because, if the applicant chooses to go to appeal, the LPA's objection will be limited to these reasons for refusal. Issues falling outside this list cannot be included at this second stage, and will have to be picked up by third parties: it is therefore in the interest of the latter, to make sure the LPA's list is as wide ranging as possible. The applicant may lodge an appeal within six months of the decision, or a longer period of time may be allowed by the Secretary of State in exceptional circumstances (GDPO 1995, Article 23).

Just a word of warning. If it was the case that officers supported the development but they were overruled by the councillors, then it will be difficult for those officers to argue the case against, come an appeal. Many officers would argue that this happens all the time and that it is their job to support the views of their members. However, the problem arises over their credibility as witnesses.

Counsel for the developer is liable to put questions like 'Well, Mr Snooks, did you not recommend that this proposal be accepted, citing A,B & C as good reasons for its being allowed? In your professional judgement, do you not still support this application?'. Difficult, given that the value of an expert witness, from the point of view of an inspector, is the soundness of his or her professional judgement. Members and objectors concerned about the erstwhile stance of officers, over a given case, should make sure the job is delegated to other officers, or recruit consultants to fight the appeal. It has even been known for the Chair or other member of the Planning Committee to be fielded to defend their decision.

In the mid nineties one in four refuseniks went on to appeal, whereas in the mid eighties it was one in three. Thus for the majority of applicants, the buck stops with a refusal. From the point of view of those concerned about the fate of a given site, a negative decision will be useful ammunition if a similar application arrives at a later date: it will be a 'material consideration'.

CPRE, Responding to Planning Applications, 1993
Roy Speer & Michael Dade, How to Stop & Influence Planning Permission, (London, J.M.Dent, 1994)
Antony Jay, How to Beat Sir Humphrey,(Long Barn Books) 1997
Your LPA's own literature on their way of operating the development control system.

 ROADS AND THE DEVELOPMENT CONTROL SYSTEM

Trunk roads and motorways are outwith the development control system. The Highways Agency of the DTp consults the public on alternative routes for a road scheme whose objectives, purpose and standard it has already set. The public consultation process is not true public participation as required in Plan preparation. Until very recently the glossy brochures, exhibitions and questionnaires failed to ask the public their views on the need for the road, limiting them to 'which route do you prefer' type questions. While 'need' is now more open to challenge, a pro-road bias of HA information is inevitable.

Moreover DTp will have already consulted, on a confidential basis, County and District chief officers (so that elected members do not know officers' views until they have already been given to DTp), and bodies such as the Environment Agency and Countryside Commission. The latter are overworked and unlikely to raise major difficulties until the public knows enough to lobby them. Thus DTp road schemes can get up some speed before the public or councillors know of them.

New procedures to bring DTp road planning into the Regional Planning Guidance process may prevent such a 'head-start' in the future. But it is unclear how it will affect road schemes listed in the DTp's national road programme but suspended for many years to come.

DTp trunk road and motorway schemes are proposed and promoted using the 1980 Highways Act, except for toll-roads which also require use of the New Roads and Streetworks Act 1991. Promotion is by the DTp's Highways Agency and decisions are made by the Secretaries of State for Transport and the Environment jointly. Apart from exceptions where DoE is seriously opposed to a road scheme, it is a 'sleeping partner' and the decision is that of the DTp. It is thus judge and jury in its own cause; the HA has no legal separate status, and is part of DTp. The Welsh and Scottish Offices both propose and make the decisions on their trunk road schemes.

For **trunk roads and DTp motorways**, no planning permission is needed. The Highways Agency publishes, in the Secretary of State's name, draft 'Orders': an appropriate term for an authoritarian system. The line of a trunk road is published as a Draft Line Order. Technically this makes the road to be built a Trunk Road, the 'general power to construct a highway' existing under a separate clause. For a Motorway this is called a Draft Scheme, and legally the motorway is called a 'Special Road' because it is restricted to certain classes of traffic: no learners, horses, cyclists, farm traffic etc.

Line Orders and Schemes have to be supported by Side Road Orders (SROs) which cover diversion of existing roads, stopping-up accesses, footpath diversions; and Compulsory Purchase Orders (CPOs) for land acquisition. Normally SROs are published with the Line Order, and CPOs after the line is fixed: however, CPOs may appear with the Draft Line Order. There may be a 'detrunking' Order to reduce the bypassed stretch of road to local authority status.

Environmental Assessment requirements apply to certain types of road scheme. For some arcane reason, the DTp's terminology, *Environmental Appraisal*, differs from that of DoE. EA is mandatory for:

(1) all new motorways and roads of similar status ('expressways') and toll-roads

(2) any new road more than 10km in length

(3) any new road over 1 km in length which passes

   (a) through or within 100 metres of a National Park, a Conservation Area, an SSSI or designated nature reserve;

   (b) through an urban area where 1500 dwellings lie within 100m. of the centre of the road.

However see Appendix III for the requirements under the new E.C. Directive.

EA can be declared necessary for any road scheme where the relevant authority, effectively the Secretary of State, determines that it would be likely to have a significant effect on the environment. A proposal for a Motorway Service Area can be determined to require EA by the local planning authority as it is the receiver of the planning application.

Generally the HA will undertake an EA for all but small schemes. If one is not undertaken, you will need to convince the relevant Government Office, the Welsh or Scottish Office, or the respective Secretary of State, that one is necessary. DoE Circular 15/88 is the key document.

The quality of Environmental Statements can be disappointing. They should be scrutinised with care, but it is questionable how much influence they have on the decision, which can turn on a few key issues. For roads, the EA is undertaken after the route has been selected. It may not cover all alternatives, especially non-road building options. Secondary effects such as land-use changes and development pressures arising from a major new road do not get analysed in EA.

Objections to published Draft Orders have to be made to the Secretary of State for Transport at the HA office which is publishing them. The objection period can be up to 3 months but as short as 6 weeks; and only 3 weeks for CPOs. If there are no objections, the Secretary of State 'makes' the orders. If there are few objections, and none from affected owners, there may be some negotiation but he has the power to make the order without an Inquiry. But for nearly all roads schemes now, there will be an Inquiry. The DTp tends to be poor at negotiating to meet objections. To obtain withdrawal of objections, it may have to give way on key matters, whereas trunk road inquiry inspectors are regarded as likely to back its case, rather than the objector's. So it has no incentive to settle before an Inquiry.

The road inquiry is covered in Section IV. It does not bear much resemblance, except in outward appearance, to an inquiry in the town and country planning system.

The processes for **local authority road schemes** are somewhat different. In the 1990s, there has been a drastic reduction in trunk road schemes being promoted. Motorway proposals have almost vanished, except for motorway widening. Local authority road schemes have thus become more noticeable, and attracted more attention. Public concern arises most often where private finance from a developer appears to be driving the plan.

The procedures require an 'application for deemed planning permission'. This is made by the local authority to itself under S.I.1992. No.1492 (see pp 49, 50) In form, the Committee responsible for roads approves a planning application and the same authority's Planning Committee receives a report from the authority's Planning Officer which appears to treat his colleagues from the highways department as an applicant. In principle councillors on one Committee should not sit on the other, but not all local authorities follow this principle.

If the scheme has been included in an adopted Structure and Local Plan or UDP, s.54A of the 1990 TCP Act requires consent to be granted unless there are 'material planning considerations' which indicate otherwise. Even if it has not been so included, the process is so obviously incestuous that the public places little confidence on the process. Notwithstanding, there have been cases of County or Unitary Authority Planning Committees, pressed by the public, rejecting their authority's application for deemed planning consent.

If the road scheme is not included in an adopted Plan, the application must be referred to the Secretary of State for the Environment as a 'departure' (see Fig.8). The DoE may call it in for an Inquiry. If it is a small scheme or there are few objections, DoE may return it to the local authority to determine it itself. Pressure on the Government Office, the MP and Minister can be effective, as can national amenity organisations where 'heritage' issues arise.

If the road scheme is called-in, the DoE is likely to invite the local authority to submit its Side Road and Compulsory Purchase Orders to the DTp and invite objections (see below) so that these can be heard at the same inquiry. The Inspector then reports to both Secretaries of State.

Where a scheme has been granted deemed consent, the authority cannot build the road unless it owns all the land and requires to alter no side roads or footpaths. It must 'make' a Side Road Order and a CPO by resolution of the relevant Committee, submit these to the DTp and advertise them for objections. In the local authority case, you object to Orders which have already been 'made' but do not come into force unless the Secretary of State for Transport 'confirms' them. Six weeks is the objection period for for SROs and 3 for CPOs. Objections (to English schemes) have to be sent to the DTp Local Authority Orders Section in Newcastle-on-Tyne (see Appendix IV).

The DTp then copies objections to the proposing authority inviting it to negotiate with objectors. In the past this would happen and objections would be met so that the DTp could confirm the Orders. Nowadays local authorities, like the Highways Agency, seem to prefer to go to an Inquiry instead.

As is made clear in *Notes for the Guidance of Inspectors holding Inquiries under the Highways Act 1980*, the fact that a road scheme has been granted deemed planning consent does not mean that objections to its need or route cannot be heard at the SRO/CPO Inquiry. Except in the most unlikely event that a fully designed road scheme was considered and approved by a Local Plan Inquiry procedure, objections to the need for and route of a local authority road scheme will be heard at the SRO/CPO Inquiry. On the other hand, with regard to a Trunk Road or Motorway Line inquiry, the Highways Act 1980 does enable such objections to be disregarded at CPO stage where a 'Line' has been 'made'.

Environmental Assessment for local authority road schemes should follow the same principles as that for trunk roads. However the generally smaller scale means that a greater proportion of local authority road plans will fall outside the 'mandatory' category for EA. The authority may assert that it can use its discretion not to undertake an EA in other cases on the ground that the scheme does not have a 'significant effect on the environment'. The DoE does have reserve power to require the authority to do one and there is precedent for DoE serving a 'direction' that one be done. So influencing the Government Office in your region (see Fig.2) is worthwhile, but better to persuade councillors that they should ensure one is done anyway.

Campaigner's Guide to Road Proposals, CPRE, 1993
Circular 15/88: Environmental Assessment, DoE, 1988
Environmental Assessment under EC Directive 85/337/EEC, DTp (published by DTp as Departmental Standard HD 18/88, July 1989)
Environmental Statements: Getting Them Right, CPRE, 1990
Manual of Environmental Appraisal, DTp Design Manual Vol. 11, 1993

ENFORCEMENT

Readers who have laboured thus far through the text may be astonished to know that it is not a criminal offence to carry out development without planning permission, or to contravene conditions attached to an existing permission. One hastens to add that this does not apply to those who ignore the need to apply for listed building consent or who wantonly fell protected trees: prosecution is then the order of the day.

Although there is no point in having a planning system, if development control is not imposed, enforcement is wont to be the Cinderella of the system within most LPAs. This situation is not helped by PPG18 on Enforcing Planning Control, which makes it clear that serving an Enforcement Notice is a last resort rather than the immediate reaction to suspicion of non compliance. The preferred approach is 'Softly, softly catch your monkey'. All reasonable means of persuasion have to be seen to have been employed. This is not just a gesture towards civil liberties but also a means of protecting the lives of enforcement officers: since such an officer was shot dead by an irate landowner, it is a sad fact that courses on how to diffuse tense situations are now offered by the RTPI to their members.

CROWN LAND

As one might expect from the Crown's place in the Planning Pantheon, LPAs cannot take enforcement action against it, or its agents. However, the LPA can, with the Crown's consent, take enforcement action against lesser mortals on their land.

Background Information

How can officers be helped by those safely beyond the firing line?. Given staff shortages etc., it is hard for the LPA to monitor what it happening in its area. Without indulging in witch-hunts, it is useful if members of the public alert the LPA to any breaches of control they may suspect. It is often difficult for an officer on a flying visit to ascertain whether or not there is a problem, and what exactly it is. Those who live in the vicinity can help by keeping diaries of activities, the comings and goings, and the ways in which their amenity is diminished e.g. noise levels at unsocial hours or the movement of heavy vehicles through a residential area. If the problem involves a business operating from residential premises, then any advertising material (free local newspapers, notices in newsagents etc.) can be very useful in establishing an unlawful change of use. However, it is necessary to take action reasonably quickly. This is particularly so with contraventions involving the building of new structures or change of use to residential: the LPA cannot take action if more than four years have elapsed.

Information gathering can be supplemented by the LPA issuing a Planning Contravention Notice. This is the new s.171C of 1990 Act, not that you will find it there: in the cack-handed way in which the legislation was introduced, it is to be found in the 1991 P&C Act, s.1. Obvious, isn't it? The Planning Contravention Notice is an effort to ascertain what is going on on site, what permissions exist and who is involved. The LPA may make an offer of talks. Such a civilised approach may be of limited use in practice: the street-wise treat it with contempt, and the opportunity may fail to register with the 'nice but dim'. Either way, the offer of talks to get to the root of the matter, is not usually accepted with alacrity. The LPA is back to relying on the community.

Gentle Persuasion

Given what they know, the LPA may decide that the although the development has occurred without permission, it would be accepted if an application were made retrospectively. The carrot to be used is the fact that the owner may find it difficult to sell the property without a permission, but the owner may choose to ignore the LPA, and PPG18 suggests that an Enforcement Notice would be too heavy-handed an approach. Gentle persuasion is also to be applied to those whose development would be acceptable if certain conditions were observed e.g. in terms of timing or intensity. This is particularly the case where employment is at stake. In some cases a move to a more suitable site might be an option. Where persuasion fails, an Enforcement Notice would be appropriate if neighbours are suffering or a designated site, like a conservation area or nature reserve, is being damaged. Some LPAs have enforcement policies that focus on listed buildings, conservation areas etc., and so the presumption may be in favour of enforcement. You will find such policies in the Development Plan.

Breaches of Conditions

Much enforcement work is concerned, not with the failure to apply for a change of use or permission to build, but with breaches of conditions attached to a permission. Enforcement Notices are cumbersome and give the appellant the chance to argue the toss over conditions imposed. The 1991 P&C Act, s.2 (alias s.187A of 1990 Act) introduced the Breach of Condition Notice. Clearly such a Notice is geared to the conditions imposed. It outlines the steps to be taken and/or the activities to be attenuated or stopped. The minimum response time is 28 days but this may be varied to allow a realistic time for compliance. One advantage is that there is no recourse to appeal: aggrieved parties would have to go to judicial review to get the Notice quashed. On the other hand, there can be problems: the party concerned may have lodged another planning application to legitimise the development or vary the conditions. A benefit of the Enforcement Notice route is that it allows Stop Notices to be used if the breach of condition is causing serious harm to a local amenity

Planning Policy Guidance Note No.18 (PPG18), entitled Enforcing Planning Control, explains how local planning authorities should assess whether it is expedient, in certain areas, to take formal enforcement action to remedy an alleged breach of planning control. Paragraph 5 of PPG 18 states that nothing in the guidance should be taken as condoning a wilful breach of planning law.

When a planning authority have specifically imposed conditions on a grant of planning permission requiring the development to be carried out strictly in accordance with the submitted plans and elevational drawings of the proposed structures (including details of any landscaping or materials), we would expect the developer to comply fully with all the relevant conditions. There is a statutory right of appeal against any planning condition with which an applicant is aggrieved.

If a developer deliberately fails to comply with such conditions, without seeking to appeal against them, because he considers that an alternative approach or design is equally acceptable to what has been approved, and is warned by the planning authority that he must comply, we would normally expect the planning authority to take formal enforcement action.

Where appropriate, planning conditions can now be enforced by serving a breach of condition notice, by virtue of s.187A of the TCP Act 1990. there is no appeal to the Secretary of State against this type of notice. A failure to comply with it can be enforced summarily in a Magistrate's Court.

In deciding enforcement appeals involving an alleged breach of an essential planning condition, Planning Inspectors will have regard to this policy statement.

Lord Lucas in reply to a Parliamentary Question
DoE Press Release, 20th July 1995

The Enforcement Notice

The decision to issue an Enforcement Notice should be made by the councillors on the Planning Committee, on the basis of an Enforcement Report, compiled by the officers on the story so far. If they decide to proceed, the LPA has to identify all the parties with an interest in the land: copies of the Notice have to be served on all of them. Often this involves a search of the records in the Land Registry. Almost always the LPA has to serve a formal Requisition for Information, under the 1976 Local Government (Miscellaneous Provisions) Act, on the owner or occupier. Then the LPA has to decide on the steps necessary to rectify the situation, and specify them in the Notice. If this involves re-designing buildings, specialist help may be required and more time is taken. Finally there is the matter of the formal reasons for serving the Notice, and deciding on a reasonable time for compliance. Only after that has expired can the LPA move towards prosecution.

It should be noted that non-compliance with an enforcement Notice is a criminal offence. The LPA will invariably ask local residents who have kept diaries etc. to act as witnesses in order to inflict a high fine on the offender. The Magistrate's court will only appreciate the 'criminality' involved if they hear from the 'victims'. So be prepared to stand up in court!

However, proceedings are liable to go into abeyance because most offenders take the opportunity to appeal against the Enforcement Notice. As such appeals are primarily concerned with past events, rather than future intentions, witnesses may be required to take an oath, either by swearing on the Bible, or other Holy Book, or by affirming the honesty of their statement. Enforcement inquiries are the only type of proceedings where witnesses are required to take oaths.

Stop Notices, Injunctions etc.

If an activity is particularly damaging, the LPA may issue a Stop Notice, but there is a sting in the tail: if the Enforcement Notice is quashed on appeal, for any reason other than the fact that planning permission should be granted, the LPA becomes liable for compensation. Consequently Stop Notices are used very sparingly. In fact the compensation risk is very small: LPAs are wont to exaggerate the problem, despite advice from DoE. An even rarer animal is the injunction. The LPA now has the opportunity to ask the Courts to issue a special planning injunction. The case-law on this particular animal indicates that it will be given much more readily than those injunctions which were available before this new form of remedy.

However, if all else fails, LPAs have powers to enter land and carry out the works themselves, charging the owner for the privilege. Whilst the attendant publicity can send the right signals to the community, there are occasions where it might be wise if the LPA served an injunction to prevent wilful obstruction by the irate owner.

> *'I cannot believe that the purpose of planning control is to enforce a boring and mediocre uniformity ... Any system of control must make some space for the dynamic, the unexpected and the downright quirky, or we shall all be the poorer for it. I believe this is one case where a little vision and imagination is appropriate.*
> Inspector's Report on the Enforcement Notice Appeal into
> the fibreglass shark plunging into a roof in Oxford

Conclusions

Thus enforcement of planning control is a tortuous business. Time-consuming though it is, action does have to be taken within a statutory period: four years since the completion of development or change of use; or ten years since the breach of other planning controls. So don't hold your breath! The average citizen would be excused for being both infuriated by the snail's pace at which the LPA is obliged to proceed, and reassured by the strength of the law protecting his liberties as a property owner.

PPG 18, Enforcing Planning Control
Denzil Millichap, The Effective Enforcement of Planning Control, 2nd Edition, Butterworths, 1995

REDRESS

If you wish to question the validity of any decision, on development control, in terms of the procedure by which it was reached, there is provision for this under the 1990 TCP Act s.288. For further detail see Section V on Redress.

Section III

Mounting a Case

INTRODUCTION

Methods of influencing development plans and development control have been discussed in the previous two Sections, and effective participation in various types of inquiries will be the subject of Section IV. Whatever the level of decision-making, success is dependent on your presenting a good case. How do you do it? It amounts to three things: good organisation; a well focused case; and professional documentation. Clearly these issues are generic to all levels of the planning system, and hence, the central position of this section within the book.

GETTING ORGANISED

Allies & Offices

If the proposal in question has something of a history, then you will have had the chance to identify the other interested parties through public meetings, letters to the press, etc. On the other hand, if the issue looms up out of the blue, you may have to organise a meeting at short notice, which must be well publicised, in order to attract sufficient support from key parties and the general population, to get the campaign off the ground. Preparing a case of any complexity requires both manpower and money, which may exceed the resources immediately available. A public meeting is a way of recruiting extra hands, some with access to new funds. At the meeting, or afterwards, people may well come forward who prove to be invaluable in terms of their knowledge or skills.

Another method is to form an alliance with other groups which share a common interest. That said, it is important that any gains in resources should not be offset by lack of coordination, or any of the parties having to dilute their stand to any extent. Remember infighting is out of order, a united front essential. The objective is to create a team which, under suitable leadership, will present your case to those who make recommendations and decisions.

Mundane realities include someone running an 'office', be it in the spare bedroom or in a shop with a short lease. It should be equipped with an answerphone, word processor and xerox. Access to a fax is essential to communicate with key individuals based elsewhere e.g. professional advocates or witnesses. Sometimes a business, supportive of your objectives, can be persuaded to provide xeroxing and facsimile facilities. Of central importance is the filing system for material gathered on the various topics to be covered: everyone involved should both understand and use it, or hard gleaned material goes astray.

Funding

An immediate concern is raising money to fight an undesirable development. Outside metropolitan areas there are local councils, the generic name of parish, and town councils in England: the former are called community councils in Wales. These comprise the lowest tier of local government and can levy a precept on the community charge, proportionate to their population. They vary enormously in size from parish councils of 200 souls to town councils of 15,000. Unfortunately development proposals are no respecters of the size, or affluence of communities.

The first step is to make an estimate of how much money you will need to raise: if you are intending to use professionals on the case you will need to obtain some ball park figures from them and then add on other costs. You will then have a target to be used when fund-raising. If the resources of a community are insufficient, then you should form a consortium of local councils which would be affected by the development: this will increase both the funds and your political clout. Mainstream or supplementary funding can be provided by action groups, monied individuals in the locality, and businesses, ranging from the corner shop, to national food retailers, and multinational companies: large companies may have good commercial or operational reasons for not wanting the development, but not want to say so publicly, so find it politically convenient to use a community organisation as a 'front', provided it can be done discreetly. On the other hand, clearly any community group or local council have to be careful not to be 'used', and even reputable companies may be a little unscrupulous at times.

Techniques of find-raising are beyond the remit of this book, but the NCVO library may be a source of inspiration (see Appendix IV).

PROFESSIONAL REPRESENTATION

The decision to retain professional help should be taken at an early stage. It will affect not only the amount of money to be raised, but also the collection and collation of material to be given in evidence. However, there can be logistical problems in getting the back-woodsmen to take action sufficiently early to make the most effective case: they prefer to wait until the axe falls before committing themselves. Whilst it is natural to exercise financial prudence, the cost of doing nothing should be borne in mind. The few thousand pounds spent fighting the development may be nothing compared with long term damage to the whole area, and the deleterious effect on property values, should the development go ahead.

> *'When people are successful, [or] retire with money in America, they use it to set up foundations for charitable purposes. In France they spend it on their mistresses (or their mistresses children). In Britain they very often use their time and money to protect or preserve a bit of England, Scotland or Wales. by buying it, giving money to the National Trust, or fighting developments threatening it. Is "Estuarine Man" so very different?'*
> Mark Sullivan, Transport Consultant

Under what circumstances do you need professional help? The following checklist of questions might guide you in your response:

1. Given the substance and complexity of the case, do you need an expert in planning and/or other fields?

2. Are you familiar with the network of bodies which constitute central and local government, and know who has the power to do what?

3. Are you used to marshalling arguments, and slotting them into letters and reports?

4. Have relationships broken down between you and your opponents, thus creating the need for a go-between?

5. Are you familiar with the procedures connected with the development plan, development control or the appeals system?

6. Do you need a legal opinion on local government procedures or environmental law? Could the case involve judicial review? (see Section V)

7. How relevant are the above questions to the problem facing you?

Whether the issue is still at the level of development control, or has moved on to a public inquiry, professionals can help in two ways: the procedural and the substantive.

The Team Leader

For the purpose of the ensuing discussion, those in charge of a case shall be called the 'team leader'. They see both procedure and substance in terms of a winning strategy. They therefore need to know how to use procedure to best advantage, and have a 'nose' for detecting the key issues upon which the case will hang, from amongst the material put forward by their witnesses.

The land-use professionals, such as lawyers, planners, architects and surveyors, are familiar with the procedures of the LPA with regard to development control. They may also be well placed to advise you on having an input into appeals handled by means of written representations and hearings: owing to their greater speed and economy these now account for 93% of appeals. As the substantive issues should be familiar to them as well, they are ideally placed to help with these cases.

It is only the remaining 7% of appeals and the called-in cases (858 in total, 1995/6), which now go to a public inquiry. As one might expect these are the longer, more controversial cases, where there are big financial interests at stake. As the procedure at a public inquiry resembles that of a law court, barristers are much in evidence, particularly on the side of the appellant, and therefore other parties feel that they have to follow suit. At local plan inquiries LPAs usually retain counsel to fight their corner because they do not want their in-house lawyers tied up for months with the inquiry, and thus unable to get on with LPA business. At road inquiries, which also tend to be lengthy, counsel are always retained to put the DTp's or LPA's case.

The question is, does the ordinary objector need a lawyer to represent them at a public inquiry? The answer to that, is not necessarily. As third parties they are unlikely to be repairing to the High Court, in the middle of the inquiry, to settle a point of law. As for knowledge of procedure, asking pertinent questions of the other side, protecting witnesses, and re-examination, these are skills which come with experience of attending inquiries, and a number of expert witnesses and lay people have learnt the ropes. However, if you cannot find such an individual, and complex cross-examination is required then lawyers, but particularly barristers, have the advantage over normal mortals, because, as is shown in Section IV, it is an art form for which training, and a certain elan, are prerequisites.

If you do decide that your case needs a proper advocate, then it is advisable to retain one with planning experience. They will be familiar not only with the procedure, and the policy documents, but also with the etiquette: a criminal barrister who reduces the planning witness to tears in an attempt to extract a 'confession', can prove counter productive by alienating the inspector. As in any other field, some lawyers are better than others, so ask around: whereas the inspector might help a layman put his case, he will expect the professional advocate to know his job. The other consideration is that the lawyer be appropriate in terms of seniority and expense. It is a waste of time and money to retain a QC, if you cannot afford sufficient of his time to benefit from his expertise.

How much will legal representation cost? Barristers are the branch of the profession which specialises in advocacy, although latterly solicitors have won the right to appear in court. Until the late eighties barristers always had to be instructed by solicitors which meant that there were two sets of fees to pay. Now they may be instructed by planners, surveyors and architects, in areas of their professional expertise, for public inquiries. Rules of Access have been drawn up for these professionals, so practitioners are advised to contact their respective professional bodies before assuming their expert witness will be able to save them solicitor's fees. The most junior barrister will charge £400–£500 and a QC in the region of £2,000 per day to appear at an inquiry plus a fee for preparation determined by the complexity of the case and the seniority of the barrister. There are chambers in the Inns of Court in London which specialise in planning, but there are reputable ones in most provincial cities.

Queens Counsel are the crème de la crème amongst the barristers: they are said to be 'learned in the law', and are appointed by the Queen on advice from the Lord Chancellor. They are sometimes known as 'silks' because they are entitled to wear silk robes in court. They take precedence in court over 'utter barristers' i.e. outer or junior barristers.

At public inquiries QCs may be recognised immediately by their portable lecterns, from which they deliver their speeches. Also by the deferential behaviour afforded them by lesser legal eagles, not to mention the inspectorate.

Unless you need a member of the planning bar to deal with a specialist issue, the alternative is to employ a solicitor who specialises in planning and is more than capable of advocacy at a public inquiry. They are likely to be more locally based and cheaper than the bar, with rates more akin to the latter's junior members. There are directories of solicitors, which list specialisms such as planning. These are likely to be available in your local public library or you could contact the Law Society [see Appendix IV]. Otherwise ask a tame solicitor who doesn't feel threatened by the fact that you are looking for someone else to do the job. Having penetrated the network, it is a matter of discovering who, within the planning section of the firm, is competent at advocacy.

If the above fees sound terrifying, do not despair. If you really need a lawyer, contact the Environmental Law Foundation (ELF) (see Appendix IV), and they should be able to put you in touch with someone suited to your case, in your locality, and if your case requires a QC, they may well be able to find you one. Either way, charges are kept to a minimum.

'Can any good thing come out of the Inns of Court?'
The Archdeacon of Canterbury applauding
the existence of ELF

The Expert Witness

With regard to expert witnesses, their most important attribute should be an in depth knowledge of their subject. They should be able to research and present your case, defend it under cross-examination, and be able to draw from their experience when confronted with new evidence served up at short notice by the other side. Here again it is a good idea to consult other groups who have retained an expert in the same field. If a lawyer is being retained as a team leader, he might know of a competent individual.

Fees for an expert witness are in the region of £75 per hour, in or out of the inquiry, plus expenses. It is a good strategy to offer a net fee and ask for work to be done up to that amount, assuming the amount is realistic in terms of producing sufficient material of the right quality. The relationship between groups and expert witnesses can be delicate on the subject of time and money. Often the case requires more work than the group can afford with the result that the work is either half done, or the consultant is out of pocket. To prevent one side or the other losing out, with the consequent souring of relationships, contact your witness at an early stage, send them the paperwork, have a meeting to allow them to get to grips with key issues, and then ask them for an estimate. The latter will be based on informed guesswork, so some allowance must be made for the unexpected increasing costs over the original estimate.

Give your expert witness adequate time to prepare a case: they may have difficulty extracting information from a suspicious or inefficient source; they may well have other work in hand; and sufficient time may lead to reduce costs because the clients themselves can do some of the leg-work. If you need more than one witness it is as well to choose people who have worked together before, or at least are not incompatible with each other, or with the leaders of the group to be represented.

Academic institutions are a great source of specialists, who often welcome the opportunity to apply their knowledge to an actual case. Furthermore universities now give them Brownie points for doing so. Write to the head of department, or ring their secretary, and enquire whether there is anyone on the staff who specialises in the subject, or whether they know of anyone outside with the appropriate expertise: it is a matter of plugging into the network. Despite the business ethos which is being forced down the throats of academic institutions, most worthwhile academics are more interested in their subject than making mega-bucks, so they are unlikely to charge more than a modest fee, plus expenses.

ELF may be able to help here too, as they have a list of specialists in various aspects of the environment. The parish town and community councils of England and Wales also have access to a consultancy service in planning and other land use matters: this is accessible via the National Association of Local Councils (NALC). Planning Aid, contactable through the RTPI, may also be able to suggest or supply witnesses who are sufficiently knowledgeable to put up a good case. Alternatively you could try advertising for an expert with some spare time: in these days of under employment and early retirement there is expertise to be tapped via the Personal columns of the press, or even the Internet. Lastly, there are interest groups and pressure groups which are well informed in their respective fields. This is both helpful to groups, and gives publicity to their cause. (see Appendix IV details).

Thus it is possible to acquire top quality advice and not be charged commercial rates. Such experts also have the advantage of being professionally independent i.e. they do not depend for their bread and butter on getting contracts from those who you might be opposing. This can be particularly difficult if there are only a restricted number of qualified and experienced people in the field and they all seem to work 'in the industry' e.g. nuclear power; noise related to motor racing; or waste disposal. A community group or parish council may find that the person with the right qualifications may back off from getting too involved in their case because they do not wish to offend existing or potential clients. On the other hand such people may be prepared to help an independent team leader behind the scenes: quite understandably, they just don't want to front the operation and upset their paymasters.

Whoever your chosen professional advisor, if they are still beyond your pocket, or perhaps unavailable at the right time, they may be prepared to help you behind the scenes by submitting written evidence (which is cheaper than paying them to appear as well), vetting the evidence of a competent lay witness, or giving tips on presentation, so that you are better equipped for a DIY job. Indeed, this approach can save time, trouble and expense of briefing someone unfamiliar with the case, its history or the area in general. There are other advantages too. At times the whole point of participating, is to demonstrate the feelings of those living in the locality, even if one has to make a nice judgement between demonstrating the widespread concern of the community and boring the decision makers. The wealth of background knowledge to be found amongst the best local witnesses means that they are not caught out by questions about their own patch.

Whether lay or professional, witnesses should be chosen according to the following criteria. They must know their subject off backwards. They should speak clearly; heavy accents may add local colour but their presence is in vain if they cannot be understood. Their delivery should be sufficiently slow to enable note taking by those listening. Temperamentally witnesses must be capable of staying cool, calm and courteous no matter what tricks of the trade or general provocation is being served up by the opposition. If an inquiry hoves in view, it is a good idea to practice before hand with the points likely to be put by the opposition plus a few unfair allegations, for good measure.

The Advocate/Witness

Another means of economising on fees, but getting the best of both worlds is to retain, say, a planning witness, who will organise the whole campaign: they will take responsibility for the strategic aspects of the case, and organise local people to help assemble evidence. Their professional knowledge and experience enables them to pinpoint the key issue[s] on which the case will hang, and also relevant subsidiary matters. They will decide whether research on local conditions is necessary and help people to adopt as professional approach as possible. They will probably be responsible for sifting through all the documentation relevant to the case, tracking down government publications and academic research, and integrating local research into the case to be presented. As team leader they will be responsible for all written evidence to be put before the decision makers. Temperamentally they should be capable of keeping up the team's morale during low moments or when disaster strikes.

What is the role of local people? They are experts on their own locality and can point out key issues to the advocate/witness imported from outside. Very often there are people with relevant professional skills who are able to guide the advocate/witness in the direction of pertinent publications, and other important documents. They supply the person-power for surveys, video shooting, and compiling a photo album, for example. They will also select from amongst themselves, witnesses to testify as to the existing situation, and how the proposal will affect them, and prepare short statements for the LPA or inquiry. They can play an invaluable role reproducing all the documentation to be submitted by the appropriate date.

At any inquiry the advocate/witness will explain to the inspector, and others present, about their dual role: they will play the team leader in terms of outlining the case; introducing and protecting their lay witnesses; cross examining the opposition; and summing up. As the chief witness, they will present the strategic part of the case and be subject to cross-examination. They will also give their lay witnesses the confidence to appear at the inquiry, read their statement and answer any questions from the inspector. Opposing counsel rarely cross-examine local people. It is not just bad form. As one QC put it, 'My dear, you never know what they are going to say!' The truth of this remark will be explored in Section IV. Last but not least, it is very important that there be a good attendance by the public any council meeting, or inquiry: such support gives silent testimony to the decision makers of the depth of public concern.

This approach to fighting undesirable development can really make an impact on decision making because it combines the strategic approach on policy with local knowledge. It is cost-effective too, so this technique has been adopted by various planning professionals, especially those involved in Planning Aid, and the NALC consultancy service. Allow a few weeks for making contact with your advocate/witness, in addition to the time needed to prepare the case.

SUBSTANCE

The Realpolitik Behind Case Presentation

In any environmental controversy, there are certain political realities involved, which affect the character of one's evidence and the spirit in which it is presented. The following sets out the most common of these.

Representing a coalition of groups should increase political clout, but it can be difficult to get people to agree on either what they want, or what they would find acceptable. To avoid this, LPAs, NGOs and local groups are usually better off coordinating their efforts, with each ploughing its own furrow in parallel with the others, so that there is no repetition to bore the inspector, and the work-load is reduced all round.

However, there can be the problem when that vital point gets omitted or fails to make the requisite impact. Much hand-wringing after the event may be prevented by asking two questions, and taking appropriate precautions:

a) How committed is Body X to winning the case? A statutory body may be doing its bit for 'political' rather than substantive reasons. Similarly, at an appeal, an LPA's officers may be present in body but not in spirit because they recommended the development but were overruled by their councillors. Thus although, nominally, you are not alone, the reality of fighting off the opposition may be left to you.

b) Will they actually 'deliver the goods' at the appropriate time? Do they have the the resources to do what is promised? What has been their track record in comparable situations? Even if you feel sure that all will be well, it is sensible to allow for the unexpected e.g. paperwork arriving too late because of illness or business commitments, counsel being ineffectual, or witnesses stranded in blizzards. Make sure you mention all vital points in your proof so that you can supplement your evidence at the last moment: if you say nothing at all, you cannot suddenly introduce a new subject without wild squeals of protest from the opposition.

A key decision is whether to support or reject the proposal, and if the latter, do you oppose it completely, or are you just objecting to part of it, or the conditions, or the proposed s. 106 planning obligation? There are times when one has to accept the unpalatable, but it can be made more bearable by scaling down the impact. In any case it is advisable to think about conditions: the LPA may accept the application, but could impose restrictions in the form of conditions, a s. 106 planning obligation, or, indeed, a bye-law. At any inquiry, inspectors are likely to ask you what would be acceptable 'were they minded to allow the development', but stressing that this in no way implies that they are prejudging the issue.

Bye-laws are means by which local authorities can exercise their regulatory functions e.g. under the Public Health Acts, and they are binding on everyone who comes within their scope. To be valid, bye-laws must be within the law of the land, and usually have to be confirmed by the Secretary of State.

What about an alternative site for the development? With regard to appeals and call-ins, the focus has to be the application in question: your proposal would require another application, and the likelihood is that the developer has no interest in that site. However, you can use your alternative as an analogy, a means of highlighting the disadvantages of the proposal under consideration. Of course, at Local Plan Inquiries, the situation is different: wrangles over alternative sites constitute much of the substance of the proceedings.

Planning decisions are made within quite narrow parameters. The discussion is on the proposal before the planning committee or the inspector, and the terms in which it is couched are likely to determine the definition of the problem, and the yardsticks for solving it, as well as putting forward *the* solution. Unless the decision makers dismiss the case completely, they will either accept it outright, or with conditions and/or a planning obligation. Thus, conservatism is built into the the planning process. Objectors must recognise this, and fight within these constraints. For example there is no point in saying that the money would be better spent in the Third World, or using the forum as a platform for railing against the privatisation of utilities.

The fora in which planning decisions are taken are not supposed to be political arenas. Clearly they are, because they are concerned with the allocation of resources, and there are bound to be winners and losers. However the apolitical fiction is maintained by the unwritten rule that the decision is made *'in the public interest'*, and therefore all evidence before the committee or before the inspector, is divested of its personal or party political trappings. This leads to untold hypocrisy e.g. Nimbyism dressed up as a problem about access, or Greed masquerading as public amenity. Therefore, it is not done to complain that the railway link will bisect the backyard, or the neighbourhood's very own international airline terminal will knock thousands of pounds off the value of the family schloss. Neither is it acceptable to say that the only reason for filing this application is to increase the paper assets of a company which is in the hands of the receivers.

'You are pressing this claim ... with greed and aggression rather than decency and fairness, and for that reason I intend to resist it. You have not got your hands on the money yet: it is still in my possession. I declare, and let all those at the Law Rock be witnesses, that I challenge you, Mord Fiddle, to single combat. ... I myself shall stake an equal sum, the winner to take all.'

Njal's Saga, Chapter 8

In any given case, there can be a lot at stake for both people and institutions: feelings can run high. There may also be a history of bad blood between organisations, and long running feuds between professionals in the same field. The *public interest syndrome* also affects the atmosphere in which issues are debated. As everyone is supposed to be arguing about what is best for the area, rather than for themselves, politeness towards opponents and adjudicators is the order of the day. This manifests itself in terms of your approach to procedures and players.

A really strong case, with the best advocacy and expert witnesses lined up to present it, can be ruined if the correct procedures are not observed. Whilst Sections I, II, IV and V deal with these in detail, a general observation on the subject is appropriate at this juncture. A theme common to all these procedures is a strict timetable, necessary because otherwise the system would grind to a halt. Do not, therefore, try to 'box clever' and withhold information beyond the time limit allowed for its submission in order to catch-out the other side. It might work in TV court-room dramas, but it doesn't redound to your credit if something goes wrong: if it comes to light that you have indulged in a little gentle skulduggery, it detracts from your case, and, in certain instances, it may mean that you have denied yourself the opportunity to put your case at all.

Even if you have good reason to be gravely suspicious of the conduct or tactics of your opponents, play it by the book in terms of observing the usual civilities and correct procedures. Then, if your worst fears are realised, you can legitimately claim to be the wronged party to the relevant arbiters: the officers/elected members of the LPA, the Inspectorate, the Secretary of State or the Courts. Your virtuous conduct will mean that you will have the satisfaction of putting your case, having invested time, effort and money in mounting a campaign. It will also enhance your reputation with the decision makers, thus influencing the view they take of the substance of your case. Being 'good' might be boring, but, it is effective. You play to win: there are no second prizes.

In a similar vein, it is *not done* to ask witnesses to give evidence on oath. The only occasion when this is officially considered to be appropriate is during an appeal against an Enforcement Notice. This is because it is primarily concerned with past events and existing development rather than speculation about the future. However, past events and assertions inevitably play a part in other disputes, yet one cannot be seen to query directly the good faith of the other side: one has to confound their arguments on substantive grounds.

The assumed good intent of the other side is also the justification for unfailing courtesy towards your opponents. Lay people can be disconcerted by fraternisation between professionals on opposing sides. They have to understand that conflicts in the ring do not necessarily mean bad relationships at a personal level: professionals never know when they will have to work together on the same side, and they have probably learned what lies behind that aggressive 'front' because they have served on some professional committee, or were marooned together in the some one horse town during a long running inquiry. In any case, a measure of cooperation is helpful in terms of the exchange of information and means that the argument is restricted to the matter in hand, and does not become personal.

> *To be born a gentleman is an accident, but to die one is an achievement.*
>
> Christopher Lee

Thus, environmental conflicts are intensely political in terms of the relationships between the various participants, the substance of their cases, and the final outcome. On the other hand, the myth of the *public interest* expedites the proceedings by taking the sting out of the debate – most of the time! If you are a serious player in environmental decision making, the realpolitik of the situation has to be taken on board: it is likely to affect, at a fundamental level, both the grounds upon which you fight your case, and the spirit in which you play the game.

Getting to Grips with the Issues

With regard to the determination of planning applications, or inquiries resulting from call-ins and appeals, the focus of your case is the planning application, and the issues arising from it. Technically the local plan inquiry is an inquiry into objections, but this only means that the subjects discussed are limited to the objection sent in during the six week consultation period on the deposited plan: the latter is still the focus of attention at any given hearing. With regard to road inquiries, there are no 'terms of reference': the central issue will be the orders before the inspector, but the scope of the inquiry will be thrashed out at the pre-inquiry meeting between the Objectors and the inspector. Thus, the substance of a case will be issues relating to the road proposal, the deposited plan, or the planning application: hereafter these three are known as *'the proposal'*. Appeals against the refusal to license an activity, under the EPA 1990, focus on the pollution rather than the planning aspects of the case.

The type of expert witness being retained by the opposition, and their status within their profession, can give one clues, not only about the subjects they consider to be important, but how much they are prepared to pay to put forward their point of view. The likely view of their professionals might be deduced from their stance at previous inquiries, and this is useful when compiling your own case. A perspective on the proposal will also be given by the views put forward by the statutory and non-statutory consultees (see Appendix V). In addition, there may be an Environmental Statement, a proposed s.106 agreement or unilateral undertaking (see Appendix IX), and visual material, such as maps, plans, photographs and models. With regard to appeals and call-ins there will be Statements of Case put forward by the local authority and developer. From the point of view of third parties, all the documents will contain references to the key policy issues involved, and the documents with which you will be obliged to become familiar.

> *'In principle, it seems to me that any consideration, which relates to the use and development of land, is capable of being a planning consideration. Whether a particular consideration falling within that broad class is material in any given case, will depend on the circumstances'*
> L.J.Cook, Stringer v. Ministry of Housing & Local Government 1971

Every case is unique, but there are certain factors which tend to be common to all. Let us return to basics:

> *The planning system ... should operate on the basis that applications for development should be allowed,* **having regard to the development plan and all material considerations,** *unless the proposed development would cause* **demonstrable harm to interests of acknowledged importance.**
> [PPG1, 1992, para.5, emphasis added]

The latter phrase has been recited *ad nauseam* in planning disputes, to the extent that whoever coined it must wish they could claim royalties. Unfortunately its successor, in paras.36 and 40 of the 1997 version, whilst retaining the same phraseology, puts it less succinctly, so one suspects that its predecessor will live on in live exchanges.

As Section I showed, there are various denominations of 'Development Plan': the structure and local plans of rural areas, the unitary development plans of urbanised areas; and minerals and waste local plans which come into play when dealing with these issues. It was also pointed out that up to date plans and those nearing adoption carried more weight, in the eyes of decision-makers than those in the early stages of consultation.

Thus, 'having regard to the development plan' means looking at the issues surrounding a given case e.g. employment, housing, tourism, nature conservation, the built heritage, transport, pollution etc., and seeing what the relevant policies have to say about each one:

a) To what extent do these policies support your case?

b) If your stance is contrary to the relevant policy in the development plan, are there extenuating circumstances, or other policies which support your case?

c) If the Plan is getting out of date, what do more recent plans say? Bear in mind that they carry greater weight the nearer they are to adoption.

It may just be the case that there are no policies in the development plan which are relevant to the proposal, in which case it has to be decided on the balance of these mysterious things called 'material considerations'. What are they? As Fig.12 shows, the definition is exceedingly wide. Work through the list systematically to see what factors can be cited as valid planning considerations in support of your case, whilst noting those which go against you because these will have to be played down in order to minimise the damage to your argument.

Lastly, what are *interests of acknowledged importance*? The short answer is planning policy in all its guises (see Fig.12 (1) & (2), and Appendix I). In addition, however, there are other issues which loom large in any environmental debate: the broader social and economic goals of our society e.g. employment, a clean environment, road safety, the prosperity of a town centre etc. It is no accident that these are to be found in Fig.12 masquerading as material considerations.

Constructing Your Case

In an environmental dispute, as elsewhere, facts are not free-standing entities but they are the raw material from which all sides construct their cases. When sifting through the evidence put forward by the opposition, and selecting the facts upon which you will base your case, you have two complementary objectives:

a) to prove that your position equates with government policy – unlike that of your opponent;

b) aim to prove that you opponent's stance on the issue would cause *demonstrable harm to interests of acknowledged importance.*(PPG1 1997 para.40)

If the link to the kind of material to be found in Appendix I is not obvious, think in terms of how this information squares with government policy on the issue. With regard to evidence supporting your case, does it accord with current policy objectives or can it be made to look as though it does? When it comes to your opponent's evidence, does that reflect the official line, and how do you undermine this position?

Figure 12   Material Considerations

1)   Central Government's Planning Policy.

TCP Acts. Other relevant statutes e.g. Criminal Justice Act 1994 for gypsy site disputes; wildlife legislation; local government Acts;
Circulars; PPGs; policy notes on various subjects; Ministerial Statements. [It should be noted that draft Circulars and policy guidance can be cited as material considerations because it shows the policy is under review.]

Which policy documents of central government (see Appendix I) are relevant to your case? How can you turn them to your advantage? Are the circumstances which led to the issuing of a draft policy relevant to your case?

2)   Local Government's Planning Policies.

Draft plans; other policy documents and proposals; design guides; development briefs; consultants' reports.

Which local government policy documents (see Appendix I) are relevant to your case?
How can they be used to best advantage?

3)   Amenity.

That which adds to the quality of life of the public. It should be noted that 'amenity' cannot be claimed for exclusively private interests.

Are amenity issues involved in this case?
How can these be most effectively demonstrated?

4)   Social Considerations.

These include the impact on schools, medical services, shopping and transport networks.

How exactly will the proposal affect your community?
How can this be demonstrated?

5)   Economic Considerations.

financial viability of the project; cross-subsidization between different parts of the 'package'.

Will the project be financially viable?
Is the cross subsidization between its different parts feasible?
Will the project have an adverse effect on the financial viability and therefore upkeep of listed buildings and/or a conservation area?

6)   Planning Rights.

Previous permissions, permitted development, and the planning history of the site

What skeletons are there in the cupboard?
How can past history be turned to your advantage?
What is the developer's past record regarding other schemes?

---

7)   Previous LPA Decisions.

Whilst not bound by past decisions, LPA's like to be seen to be consistent in their approach to similar problems.

Are there other planning decisions relevant to your case?
In what respects can the LPA's decision help your case?

---

8)   Precedent.

Can be a material consideration, but only if concerns are well founded.

Is there a real danger that this proposal will set a precedent?
How would it matter if it did?

---

9)   Prematurity.

This issue is raised particularly frequently when appeals are lodged in the later stages of the local plan process. (see PPG1 1992, paras.32–34)

How exactly will the granting of this permission jeopardize the provisions of the local plan?

---

10)   Retaining or Promoting Desirable Uses.

This should not be used to protect private interests but rather to show that a certain use, or mix of uses should be preserved or promoted in the public interest.

Is the existing use certain to continue if this application is refused?
Can the desirable mix of uses actually be achieved?
Why is this use needed?

---

11)   Alternative site.

This situation may come about either because of the nature of the proposed development or because of the character of the chosen site. The LPA is not obliged to look for alternative sites.

How exacting are the requirements for this proposal and could it be readily accommodated elsewhere?

Is it in the public interest that only one proposal of this type should be allowed, and therefore that the optimum situation be found?

What are the benefits and disbenefits of the respective sites?

Could you use the example of another site which highlights the disadvantages of the proposed site for this development?

12) Morality.

In terms of censuring behaviour, this is not a material consideration, but equity between different sectors of the community can be introduced.

Does this proposal raise issues of equity or fairness?
Does the developer's past conduct suggest he will abide by conditions?

 LEGAL MATERIAL CONSIDERATIONS

13) Private Law Rights. The fact that a proposal, if allowed, could lead to legal actions on grounds of nuisance in the future, does not preclude the granting of planning permission.

How can issues which could lead to future legal action be transposed into planning lingo so that potential problems can be prevented rather than cured?

14) Section 106 Planning Obligations (see Appendix IX)

Is there a s.106 obligation on the *existing* development? Can you persuade your LPA not to agree to discharge, of modify it? Was it signed before or after 25th October 1991? Will the LPA be willing to go through the appeals procedure?

Proposed s.106 obligation accompanying *new proposal*. Such a legal agreement can be weighed in the balance as a material consideration. Unacceptable development should never be permitted because of unrelated benefits offered by the applicant. Planning obligations should only be sought where they are necessary to make a proposal acceptable in land-use planning terms. In other words, the offer of a planning obligation must not constitute a bribe.

Does the proposed s.106 agreement conform to the strictures of DoE Circular 1/97 Annex B?

Are there any High Court judgements which support your position?

15) Other Statutory Controls.

Inevitably there is an overlap between planning and other areas of law affecting the environment. The rule is to choose the most effective mechanism in terms of control. According to Circular 11/95, planning conditions which duplicate other legal controls are unnecessary, and those which run contrary to them are *ultra vires*. The problem is that other statutory controls may achieve some planning objectives but not others, so it essential to be clear which regime can deliver which objective. (See Appendix IX)

Does this proposal involve other statutory controls?

Can they deliver the goods in terms of planning objectives?

Should the situation be dealt with by framing appropriate conditions?

Environmental decisions are concerned with the future, and so there are no *Rules of Evidence* or bans on press reporting. Evidence can range from massive tomes to hearsay. How much weight it is accorded by the decision makers depends on how reliable it is. The analysis of material may be divided into four sections: your opponent's case; official information; other published material; and your own data collecting.

Opponent's Evidence

Begin by looking critically at your opponent's evidence:

1. Is this proposal exactly the same as a previous one from the same developer, or are there subtle differences? If so, have these been noticed by the local planning authority and drawn to the attention of statutory consultees? Do these subtle changes have important implications?

2. Check each part of each sentence for accuracy. If the first half of a sentence is true, is the second half? Does the latter follow logically from the former? Is the statement capable of another interpretation? Is there a statement, further on in the document, or in another one, which counter-balances the quote given in their text?

3. Check the references throughout the written text. Are they being economical with the truth about the source material? Is the date supplied with extracts from letters and reports? On a key issue, is there a recent report, and if not, why not?

4. Examine most carefully their maps, plans and artist's impressions. It is not unknown for cuttings to be mistaken for embankments, the latest houses in the village ignored because the maps used are out of date, or artistic licence to overstep the boundaries of the applicant's property. What would a computer mock-up of the proposed development actually look like?

5. Look for authenticity and accuracy in the numerical material. What premises underlie the statistics? What are the parameters of the computer model? Are they looking sufficiently far into the future? Do key assumptions accord with common-sense, not to mention reality?

6. Do the proposed conditions, or s. 106 planning obligations conform to government guidance set out in DoE Circulars 11/95 and 1/97 Are there any helpful High Court cases, which further illustrate your point? (See Appendix IX).

Accept nothing at face value. You will be amazed how often there is another side to the story that they are telling. The use of your opponent's evidence has the great advantage that they will not cast doubt on the credibility of their own source material, even if they do not agree with your interpretation of it. It is essential that everyone be seen to sing from the same hymn-sheet.

There are times when even one's allies appear to be taking a rather strange view of the situation. It might be as well to check their sources to make sure that letters have not got 'lost' and that all concerned have got their facts straight, so that the true position can be put to the decision makers.

Official Information

Before embarking on a search for relevant material amongst the plethora of official information, look at that which could have a bearing on this proposal because it is related to the existing situation, both on the site and in the surrounding area (see Appendix VI).

Where an application involves environmental assessment, much additional information should be available. The Local Government (Access to Information Act) 1985 provides for the admission of the public to all council meetings, unless confidentiality is endangered, together with access to agendas, reports, background papers and minutes. If anyone tells you that you cannot see or take copies of a planning application, or a letter from a statutory consultee, they are either lying or misinformed. Quoting the 1985 Act should result in their scurrying to filing cabinet. The only proviso is that you will have to pay for the photocopying.

The relevance of the European environmental law is discussed in Fig.13. The availability of environmental information appears to have been greatly extended by the EU directive on Freedom of Access to Information on the Environment which has been transposed into British legislation in the form of Regulations, S.I.1992, 3240. As can been seen from Appendix VII, the practical effects of the legislation have yet to be tested in the Courts, but it is a move in the right direction.

The range of information available from central and local government is to be found in Appendix I. If you don't know where to start, begin with the PPGs which look as though they might have a bearing on your case, and work on to the RPGs and MPGs, if they are relevant. They will refer to key government reports, and the main statutes PPGs and Circulars involved, and often have a list of addresses of official bodies and even non-government organisations (NGOs) who may be able to give further advice. The DoE publish an Index of Planning Advice: contact the DoE Public Enquiry helpline (Appendix IV) to obtain the current edition.

There was a time when one could say that government policy could be defined as anything on sale in an HMSO bookshop. However, that is no longer the case: HMSO has been superseded by the Stationery Office. Their shops stock a wider range of goods, and, in these days of deregulation, not all agencies of government have contractual arrangements with them. Chadwyck Healy publishes a monthly catalogue of British Official Publications. If you have difficulty in acquiring, say, a copy of a report, contact the relevant body directly, ask for the publications department, and have the publication sent to you by post. It may even come free of charge, whereas you used to have to pay for it: thus, to those with initiative, it shall be given.

PARLIAMENTARY OMBUDSMAN

If you have difficulty obtaining information which should be available from central government or its acolytes, you might approach the Parliamentary Ombudsman in Millbank Tower. He can investigate claims about: undue delay in supplying the information; excessive charging for supplying it; refusal to produce material; and incomplete data. Nonetheless certain information is withheld from disclosure under the Code of Practice. Copies of the latter are available from the Machinery of Government Division, Office of Public Service (see Appendix IV).

Giselle Bakkenist, Environmental Information, (London, Cameron May, 1994) p.122
N.Lees, & H.Woolstanton, Environmental Information: A Guide to Sources, (London, The British Library of Science Technology and Industry.)
Catalogue of British Official Publications, (Cambridge, Chadwyck Healy)

Many Departments of Government are now providing a 'Who's Who' guide to their departmental structure, complete with phone numbers: this does make life easier for those tracking down the latest development in government policy. Thus encouraged, if you take the provision of information one stage further in terms of personal contact with individual Ministers or civil servants, you may still run up against personal vetting: whether you get that piece of information will depend not just on who you are, in terms of your qualifications, but who you represent. Consultants representing different interests at different times have discovered that they can become *persona non grata* with the decision-makers if they are retained by an organisation considered politically 'risque', or generally 'below the salt'. Being a citizen of Planet Earth is still inadequate in Great Britain PLC: getting that vital information can be more akin to pulling teeth. On democratic grounds the pathetic Code of Practice on Open Government is no substitute for a Freedom of Information Act. (see Appendix VII)

We do not accept the the argument (as advanced by the Water Services Association and the Department of Trade and Industry) that transfer of ownership of a public utility or statutory undertaker, to the private sector should necessarily remove that body from the ambit of the Regulations: the concept of control, as the DoE's guidance note indicates, goes wider than that of mere ownership. ... We find it bizarre that the Water Service Companies, in particular, should persist in their view that they are neither controlled (in the sense of having statutory duties) nor hold 'public responsibility for the environment'.

Opinion of House of Lords Select Committee on European Communities, Report on Freedom of Access to Information on the Environment, 1996

Environment Facts: a guide to Using Public Registers of Information (DoE 1995)
Who Does What on Environment Matters at the DoE? (DoE, Oct.1994)
Environmental Contacts: A guide for Business; Who does What In government Departments?(Dept. of Trade and Industry)

Figure 13   European Law

The purpose of the European Union (EU) extends beyond free trade: one of its objectives, almost from its inception, has been to improve the quality of life of its inhabitants, and that includes protecting their environment. Nonetheless, environmental protection can be justified in terms of fair competition between Member States: it protects natural resources, including biodiversity;   makes sure companies cannot obtain a cost advantage by being allowed to pollute the environment in States where the laws are more lenient; imposes standards on goods in transit to prevent harm to people and the environment; and minimizes trans-boundary effects by regulating activities on a given country which could affect the environment in neighbouring countries. Environmental requirements have been grafted onto other EU policies pertaining to agriculture, industry, energy, transport, the regions, and competition between Member States, although it has to be said that there is a difference between theory and practice: as in Whitehall, the big spenders in the EC are still in the process of being educated about the environment.

For some time, there were differing opinions as to whether environmental policy fell to be considered as a true European community issue. The issue was finally settled by the adoption of the Single European Act in 1986, and subsequently transposed into the Maastricht Treaty. Prior to 1986, European legislation in this field owed much to conserving a political consensus and/or securing uniform economic conditions.

Since 1973 there have been successive Community programmes on the environment, reflecting the issues of the day, and the priority accorded them by the incumbent EU Presidents: the current Programme, 'Towards Sustainability' is due to run to the year 2000, and is based on the theme of sustainability to be found in the Brundtland Report of 1987.

Whether or not a measure is eligible for inclusion also depends on whether it needs to be tackled at a community level rather than left to individual member states. Thus there has been successive legislation on all aspects of pollution: waste; water; air; nuclear safety and dangerous chemicals. Measures to protect wild birds and habitats have been justified in terms of conserving biodiversity. Town and country planning, on the other hand, is considered as a matter for Member States: as is shown elsewhere in this book the only two measures which have affected it directly, have been environmental assessment and access to environmental information.

Most European environmental legislation has appeared in the form of a *Directive*. This imposes the obligation on a Member State to achieve its aims by introducing or revising legislation, and/or appropriate administrative measures within a given timescale. European law may be invoked in two ways: interpreting national law using European law on that subject, or relying directly on European law by invoking the doctrine of *direct effect* when arguing with public bodies over their obligations, or dragging them through the courts.

Given that any given land-use case may have implications in areas which are the subject of European Directives, it is as well to be aware of them because they may have significant effects on both the procedure and the substance of the matter in question. European law gives another dimension to environmental regulation and may be invoked when dealing any 'emanation of the state', from central and local government to a privatised utility. Thus a wide range of cases may benefit from your professional advisor having a knowledge of European environmental law, or access to those who do. If you think you may need a specialist in this area, contact ELF or UKELA (see Appendix IV).

Where do you find out about European environmental law? Basically, good sources are likely to be:

a) the European Commission Offices* in the UK;

b) universities with law libraries, stocking EU and environmental law publications;

c) NGOs* with an interest in the sort of issues listed in European Issues;

d) A comprehensive list of publications is to be found in CPRE's 'A Campaigner's Guide to Using EC Environmental Law', Appendix 3 and the Select Bibliography appended to ELF's manual, 'European Issues in Environmental Litigation'.

[*see Appendix IV]

Other Published Material

Take heart. There is reputable information which may be crucial to your case beyond the reaches of Whitehall. Obviously the more 'blue chip' it is the better, and for every category of information there is a sliding scale in terms of prestige and reliability. Advice on Parliamentary material may be given by the House of Commons Public Information Office, and extracts from Hansard obtained from the House of Commons Library. In addition the Press Association will provide copies of articles from past issues for a moderate charge, and extracts of academic research may be found in environmental and scientific journals. And then there is the Internet: more and more international, governmental, and research institutions worldwide are joining the world wide web, and making their wares accessible by electronic means.

If you wish to follow up an article by reading the original research paper, telephone either the academic establishment which undertook the research or a local academic centre with an interest in the subject: they just might have a copy of the document in question which you can read in the university library, or have copied for a moderate charge. With a little charm you may even obtain an interview with the researcher: academics enjoy explaining their work. It is advisable to read round the subject and compile a list of questions beforehand, so that you get the most out of the interview, and at least appear intelligent however inadequate you feel.

Your Own research

At an early stage you may have to consider embarking on your own research, because you know that a vital piece of evidence does not exist elsewhere. The danger of undertaking your own data collection is that your opponent will endeavour to discredit the methodology you use, and therefore the results you get. It is, therefore, imperative that you use a nationally recognised basis for your research. If in doubt take advice from academics or professionals in the land use field: they may be able to point you in the direction of the methodological bible on the subject. A word of warning: if you are not able to produce top quality results, you would be better off relying on allies who have the resources to do the job properly, because you will be taken apart in correspondence or cross – examination for pretending to expertise you don't have. That said, lethal results may be achieved by using a combination of the evidence given by your opponent, and a nationally recognised research tool, and laced with a little of your own initiative: see Fig.14.

Figure 14   Researching Your Case: Examples

Example 1. Proposed Park & Ride site, on Green Belt.

A social survey, according to recognised methodology, was undertaken of all the villages thought by the LPA to be the catchment area for the P&R. the objective was to find out whether, and to what extent, there was a demand for the facility. The survey showed that demand would have been too low for the P&R to have been economic.

Example 2. Proposed expansion of industrial site in rural area.

A traffic count was undertaken, using the approved DTp methodology, to illustrate the existing nuisance from heavy vehicles, particularly in the early hours of the morning. The survey was conducted between 3 am and 8 pm., and proved the high incidence of existing traffic in the early hours.

Example 3. *The impact of a new superstore on a town centre*

Objectors acquired the most recent Goad* Plan of the town centre; categorised and colour coded the shop into 'convenience'; comparison; charity; restaurants etc.; and vacant premises. Using the superstore's list of goods which they planned to sell, they illustrated by use of coloured stickers, those town centre shops which would have been in competition with the super store. For comparison, they acquired an historic Goad Plan of the town which illustrated how many more convenience shops there were before the existing supermarkets arrived.

* Goad Plans are sold by Charles Goad - see Appendix IV.

Example 4. *Estate of houses on prominent location*

A computer mock up of a proposed estate, produced from developers plans and architect's drawings, was super-imposed on existing photograph of site, which was a view of the village well known to all those approaching it by road from that direction. At the appeal the developer could only quarrel with the colour of the bricks: it looked like the eyesore it would have become, had it be allowed.

There are occasions when someone with a key interest in the ultimate decision cannot be seen to participate openly in the debate because they will have to continue to live with their landlord, or will be neighbours to the new development if it goes ahead. In such a situation, they can feed information to a broader interest group to augment their case: if it is somewhere in the public domain no one will ask about its source.

A common local initiative is to demonstrate local opinion through signing petitions. These and preform letters are only of value if the case is well supported by government policy: they reinforce a good case. If, however, government policy is contrary to your position, then collecting signatures or exhorting people to send in letters is a waste of time. The reason is that policy is the product of a democratically elected government. Thus policy is equated with the 'public interest', which should override narrower local or sectorial interests. In the mid nineties this may be difficult to accept, but the fault lies beyond the planning system. Further discussion of this important issue is to be found in Section VI.

Videos are now accepted as part of modern life, apart from the old school amongst decision makers. If you do decide to make a video, have it edited by a professional: minutes spent gazing at an empty road, do not help your complaint about traffic. It is essential to provide a commentary to make sure those watching understand what they are looking at. Having obtained the permission of those adjudicating, make sure someone knows how to work the video player: there is the true story of the road inquiry where the inspector and all participants were treated to a sizable extract of a Tarzan film on television, before someone was found who could work the video! Lastly, having got your message across on celluloid, have a duplicate video the decision-makers can take away for private viewing.

Leaving aside the home movies, there can be a tendency to be too academic when trying to present evidence. It is sometimes better to let the experts churn through the technicalities and apply your imagination to how the development will affect you and your community. A few well chosen words can paint a picture in the minds of the decision makers. Yes, they will be interested in the distress to domestic animals caused by explosions on a nearby MOD property, or fears of baby and buggy being mown down by HGVs. This type of evidence will be just as valid, and even come as a welcome relief, after the volumes of statistics produced by those who will not have to live with the development.

Organising the Evidence

Once you have decided on your stance, set about constructing your case. It is never to early to start, because there is never enough time before you have to present it.

How do you decide which points are of strategic importance and which should play a supportive role? The former underpin the whole case being put forward by your opponent because it is of fundamental importance to either the site, or the development. As recognising a strategic issue is rather akin to the proverbial elephant, difficult to describe but easy to recognise. However, the examples included in Fig.15 may help.

Figure 15   Pin-Pointing the Strategic Issue

Example 1. *Building an estate of houses amongst woodland.*

At a previous inquiry an inspector granted outline permission for build-ing an estate of houses on a wooded slope overlooking an industrial town. Permission was conditional on a substantial number of trees being left on site after development. Objectors set out to prove that the proposed plans, now subject of an inquiry into reserve matters, would not fulfil that condition: this was the key to winning the case.

The trees on the site were mapped; the developer's own plans and a publication produced by the House Builders Federation, were used to calculate the number of trees which would have had to be lost on this site. Overlays were used to show how more and more trees would be lost by the building of the access road, the construction of the houses, the provision of service trenches, providing daylight round the houses etc. Objectors proved that a mere 13% of the tress would be left. Hardly the 'substantial proportion' required by the outline permission. The appeal was dismissed. The land has never been built on because it is not an economic proposition to build the few houses required to fulfil the condition.

Example 2. *Constructing a marina in a Ramsar Site*

The proposal was to build a marina for 300 boats in a small embayment in an extensive natural harbour in the south coast. The harbour was renowned for its bird-life, and had been designated as an SSSI as early as 1958. In 1986 DoE designated it as a Ramsar site, and it is now a Special Protection Area (SPA). The EC Habitat's Directive says that development is not debarred from an SPA but it does make it difficult. There was certainly an economic case for the development: demand from boat owners in a traditionally tourist area, with high unemployment. On the other hand, it is a wildlife site of international importance.

The DoE's policy on nature conservation is set out in PPG 9. Annex C details the issues which should be taken into account in controlling development in SPAs: whether the proposal would have a significant effect on the SPA; the site's conservation objectives; the effect on its integrity; whether or not it hosts priority habitats and species; the out-come of an assessment by English Nature; alternative solutions; and whether the development is of overriding public interest for social or economic reasons. A flow chart is provided as a visual aid. This policy statement provided the key to winning the case.

All sides to this dispute had to examine these issues systematically. Some were more cut and dried than others, but the outcome of the dis-pute was determined by means of working through the checklist of strategic issues. The application was refused because: the embayment was of key importance as a feeding area within the harbour; no mitigating measures suggested by the developers could safeguard it; and the argument that this economic development was 'imperative, for reasons of overriding public interest', could not be sustained.

Example 3: *A Pets' Incinerator in Remote Tourist Area*

An appeal was heard against the non-determination of an application to install an incinerator for pets, in a farm in remote hill country, in the north of England. The incinerator was already in use, and local people were experiencing the nuisance of smell from the plant: deep frozen great dane, and other dear departed creatures, were wakening the entire populace in the early hours.

The bypassing of national public health regulations constituted the strategic issue in this case: the inability of the appellants to conform to the DoE code of practice on clinical waste in terms of transport, storage, trained personnel, drainage, the disposal of plastic waste, and the incinerator design. The £1,600 chicken burner from the USA did not conform to British Standard 3316: it burned at too low a temperature to consume the smell. An incinerator, adequate to the task, of disposing of animal carcasses without smell nuisance, would have cost £21,000, at the time, and would have come equipped with a 30 foot chimney. This would have been visually intrusive in an area of High Landscape Value, attractive to hill walkers and adjacent to a National Trust property visited by 140,000 visitors a year: the key role of tourism in the local economy was enshrined in the development plans for the area.

Whilst one cannot imagine that too many private households would wish to set up an in-house crematorium, the refusal of this application avoided an unfortunate precedent.

Sometimes the central issue is given prominence by those putting forward the scheme, but not always: it can be hidden in the documentation, and occasionally it is omitted altogether either through ignorance or design. Tracking down the key issue only appears to be an art-form: in fact it is defined by the extent to which the whole case hangs on this one point. If it does and you can manipulate it to your advantage, then you are likely to win your case. It is also necessary to have a yardstick by which it will stand or fall because all sides assent to it e.g. a key phase in law or policy, or the conditions imposed by the inspector when granting outline permission.

Unfortunately some cases are difficult to fight because they do not present specific targets e.g. one more housing development when a community is already coping with the traffic problems and pressure on social facilities or physical infrastructure, because of the cumulative effect of a series of previous permissions. In such a situation you just have to produce the best evidence you can about the known pressure points. If you can document your concerns, there is no reason why you should not persuade the decision-makers: it is a matter of patiently turning round the evidence on every point, major and minor.

Disputes over development are a zero sum game: during the proceedings, a point to one side is a point lost to the other. In the circumstances you would be foolish not to recognise the strengths in your opponent's case, and thereby lose the battle, all because you assumed the decision makers would share your blindness. What can you do beforehand about the strong arguments in their favour? Basically it is a matter of minimising the damage by any means available. Procedures for doing this are the same as those use in mounting a critique of your opponent's evidence, or deployed by an expert witness defending his position. The repertoire of respectable techniques include: enlarging the context of the debate, pointing out omissions in the evidence, and the questioning the credibility of the source. Just be sure that whatever you say in your proof or on your feet, is true: someone may be applying these forensic methods to *your* case.

As the discussion proceeds in a dispute of any length, its focus can change, and a subsidiary issue can suddenly loom large, so don't neglect them. It is essential that you have given them some thought beforehand, or you will be caught unawares and unable to develop your case. Flexibility and adroit manoeuvring are the name of the game if you are to stay the course, and achieve victory at the end of the day.

CONCLUSIONS

Clearly land-use proposals come in all shapes and sizes, from the house extension to the airport. The larger the proposal, the greater the level of input by official bodies and qualified personnel. If you are to make any substantial input into the proceedings, it is essential to build alliances with other like-minded bodies, and choose the right people, professional and lay, to put across your case to best advantage. Other Sections in this publication deal with specific procedures, but all of them operate, officially at least, in the spirit of *the public interest*, and this ethos has to be respected by your representatives if they are to acquit themselves well in the eyes of the decision-makers.

The overall objective is to win your case by proving that your position, unlike that of the opposition, is supported by government policy and the broader objectives of our society. Therefore, having reviewed all the evidence available, and selected the facts to support your case, you boost the arguments in your favour and undermine those of your opponents. This is not an occupation for those of a genteel disposition. Truth, in the sense understood by academic scientists, is an early casualty in the battle for a decision in your favour. You will find that all is fair in Love, War and Environmental Disputes.

Section IV

'Public Inquiries'

INTRODUCTION

This chapter could, with more accuracy, be entitled 'Planning Decisions by the Secretary of State' but it is doubtful whether this would mean much to readers, whereas 'the public inquiry' epitomizes the land use planning system for many people. In fact, it is the public face of a complex administrative system outlined elsewhere in this book, but public access to a drama concerning local issues is guaranteed to attract media attention.

Public inquiries can be categorised according to their legal origins: applications called-in by the Secretary of State; various appeals against refusals of planning permission; inquiries into the objections to local plans; road inquiries, and 'pollution' appeals (see Fig.16).

The reason why the title to this chapter is in parentheses is that not all disputes which could go to inquiry, actually make it. In terms of numbers, the various denominations of appeals still dominate the system, but these days few of them are given the full 'wig and gown' treatment. Since the early sixties there has been pressure to speed up appeals, and those in charge of the inquiry system devised simpler mechanisms to deal with the flood of appeals: the written representations procedure, and informal hearings. The former are no longer classified as public inquiries. Thus there is not generic name for planning decisions by the Secretary of State: all appeals do not go to inquiry, and the inquiry format is applied to matters other than appeals. Nevertheless this chapter sets out the ground rules for participating in the main classes of fora.

It begins with the key actors in these land-use dramas: the Inspectorate. It proceeds by dealing with written representations and hearings, before moving onto the salient points of various types of inquiries. The final section sets out how to make optimum use of the moves in the game at an archetypal inquiry, with suggestions as to how to simplify the procedure for use by parish councils and community groups.

THE INSPECTORATE

Like other branches of the Civil Service, the Planning Inspectorate has become an Executive Agency. Its inspectors can be divided in two: those under the aegis of the DoE and those forming part of the Lord Chancellor's Panel.

> *An interviewee for the roads Panel was grilled for two hours on how she would handle a riot at an inquiry. On returning home she recounted the tale to her son, a seventeen year old Harley Davidson devotee. 'Don't worry Mum. Any trouble, I'll send in the Hell's Angels!'*

The latter are concerned predominantly with road inquiries, although the odd light railway, pipeline or airfield or may come their way (see Fig.16). The Panel was created in the 1970s after there had been riots at motorway inquiries because it was felt that the DTp were judge and jury in their own cause: their own inspectors heard objections and reported to 'their' minister. The new Panel became known as the *Independent Inspectors*. It is comprised, mostly, of recycled military men: retired air marshals, admirals and colonels. They are contracted to take individual inquiries, rather than being salaried. With the demise of the road programme, they are becoming something of an endangered species.

Ascribing independence to the Panel is rather resented by the DoE inspectors who jealously guard their autonomy from Whitehall: their headquarters in Bristol are symbolic of a professional, not just a geographical distancing from London. The DoE inspectors have usually had a previous career in one of the land use professions: town planning, engineering, architecture, or surveying. Inevitably this influences their approach to problem solving e.g. engineers are concerned with technical feasibility whilst architects are likely to know less about nature conservation than aesthetics. Then there is the question of their personal background and interests. There is the tale of a minerals local plan inquiry, where a local archaeological trust was objecting to the possible destruction of the site of a Romano/British battlefield. The Director of the trust read out, in Latin, the account of the battle given in Caesar's Gallic Wars. As a good classicist, the inspector duly deleted the site from the plan.

As can be seen from Fig.16, the number and type of inquiries varies from year to year, so in order to deploy their staff to best effect, there is a hard core of salaried inspectors, to provide stability

Figure 16 Types of Public Inquiry: England 1995/96

The Inspectorate's Casework

CASE TYPE	1994/95	1995/96
Planning Appeals	12,236	11,214
Enforcement Appeals[1]	2,953	1,886
Development Plan Inquiries	66	91
Listed Building & Conservation Area Consent Appeals	656	608
Rights of Way Orders[2]	486	430
Listed Building Enforcement Appeals	215	129
Environmental Protection Act & Water Cases	47	49
Compulsory Purchase Orders	42	31
Drought Order applications	–	16
Applications for costs	1,593	1,227
Advertisement Appeals	–	1,655
Called-in Planning Applications	92	76
Transport and Works Act Cases	3	2
Certificate of Lawful Development Appeals	121	116
Hazardous Substances	1	1

[1] Includes appeals under section 174 and section 39
[2] Includes Public Path and Definitive Map Orders

The Lord Chancellor's Panel cases

DEPARTMENT OF TRANSPORT	
Trunk road orders	13
Local authority SRO & CPO	38
Stopping up of highways	13
Harbour Revision Orders	2
Light Railway Orders	3
Cycle Track	1
Civil Aviation Authority	1
Non Statutory	1
National Rivers Authority	1
Total	**73**

DEPARTMENT OF ENVIRONMENT	
Planning appeals	11
Circular 18/84	3
Rights of Way orders	1
Total	**15**

and specialists in certain areas, plus a floating population of contract and fee paid inspectors who are brought in during times of peak demand, to do appeals. Unlike the Panel, the DoE Inspectors undergo regular training to keep abreast of developments in their chosen field. Even so, they may need the help of an assessor over some technical matter e.g. appeals under the EPA 1990. For major inquiries, such as into an international airport or nuclear power station, a senior member of the planning bar is usually appointed for the duration.

Whatever their denomination, inspectors are not assigned to cases in the area in which they live or have some personal interest. This should be borne in mind when preparing and giving your evidence, and going on the site visit: it is a matter of explaining things clearly to someone who is a stranger to the area.

GOING TO APPEAL?

Those contemplating going to appeal, having had an application refused, should continue or initiate discussions with the LPA in the hope of reaching an agreement thus eliminating the time and expense of going through the appeal process. Objectors are often suspicious of these discussions, but they should understand that public bodies are obliged to go on talking to appellants because government has made it plain that the appeal procedure should only be used as a last resort.

Although the decision to go to appeal can be made any time within the six months after a refusal, if you opt for written representations, you effectively have only three or four months in which to make all the arrangements which might be involved. This is because, under DoE Circular 15/96, one is required to supply one's *full case* on the appeal application form. Thus the time is reduced for negotiating with the current owner of the property, raising the money, and taking the final decision to go ahead with an appeal. If you do not allow for all of this, you could find yourselves opting to be heard because then you only have to outline your case on the appeal application form! If you find yourself putting your case to an inspector, by intention or default, the DoE has the final word on whether it will be by means of a hearing or an inquiry. However, the views of the main parties e.g. LPA and appellant, will be taken into account.

Whichever side you are on, the techniques for optimizing the use of each procedure are set out in full in the remainder of this Section.

WRITTEN REPRESENTATIONS

All classes of appeals, under the Town & Country Planning Acts can be conducted by means of written representations: in 1995/6 they comprised 82% of appeals. There is now a presumption in favour of appeal by written representations. Government advice to appellants is that inquiries should be limited to those cases in which the evidence needs to be tested through cross-examination. Both appellants and LPAs tend to favour the procedure because of the reduced costs and greater speed with which the decision can be taken.

Nonetheless, if either party wants a full inquiry there has to be one. Third parties anxious for an inquiry because they fear that the full facts will not emerge otherwise, should ask their councillors to lobby the LPA for an inquiry. If the appeal proceeds by written representation, then the LPA is only obliged to contact third parties who objected at the application stage – which goes to prove how important it is to watch out for contentious planning applications at the early stages. Once notified, third parties have only 28 days in which to submit their case to Tollgate House, the Inspectorate's office in Bristol. (see under 'DoE', in Appendix IV)

Given that the original objection will be sent with the LPA's material to the Inspectorate, the opportunity should be taken to furnish new evidence e.g. circumstances which have arisen subsequently. Photographs or other visual material could also be included, but remember to send copies to the LPA and appellant if they have not seen them. Third parties can be of greater assistance to the inspector if they can complement the LPA case by putting forward specialist evidence, or the view from the grassroots. Requests for the inspector's or the Secretary of State's decision should be made at this stage.

The comparative speed of the written representations procedure is very much dependent on all parties keeping to the timetable of events. Indeed there is a Penalty Clause in para.16 in DoE Circular 15/96 Annex 1, stating that the Secretary of State is at liberty to disregard late representations, if he feel he has enough material upon which to base a decision.

Within 14 days of the receipt of the appeal the LPA is required to send to the Inspectorate and the appellant all the documents specified by the DoE's questionnaire, such as relevant plans and policies, the planning officer's report, and objections received. It is not necessary to send a specially prepared statement augmenting the LPA's case, but such a statement would elaborate on how exactly the application would contravene policies and damage interests of acknowledged importance. LPA statements should arrive with the Inspectorate and the appellant within 28 days.

The appellant is required to respond within 17 days of the receipt of all the LPA's documentation. In rebutting the LPA's case, the techniques used will be those detailed on pp.171, 172. If the application is for outline permission only, then too much detailed material could have the case refused on the grounds of 'over-egging the pudding', and plans and illustration should be marked as 'illustrative only'. For both the LPA and the appellant, this first stage is the crucial one. The LPA is not expected to reply, but if it chooses to do so it should be with new material and submitted within 7 days of the appellant's response.

In order to speed the decision, the Inspectorate favour unaccompanied site visits. If the site is not on view from public land, the inspector is not allowed access unless accompanied by the owner or his agent, plus a representative from the LPA to see fair play. Accompanied site visits are only appropriate if there are features on or near the site which are germane to the decision. The usual rules about both parties being present and neither being able to argue their case, apply.

Unlike hearings and appeals, no costs can be awarded for an appeal using written representations, unless it is an appeal against an enforcement notice. This gives local authorities the incentive to opt for this procedure because they are often paranoic about costs being awarded against them, despite the fact that they have nothing to fear if they have good planning grounds for refusal and have observed the usual courtesies (see Fig.10). The result can be that written representations are used in cases which ought to have allowed local people their say at a public inquiry.

DoE Circular 15/96 Planing Appeal Procedures, Annex 1
DoE Circular 11/87 TCP (Appeals) (Written Representations Procedure) Regulations 1987
DoE Circular 8/93 Awards of Costs Incurred in Planning and Other Proceeding

HEARINGS

These were introduced in the mid-eighties, and were formerly known as *informal* hearings. They have increased in popularity and now form 12% of appeals. The hearing is the most informal type of inquiry, and is characterized by cases which do not evoke widespread public interest, nor do they require cross-examination, discussion of complex policy issues, or raise points of law. The Secretary of State, as represented by the Planning Inspectorate, decides whether a hearing is appropriate before offering it to the parties, and both the LPA and appellant have to be agreed to its use. Typically they involve small scale applications, where the parties feel negotiations would benefit from a face to face meetings attended, perhaps, by the immediate neighbours.

As befits such an arrangement, hearings are non-statutory, the procedure is guided by a code of practice, but costs can be awarded. The hearing will take place within 12 weeks of the Secretary of State's decision, with 28 days notice being given of the date. The LPA will notify all those who have an interest in the land and/or objected to the application. Any other publicity is at their discretion.

The LPA will send details of the arrangements to all those, other than the appellant with an interest in the land, and to all who wrote in at the application stage. Here again, third parties will benefit from being alert earlier on. The LPA may also use its discretion over further publicity. Those notified will be sent a copy of DoE Circular 15/96 Annex 2, containing the Code of Practice for Hearings, and told where they can inspect the papers pertaining to this case. They will be informed that they can participate in the discussion on the day, at the discretion of the inspector.

A feature of this procedure is that the inspector leads the discussion, and thus must be aware of all the issues involved. It is essential, therefore, for both parties to send in their respective written statements and a list of documents cited, to the Inspectorate, at least three weeks before the hearing. At the same time they should exchange statements. If documentation is late then the hearing may be deferred, in which case the objective of a speedy decision is defeated.

If at any time the appellant or the LPA decide that this forum is inappropriate, they may inform the DoE, and a local inquiry, with its more formal procedures, can be arranged e.g. if it becomes clear that evidence needs to be tested by means of cross-examination.

At the hearing itself, the emphasis is on informality. Government advises against the use of council chambers and other official settings. Participants should be able to sit round a table to discuss the issues. At the time when hearings were being introduced a cartoon appeared in one of the professional journals, depicting a hearing in the saloon bar of the local hostelry, and the general approval of all concerned. Meanwhile, back in boring reality, the inspector commences with a review of the case from his understanding of the paperwork and his pre-hearing site visit. He outlines the main issues, and indicates the areas where he needs further clarification or explanation. This does not prevent the other parties raising issues which they consider to be relevant.

The appellant will be asked to start the discussion. They may choose to be represented by an agent or advisor, but this is not essential. As all documents should have been circulated beforehand, there should be no need to read them out. It is frowned upon to introduce new material at this stage as it could cause an adjournment, and thus a delay. Within the bounds of good order, everyone participating will be encouraged to ask questions, informally, throughout the proceedings, but the appellant will have the final word. Sometimes, with the approval of all involved, the later stages of the hearing might take place on the actual site. If not, the inspector will suggest that he be accompanied on a site visit at a future date. Unlike site visits connected with public inquiries, it is permissible to continue the arguments on site.

All hearings are decided by the inspector, and he may offer to give a decision within 24 hours of the hearing, but only if both parties agree. He will write to them indicating his intentions but no action should be taken until the decision letter proper is received.

Before any adjournment to the site, either to continue the Hearing, or for the site visit, the inspector will invite any applications for costs. Parties putting in late submissions and causing unnecessary expense to another party, is liable for costs. It should be noted that third parties could ask for costs under these conditions.

DoE Circular 15/96 Planning Appeal Procedures, Annex 2, Code of Practice for Hearings
DoE Circular 8/93, Award of Costs incurred in Planning & Other Proceedings, Annexes 4 & 7

POLLUTION APPEALS

The nineteen nineties have seen the extension of the appeals procedure into the field of pollution control: discharge consents and abstraction licenses under the 1991 Water Resources Act; authorisation to carry out prescribed processes under the IPC and LAAPC regimes of the EPA 1990, Part I; applications to deal with waste on land under Part I of the EPA; remediation Notices pertaining to contaminated land under s.57 of the 1995 Environment Act (alias s.78L EPA 1990!); hazardous substances consent under the Planning (Hazardous Substances) Act 1990. This plethora of legislation has presented a steep learning curve to all parties, including the Inspectorate. On the substantive level there have been two problems: giving inspectors adequate training to ask the right questions; and the recruitment of assessors who are professionally independent of those appearing at appeals. The gravity and complexity of the issues has meant that it has been a matter of devising procedures ensure a thorough investigation of the arguments before a decision can be made which is likely to be both equitable and safe.

As with the appeals system used in planning disputes, many of those brought under the EPA 1990 and the Water Resources Act 1991, are settled by written representations. That said, there are times when, perhaps after the site visit, the inspector comes to the view that the issue is more complex than he had first thought, and decides to escalate the proceedings to an inquiry.

For cases like these, and those which were always known to be complex, the question is what which procedure to use? At first blush it may seem surprising that the Hearing seems to be the favoured choice: in planning cases these tend to be used for the less contentious issues. However, as in the planning scene, one of the reasons for using it is because there is little wider public interest, although this is changing now, as people get to know about the appeals procedure in which they can actually discuss *pollution* per se..

The other is that the full inquiry procedure induces a battle between entrenched positions, with counsel vigorously defending their position and attacking the other side. This is counter-productive if what is required is a creative discussion between experts: indeed the barristers have been temporarily banished from major inquiries in times past, to allow the inspector and assessors to have a constructive discussion with the experts on either side.

Nevertheless, full inquiry procedure has its place, if evidence needs testing through cross-examination and/or there is third party interest: the public now realise that they are not confined to, say, giving evidence at the Waste Local Plan Inquiry, the submission of the planning application, or the planning appeal. Perhaps not surprisingly, appeals concerned with hazardous substances are always dealt with using the full inquiry procedure!

THE FULL PUBLIC INQUIRY

Preliminaries

With 82% of appeals being heard by written representations, and 11% by hearings (1995/6), the number of cases going to a full inquiry is much diminished. On the other hand they do tend to be the more complex cases, and thus require assiduous preparation by all sides. If you are unable or unwilling to appear at a public inquiry, you can still send in written representations, but do go if you can because it will make much more of an impact. It is the difference between receiving a letter and meeting someone, added to which the inspectorate now take the majority of decisions: in recent years only 13% of inquiries have been 'recovered' by the Secretary of State.

Preparing Your Evidence

Strategic and subsidiary issues should be marshalled into an elegant whole. Where a team consists of a lawyer and expert witnesses, the latter will advise the former on the issues involved, and the lawyer will decide how the case can be presented to best advantage, and devise a framework to which the expert witnesses will work. This is not a once and for all decision, but basically it is the job of the lawyer to have an eye to the overall design, whilst experts focus on the details. Where a case is to be presented by members of a local group, the general thrust of the case has to be agreed, and then the homework done. The difference is that the team leader will be as well acquainted with the material as the witnesses, and there may well be others feeding information into the filing system.(see Section III)

Although collecting information may be a group effort, the actual writing up into a proof of evidence is done by the witnesses who will be appearing at the hearing. No one is obliged to produce a proof of evidence for a public inquiry, but it does provide a record of your case which the inspector and others can take away with them. It should therefore be written with your readers in mind. They will be busy people with a limited amount of time to spend absorbing material which they are seeing for the first time: it is easy to forget this when one has been living and breathing a case for months, if not years. Clarity of presentation has to be paramount.

Even if you are sure an ally will deal with an issue thoroughly, it is a good idea to mention it in your proof: for perfectly understandable reasons, your ally may not deliver the goods on the day, and you can step into the breach. If you have not mentioned the issue, you cannot suddenly introduce it into you case at such a late stage, without howls of protest from the other side. Also, do not be tempted to withhold information in order to spring a surprise when you are being cross-examined: a canny barrister will not ask you *the* question which would trigger that response, and so that gem will be omitted from you case altogether. Thus it will save much gnashing of teeth afterwards if all your material is included somewhere in the proof. That said, never include anything which you could not defend under cross-examination: it is for this reason that the person who has done the reading and written the proof should appear on the witness stand. Even the most experienced professionals can look like idiots trying to defend someone else's proof because they may not be well so acquainted with the background reading, or the underlying rationale of the argument.

Having done your research, and decided on the primary and subsidiary issues, it is essential to do your case justice by laying out your results in the most accessible and appropriate form. Proofs should be printed or typed. The front cover should have the title and reference numbers of the matter under discussion at the inquiry, and name of the group. The main proof should have an introduction which gives the name of the author and their qualifications and experience. Professional witnesses are used to parading their credentials before those that matter: it is a kind of war dance to impress and inspire confidence in allies (including their pay-masters) and instil terror into the opposition, but it also has a serious purpose in allowing the inspector to assess the weight he should put on that witness's evidence. Local people acting as witnesses should not hide their lights under bushels either, but not pretend to technical expertise they don't have. They should state: their name; occupation, if it is relevant to their evidence; and how long they have lived in the area. If they represent an action group or parish council, they should say how many people they represent, and their position within the organisation. If they are also an elected member of a local authority, they should state who they represent, and membership of any relevant committees, but not their political affiliation.

If you are unaccustomed to report writing, it is a good idea to divide up your material by subject, beginning with the strategic issues, following on with subsidiary issues arranged in a logical order, and concluding with a topic which shows the significance of all these issues for your community. Do not bother to quote extracts from mainstream policy documents such as PPGs, but content yourselves with cross-referencing: this takes up less space in the proof and you can be sure that the inspector and others will have copies to which they can refer. More obscure extracts of official information (see Appendix I) and local plan policies, may be included in the text: short extracts in the proof and longer ones in the appendices.

Each section of the main proof should be numbered, and each paragraph numbered within that section. Also number all the pages. This numbering fetish is essential for ease of reference, especially in the heat of battle, but it also comes in handy should you have to provide a Summary of the Proof (see below). Keep short quotes or key statistics, illustrating your points, in the proof, but shunt articles, statistical tables, and other detailed material into appendices. Make a list of abbreviations, and compile a glossary of technical terms as you go along. These should be inserted at the front of the proof, between the summary and the main body of the text, so that readers know immediately where to look for explanation. All references should be properly footnoted, whether published or unpublished, and the list of references at the back of the proof. Lastly, it is a good idea to use different coloured covers for your documents, so that you can spot them lurking beneath the welter of paper on your desk at the inquiry.

Use visual material whenever possible to illustrate your text: maps, photographs, computer mock-ups, tables, diagrams and histograms. Here again each should be numbered, and reference made to them from the main text, otherwise they get overlooked. Bind the petition or protest letters together, so that they do not collapse into an untidy heap, or worse. Put yourself in the position of the inspector who may not be as familiar as you with the subject or the area. If you need to illustrate your material with lots of photographs, put them in an album, no bigger than A4 size, number them, give details of time and date, and provide a map showing where and in which direction the photograph was taken. Also confess whether a fancy lens was used in any particular case: you may be asked because cameras can be used deceive. Colour photographs should also be taken of models on display at the inquiry, and enlargements submitted as inquiry documents.

Check all your references and cross-references for inaccuracies: it's not worth upsetting the inspector by making him or her hunt for your quotes. Draft and redraft the proof of evidence to make sure it is logical. Ask someone not directly involved to read it through to see whether it is coherent and correct the typing errors: at one inquiry there was the embarrassing incident of the HIV lorries... If different witnesses are producing their own proofs, it might be as well if someone checks that they are all singing from the some hymn sheet: if they are contradicting each other, even on less important issues, it can provoke much merriment, at your expense, come the inquiry.

During long inquiries such as those examining local plans or trunk roads, you may not have to submit your proofs until around three weeks prior to your appearance. This means you may hang onto your proof and update it. At other inquiries, if you are a main party, you will be expected to submit your proofs beforehand, and the opposition can be very unpleasant on the opening day if they reckon that you should have sent them your proof beforehand: to avoid this it is better to fax it across the previous afternoon, than not at all. However inconvenient prior exchange of proofs may be, it does have the advantage that you will be able to see what the opposition have in store for you, and you can plan your cross-examination of their evidence.

With regard to appeals and call-ins, proofs of 1500 words or more should be prefaced by a summary of the main points: as a guide, summaries should not exceed 1,500 words or 10% of the main proof, whichever is the longer. If the main body of your proof only marginally exceeds, the 1500 words, the inspector may not be too fierce if a summary is not provided. Should a Summary be required, it is this which is actually read out at the inquiry in lieu of your proof, in order to save inquiry time. It must therefore cover the main points and *not introduce new material.* If the prècis was not your strong point at school, you will not go far wrong by summarizing each paragraph of your main proof, and numbering it accordingly. There are no inquiry rules requiring summaries of proofs for Local Plan Inquiries. However, the inspector may well require require them for longer proofs, and it would be as well to check the minutes of the pre-inquiry meeting, or ask the Programme Officer. Here again, the summary is what is actually read out at the inquiry, although the inspector has discretion to ask for the whole proof, or extended passages from it, to be read out on the day.

The number of copies required depends on the size of the inquiry. This can prove expensive, and pose problems: there are always those photographs which have no negatives and one can be haunted by half sets of prints, and maps or models which cannot be mass produced. If you hope to persuade the inspector to let you show a video at the inquiry, then you will need a copy which he can take away as an aide memoire. The reality is that one usually finds oneself with full, and incomplete sets of evidence. Make sure that full sets are available for the key parties: your own team, the inspector, the appellant and the LPA. The incomplete sets, consisting of easily reproducible written material, should be supplied to the assessor (if any), the LPA inquiry library, and other parties appearing. In addition there should be some left over for the press: they may be grateful for the summary and any key diagrams, and it helps in giving an accurate picture of your case to the wider public. It is also good for public relations to have some over for members of the public attending the hearings, particularly if they are funding professionals to represent them.

If some major event, like the publication of an important and relevant PPG, transforms the situation between the time you submitted your proof, and your actual appearance, then ask leave of the inspector and your opponents to amend your proof or summary. It will probably be granted because it would expedite the conduct of the inquiry, and will not catch anyone off-guard. Should the supplementary proof exceed 1500 words, that too will have to have a summary. Reproduce enough copies to furnish all the main parties, the press and the public. In terms of the great exercise of reproducing sets of evidence, this is the least of your problems.

All the responses and views you receive post submission will enable you to fine tune your arguments. You can augment the salient points with verbal references to the evidence submitted by others. For example you may say you support X's position on points A,B,& C, and disagree with Y's evidence on points P,Q,& R. You can also add in any new evidence, which supports your position, such as Ministerial Statements or extracts from new policy documents e.g. a brand new PPG. If there has been a fundament shift in government policy, or other major event since you wrote your summary, tell the Programme Officer you are rewriting the Summary and circulate it as soon as possible, if necessary by fax, before the inquiry. At worst it can be handed out on the day, but afford all concerned a few moments to glance through it before you speak. You do not want to cross the inspector, and opposing counsel are paid to stand on their dignity whenever their clients are to any disadvantage, real or imagined; this can be a discomforting experience, even if undeserved..

DoE Circular 15/96, Planning Appeal Procedures, Annex 5

Count Down to the Inquiry

Once an inquiry is on the cards, the next issue is the date when it will open. Since 1986 the DoE has allowed each party only one refusal: after that the Inspectorate will proceed to fix a date, time and place for the inquiry. The period for negotiation is limited to a month, although this can be a bit tight for an LPA with a procession of appeals and limited accommodation. Once a date has been set, it will only be changed in exceptional circumstances.

For most types of inquiry, the course of action from its announcement until the final decision, is governed by statutory Rules. Local Plans are exceptions because they are supposed to be about public participation, so they have a Code of Conduct instead. The following discussion is geared to that prescribed for appeals determined by inspectors (S.I.1992, No.2039, see Appendix VIII) because they are the most common: over 98% of appeals are 'transferred' to the inspectorate. For other types of inquiries see Fig.16.

Upon hearing of the date of the inquiry the local planning authority notifies the Secretary of State and the appellant of the name and address of any statutory party who has made representations to them. Similarly the Secretary of State will notify the LPA and the appellant of any statutory party who has been in touch with him.

For those who delight in the history of such things, 'statutory parties' are born again s.29(3) parties i.e. persons other than the appellant with an ownership or tenancy interest in the land. They are 'entitled' to appear at the inquiry along with the stage army of representatives from central and local government. All entitled parties are duly notified by the Secretary of State, of the name of the inspector and assessor, if any, rather than waiting to see who will be parachuted in on the day.

Up to six weeks after the announcement of the inquiry, the LPA serves a statement of case on the appellant and the Secretary of State, which outlines the case the LPA intend putting forward. This is often little more than the original reasons for refusal, assuming there were any: if the inquiry is the result of non-determination within eight weeks, or the agreed time-frame, it is essential that the LPA take a decision which then forms the basis for the statement of case. Thus the latter consists of the reasons for refusal plus a list of documentation, and copies of relevant documents which the other parties would not possess. In a similar fashion, the appellant serves his statement of case up to nine weeks after the inquiry announcement. If an inquiry has to be arranged at short notice, then statements of case must appear at least four weeks before the inquiry commences.

It is possible for third parties to join the grown ups at this stage: if they have always taken a constructive interest in the case, they may be asked, by the Secretary of State, to serve a statement of case on the other main parties, and become one of the parties 'entitled' to appear at the inquiry. That said, it is not vital if third parties do not become one of the elect. They can request the LPA for copies of statements of case and other documents.

An inspector may, not later than 12 weeks from the announcement of the inquiry, serve on all concerned, a list of topics which he considers to be of particular interest at this appeal. If the inquiry looks as though it will last several weeks because there are several proposals to be considered and/or there are piles of technical evidence, the inspector is likely to call a pre-inquiry meeting with all parties entitled to appear at the inquiry, plus anyone else who can make a useful contribution.

The inspector will introduce himself and take appearances i.e. team leaders for the main parties will introduce themselves and name their witnesses, and other parties like parish councils, NGOs and community groups will indicate that they wish to participate. Part of the purpose of a pre-inquiry meeting is to assess the length rather than the strength of the opposition. On the procedural side, the meeting is to discuss: the submission of documents; sitting hours – including the possibility of evening meetings for the hearing of objections from the community; the convenience or otherwise of the venue; photocopying facilities; and the order in which cases should be presented etc.

In terms of evidence, it is an opportunity to air any queries you may have about the relevance of issues, sort out when proofs should be exchanged, and how documents should be numbered. If invited, do go as it is an opportunity to meet the inspector and size up the opposition. If there is any disruption, inspectors have the power to evict trouble-makers and refuse them entry to the main inquiry, or permit their appearance on condition of good behaviour. Minutes of the pre-inquiry meeting are circulated to those who attended, and can be a useful source of reference at a later date.

In the normal course of events, proofs of evidence, summaries, and other inquiry documents are supposed to be submitted to the Secretary of State and all parties entitled to appear, at least 21 days before the commencement of the inquiry, but the inspector has discretion to alter the timetable and request that documentation be in by another date. If parties fail to submit proofs on time and this results in prolonging the inquiry, they could be liable for costs.

Small objectors, who have not been drawn into the 'entitled' net, can still appear at the inspector's discretion, and this is usually extended in a liberal fashion. They also have the advantage of not having to produce evidence beforehand, but can still make copies of documents as they materialise.

In 1988, government departments and other LPAs came of age, and were allowed to appear on their own rather than at the behest of LPAs. As DoE Circular 10/88 delicately puts it, 'This overcomes the potential awkwardness of a representative, hostile to the LPAs case, being called as a witness.' In more mischievous vein the Circular continues 'Although there is no change in the rule that a representative of a government department shall not be required to answer any question directed at the merits of government policy, the inspector is no longer required to disallow such a question if the representative is prepared to answer it'. Subsequent Circulars have kept silent on this issue, but given the current vogue for equating policy with market forces, this may not be as risqué as it looks. If representatives of government departments or agencies do materialise at an inquiry, it is a sign that they feel strongly about the issue because it is usual just to send a letter to the inspector. If you want to pressurize a government Department or Agency to attend the inquiry, contact your MP or the relevant Minister: believe it or not such bodies are accountable to Parliament.

Two weeks before the start of an inquiry, the Secretary of State may require that announcements be placed in newspapers, key parties be informed and notices be posted in conspicuous places near the site. Whilst the site notice may not require an armed guard, it is as well if someone checks its existence from time to time lest the inspector mistakes the site on a clandestine visit.

The timescale for the run up to an appeal, to be decided by an inspector, is up to twenty weeks (see Fig.17). However, it may be less than that: when this timetable was introduced in 1988, developers began jumping up and down because time is money. Since then the Inspectorate have become an Agency, and even more conscious of performance targets. The net result is the 1992 Rules, which allow for greater flexibility: if the main parties are agreeable, and an inspector becomes available, the run up to the inquiry may be considerably reduced. So do not be surprised by an announcement of an inquiry short notice.

Town & Country Planning (Inquiries Procedure) Rules 1992 S.I. No.2038: these are colloquially known as the Secretary of State's Rules – TCP Act s.77 call-ins and s.78 recovered appeals, Tree preservation order appeals, listed building and conservation area consent appeals under ss.12,19 or 20 of the Listed Buildings Act 1990
Town & Country Planning Appeals (Determination by Inspectors) (Inquiries Procedure) Rules 1992, S.I.No.2039. (see Appendix VIII) These apply to s.77 appeals under 1990 TCP Act and s.20 or s.74(3) appeals under the Listed Buildings Act 1990.

Highways (Inquiries Procedure) Rules S.I.1994 No.3263
Town & Country Planning (Enforcement)(Inquiries Procedure) Rules S.I.1992, No.1903
Compulsory Purchase by Ministers (Inquiries Procedure) Rules S.I.1994 No.3264

Compulsory Purchase by Non Ministerial Acquiring Authorities
(Inquiries Procedure) Rules S.I.1990 No.3264
Tribunals & Inquiries, Pipelines (Inquiries Procedure) Rules
S.I.1995 No.1239

MAJOR INQUIRIES

It is said the 'major' inquiries, like elephants, are difficult to define but easy to recognise. They are likely to be selected from the 13% of inquiries 'recovered' by the Secretary of State, plus less than a hundred s.77 call-ins per year. By definition these tend to be the bigger inquiries e.g. a nuclear power station or airport. However, it is the prerogative of DoE to decide whether a given inquiry falls into the *major inquiry* category, and therefore become subject to the Code of Practice set out in DoE Circular 15/96 Annex 4.

The LPA is required to notify prospective participants about the inquiry: voicing your opinion at the application stage is the key to involvement later. Such parties are sent a copy of the Code, plus a registration form which covers such issues as whether your input will be confined to written representations, a simple oral presentation or your intention to go for the whole shooting match in terms of professional representation, the calling of witnesses, and cross-examination. All is not lost, however, if you failed to get involved earlier as the LPA will announce such an inquiry in the press and invite people to apply for an applications form. These should be returned to the DoE in Bristol within 21 days of the formal notification in the press.

The inquiry secretariat will compile a register of participants. This will be divided into three sections: Part 1 will contain the major players who will be required to stick to the Code in terms of prior exchange of documents etc.; Part 2 will be comprised of those giving oral evidence only; and Part 3 will list those submitting written representations. Copies of the register will be sent to all participants and should be of great interest to those involved, helping people to identify kindred spirits and perhaps amalgamate their representations. The inspector is likely to allow all those appearing in Part 1 of the register to appear, and also those in Part 2, providing their evidence is thought to be relevant and does not duplicate that submitted elsewhere. Anyone not included in either Part and without a legal entitlement to appear at the inquiry, may appear only at the inspector's discretion.

In accordance with Rule 5 of the Secretary of State's Rules, the applicant and the LPA have to provide their written statement, no later than eight weeks after the notification of the inquiry. Other major participants may be asked to produce a statement, wishing four weeks of being asked, setting out their stall in general terms: its relationship to the points set out by the Secretary of State; the number of witnesses with an estimate as to how long they will take; an indication of who they would like to call to be cross-examined; and a list of special studies to be submitted as evidence to the inquiry. Outline statements will enable the inspector to request that parties with similar cases should join together to make a single presentation to the inquiry. Obversely, the inspector may become aware that a key issue will not be discussed at all unless he himself invites expert witnesses to fill the gap. The inspector will seek an agreement between the main parties on matters such as the history of the case, site and surroundings, methodologies relating to environmental effects. These 'agreed facts' will be supplemented by 'matters under dispute'. This statement will be circulated as soon as possible.

A pre-inquiry meeting, or indeed, more than one, is certain to be held. Amongst matters likely to be reviewed are: the DoE's statement; the provision of additional material needed by the inspector; possible collaborations; progress of statements of fact; assessors; and a review of count-down to the inquiry. It may be necessary to stage a separate meeting to discuss the programme. If there is a choice of venue, for example when several LPAs are involved, then, after convenience, comfort is a factor, for one cannot have eminent sit-upons seizing up! Other items for consideration may include: evening sessions; the programming of topics and appearances; office facilities and accommodating the media; transcripts, and generally organising the paperwork. Those appearing at the inquiry will be sent copies of the minutes of these meetings plus a notice detailing the date, time and place of the inquiry. If various matters cannot be ironed out at these meetings, then informal gatherings may have to be held.

The applicant and LPA will, and other Part 1 participants may be required to produce their proofs of evidence four weeks in advance of the inquiry. If these exceed 1500 words – who is kidding who? – then Summaries have to be prepared which do not exceed 10% of the length of the proof. The Code also covers other probable occurrences like the introduction of new evidence during the inquiry.

Town & Country Planning (Inquiries Procedure) Rules 1992 S.I. No.2038
DoE Circular 15/96, Annex 4, Code of Practice on Preparing for Major Planning Inquiries in England and Wales

Figure 17 Countdown to the Appeal

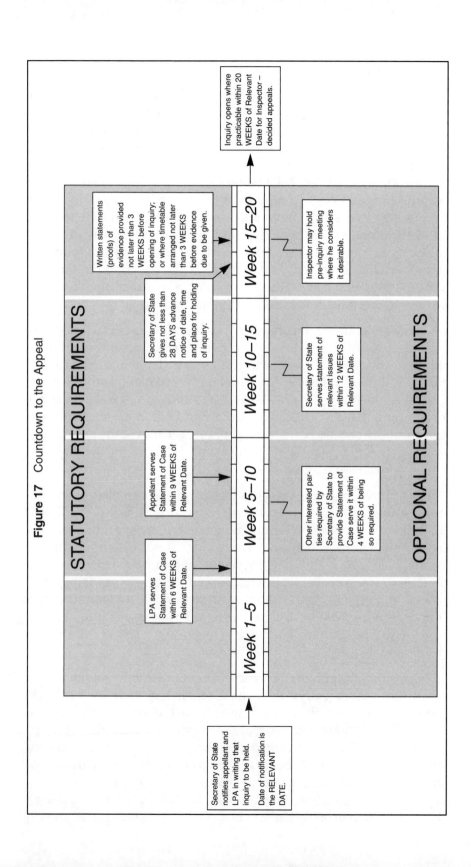

At the Inquiry

It is probable that the inquiry proper will be held in the same place as the pre-inquiry meeting. Generally inquiries are held in LPA premises: it saves money and it is convenient for the LPA, if no one else: as LPAs have grown in area with reorganisation, so they have joined the throng of out of town uses. Be grateful if your LPA does not inhabit a redundant MOD establishment, miles from lunchtime watering holes. Long running inquiries can have several locations because the owners of the premises need them, from time to time, for their intended purpose. That said, going on safari with a public inquiry is not for the faint-hearted given the amount of paraphernalia involved and the difficulty of finding suitable venues: there is the story of the inquiry assigned an infants school with its diminutive furniture, and Lilliputian loos...

It is not unusual for the inspector, counsel and expert witnesses to indulge in a little furniture shifting before the commencement of an inquiry. The typical layout of the hall in which an inquiry is to take place, is shown in Fig.19. A variation on the theme is the Council Chamber itself, with the inspector sitting in the Chairman's position, and the parties grouped around the horseshoe of fixed furniture. Advocates beware microphones geared to the users being seated rather than standing: microphones at the wrong height breed clients for chiropractors.

Whether or not one is intimidated by oak panelled chambers manifesting municipal rolls of honour, the atmosphere prevailing at an inquiry is wont to be formal. Suits are the order of the day, and even if such attire is not the norm for you, it is worth appearing to conform in order that the inspector and others will take you seriously. For practical reasons there will be no smoking, and silence will prevail, apart from the distraction of people coming and going, accompanied by low mutterings. To stand a chance of being a successful participant, you have to respect the ground rules of this public ritual.

Those unfamiliar with the proceedings are strongly advised to sit in on the inquiry before they rise to their feet: find the car park, locate creature comforts, and tune into the daily ritual of the proceedings. You will notice that the inspector is friendly but keeps his distance from the participants: fraternizing with one side or other is not allowed because of keeping the appearance of impartiality and can provide grounds for an aggrieved party to repair to the High Court. The formality is likely to be more apparent than real: the personality of the inspector and leading counsel will set the tone, and hopefully a certain measure of wit will bubble to the surface, breaking the tension. Attendance at the inquiry is the best cure for nerves, apart from enhancing the substance of your case.

The majority of inquiries last less than a week, but longer running ones sit from Tuesday to Friday, commencing around 10 p.m. and continuing until late afternoon, with an hour for lunch, and short breaks between heavy blocks of evidence. No refreshments are provided within the inquiry hall, other than flasks of water – good for the complexion if nothing else. Sometimes there is an adjournment for a week or two to enable the inspector and the main parties to recharge their batteries on the ski slopes or in the DIY store. If the inquiry goes on for weeks or months, such as those concerning roads or local plans, have a rota of people attending so that your group is kept informed of who said what to whom, so that you can interject pertinent remarks into the reading of your summary.

The Ground Rules of the Game

Much of the ensuing section is devoted to making the optimum use of the quasi-judicial process in order to defeat your opponent. Nevertheless it cannot be stated too strongly that *the objective of appearing at a public inquiry is to influence the inspector.* However skilled you are at out-flanking the other side, it is to no avail if you have failed to impress the adjudicator. During your hearing it is politic to act in accordance with the inspector's wishes: the Rules give them discretion as to how they wish to run the inquiry and whether they actually want to visit X on the site visit, or allow Y to continue with their irrelevant cross examination. Whilst you may state your point of view, it could be counter-productive to insist. The inspector also has discretion to permanently exclude disruptive elements, although they may be allowed to make a written submission.

With regard to substantive matters, watch the inspector and assessor to make sure you are holding their attention and noting your points. Decisions are made solely on the basis of evidence put forward at the inquiry and seen on the site visit: hence the importance of interesting the inspector and giving him time to write appropriate notes. Some inspectors are more interventionist than others, but it is open to them to pursue their own line of questioning. Often they pick up points made by the appellant and then put them to third parties to find out what effect such a proposal would have on the locality, or ascertain the current situation. Do listen to what they are saying to you, or to others, because it shows how their minds are working, despite maintaining a sphinx-like appearance for most of the time.

A few tips on the personal level. Call the inspector 'Sir' or 'Madam', and know the names and titles of key participants. It will help your cause if you are courteous to the inspector and all other participants no matter what the provocation: if opposing counsel is pugnacious, you will excite the admiration of all concerned by keeping your cool. Have your papers organised and know their numbers, so you can your hand on that vital document or map at the crucial moment. If a piece of evidence gets mislaid, don't panic, be assured that this has happened before, and have the confidence to ask for time to locate it. Similarly, do not hesitate to ask the inspector for time to confer with colleagues should the unexpected arise. Confidence breeds confidence.

Order of Play

On the first day of the inquiry the main parties arrive in plenty of time to take up their positions, and the erection of displays, or models must be completed before 10 a.m. Purloin a table and get unpacked: containers vary from plastic crates and cardboard boxes to empty cases of wine, from suitably prestigious chateaux.

A Question of Luggage:
Avoid cumbersome luggage. If you must take a good deal, as of course you must if your visit is to last longer than Saturday to Monday, have your boxes as light as possible, and not very large. It is better to have two small dress baskets, than one of those huge arks which are such a terror to porters and servants.
A Book of Edwardian Etiquette, 1983

Being a facsimile reprint of 'Etiquette for Women: a Book of Modern Modes and Manners' by 'One of the Aristocracy', published by Arthur Pearson Ltd., 1902

The inspector begins by introducing himself or herself, and reading out the official title of the inquiry. Next the appellant's counsel gives his name and professional rank, and names his witnesses, explaining who is expert in which field. He is followed by the LPA's team leader giving his details and those of his witnesses. If other Government Departments and/or local authorities intend giving evidence, they indicate their presence. Last amongst the statutory bodies are the parish councils. Then come NGOs, action groups and individuals.

If lay objectors have imported professional help, it is essential that the person concerned has a typed list of the witnesses to be called and their addresses: it can be very embarrassing not to be able to read a name, and not have a clue where they live. Once read out, the list may be given to the inspector. This is the time to ask him whether he will allow Mr X to give evidence on Thursday afternoon, because that is the only time he can be absent from work: inspectors are usually very sympathetic towards those who have more productive ways of spending their time than attending public inquiries.

The inquiry always commences with the appellant's case and closes with their final submissions. The typical batting order is to be seen in Fig.18. However, reality is usually less clear cut, because professional as well as lay participants may have other commitments which have to be accommodated. Thus stray witnesses will be slotted in during convenient breaks in the proceedings once the main cases have been heard.

There was a time when the opening speech by the appellants's counsel could take hours, but in the cost conscious nineties there have to be very good reasons for exceeding half an hour, during which time counsel just outlines the case and explains the inter-relationship between the evidence to be given by the witnesses. At the larger, multi-day inquiries the opening statements of all the main parties will be given on the first day for the benefit of the public and the press. Normally, however, opening statements of other parties are kept to a minimum. They are expected to proceed rapidly to their witnesses giving their 'evidence in chief'. Unless they have committed some misdemeanour in the eyes of the inspector, the team leaders of all entitled parties may cross-examine witnesses opposing their own case.

It is possible for the non-professional to raise his game by making optimum use of the various 'moves' available to him during the inquiry. It is essential to understand exactly what you can and cannot do at each stage: it is maddening to realise that you have missed the opportunity to, say, raise an issue or cross-examine a witness, because it is almost impossible to recover the ground at a later stage. The following sections set out the unwritten rules for presenting a case to best advantage. The moves are dealt with in the order in which an objector might well play them.

Figure 18   Batting Order at a Public Local Inquiry into an Appeal

1   **Appellant's Case**
Opening Submission
Evidence-in-Chief
Cross-Examination of Appellant's Witness(es) by:
>   Team Leader of Local Planning Authority
>   Team Leaders of Third Parties

Re-Examination
Inspector's Questions to Appellant's Witness(es)

2   **Local Planning Authority's Case**
Evidence-in-Chief
Cross-Examination of Local Planning
Authority's Witness(es) by: Appellant's Team Leader
Re-Examination
Inspector's Questions to Local Planning Authority's Witness(es)
Closing Statement

3   **Other Authorities' Cases**
(Procedure as for Local Planning Authority)

4   **Third Party's Case**
Evidence-in-Chief
Cross-Examination of Third Party's Witness(es) by:
>   Appellant's Team Leader
>   Local Authority's Team Leader
>   Other Authority's Team Leader
>   Other Third Party's Team Leader

Re-Examination
Inspector's Questions to Third Party's Witness(es)
Closing Statement

5   **Third Party's Case (Simplified Procedure)**
Statement combining Opening Statement and Evidence-in-Chief
Cross-Examination of Third Party's Team by: Appellant's Team Leader
Inspector's Questions
Closing Statement

6   **Appellant's Case**
Closing Statement

(i)   Cross-Examining the Opposition

Before discussing techniques of cross-examination, it is an opportune time to mention the fact that there are powers, under s.250(2) of the Local Government Act 1972, to summon a witness to appear at an inquiry. The inspector would have to be satisfied that the evidence produced by that witness was essential for the determination of the case, and that neither the witness nor their evidence could be got by other means. If the inspector grants leave for the party to summon the witness, the latter should note that they are liable for all the witness's expenses, including loss of earnings, and that even if he does appear at the inquiry, he is not obliged to speak! This power is of interest, but rarely used in practice: the professional circus make a living out of appearing at inquiries, so don't require coercion.

You should only embark on cross-examination if there are points in the appellant's or applicants case which challenge your own: it is a matter of testing the underlying assumptions or facts in your opponent's evidence. The aim of cross-examination is to manoeuvre the witness from the opposing side into conceding to your position. In order to question the contents of the opposition's proof of evidence you need to be thoroughly steeped in the subject, so that you have verified the facts, and are acquainted with rival interpretations of the evidence presented. Although the team leader will conduct the cross-examination, its planning should be a joint effort with the witness, so that the expertise is pooled.

The cross-examiner plans a series of questions on a given topic in the opposition's case. His witness should spot the weaknesses in their case and point these out to him. The cross-examiner must know what he wants to achieve before he starts. This means knowing exactly what answers *he* wants in reply to each question. This is the singularity of cross-examination: those undertaking it should never ask a question to which they do not know *their* answer. A series of say, six questions should corner the witness so that he is forced to agree with you, and a series of concessions constitute the grand design which undermines the opposition's case.

The techniques outlined above are used by the professionals, but clued-up lay people can do a sizeable amount of damage with a well-researched series of questions which undermine the opposition's case by exposing the truth of the matter. First of all, make sure that you have got the right witness: otherwise he will deny that he has any expertise in the subject and your point will be lost. Therefore make arrangements beforehand with your opponent's counsel, or the programme officer, if there is one, for the witness you want to be present at the time when you want him. Secondly, make sure that you are actually asking *questions* of the opposition rather than making statements supporting your own case: this is a common pitfall amongst lay cross-examiners and the inspector will gently stop the cross-examination, on this topic, if it occurs.

Having written down your series of questions, don't allow yourself to be thrown by the unexpected answer. It is a good idea to anticipate possible tangents which may be taken by a witness, and have subsidiary questions in readiness. Never ask a question 'fed' to you by an ally or even another member of the team, unless you really understand what it means. If it is an important point, you will look very foolish if you cannot guarantee the 'right' answer. That said, there is also a place for 'going on a fishing trip': if, having done some research, you just cannot understand the connection between X and Y, or the reasoning behind Z, then ask an innocent question. The opposition may be put to confusion, and doubts will be raised in the inspector's mind. After each question, take time to write down the response given: the inspector is likely to be taking notes, so this will not prolong the inquiry unduly. Cross-examination is likely to be rather a 'stop/go' affair, rather than an effortless crescendo.

Cross-examination is a two edged sword: it is an opportunity to undermine the case of the opposition on key issues, but if it goes wrong it gives them another chance to confirm the veracity of their case. So you have to be very careful, but with adequate preparation and a certain amount of adrenalin, you can achieve results.

(ii)   Opening Your Case

When introducing your case, your team leader should stand, stating his name and identifying those whom he represents. Parish councils have the advantage of being statutory bodies and therefore no one will query their standing. Action groups, on the other hand, are open to the charge from the opposition that they do not truly represent the community, that they are just self appointed busybodies. It is essential therefore to be able to demonstrate the extent of the membership in terms of numbers, geographical spread etc. This is especially necessary if day time meetings prevent attendance by members, although as large a number as possible should be encouraged to attend. The image to be presented is that of a large body of public spirited citizens. Convincingly done, this will obviate a possible attack by your cross-examiner when the time comes. The team leader proceeds to sketch the outline of the case and say which witness will be doing what.

If you have someone playing the part of advocate/witness, they should explain this to the inspector and other parties when introducing the case, so that everyone knows to whom they should be addressing their questions. As advocate they will stand to make their opening remarks and then sit to give their main evidence. If they then go on to call specialist or local witness, they will be on their feet again to introduce them and draw out important points. For the advocate-cum-witness it is necessary to remember which role he is playing at any given time: a matter of brain activating legs.

(iii)   Examination in Chief

Before the Examination in Chief begins, the witness will 'take the stand' i.e. move to the position set aside for witnesses in the inquiry room (see Fig.19). The team leader will introduce the witness to those present at the inquiry. Expert witnesses will state their qualifications, the firms they have worked for, and their experience. The objective is both to inform and impress, thereby lending credibility to their evidence. In the case of a very well qualified witness, the effect can be almost liturgical. On the other hand such a witness should be sensitive to the scale of the inquiry: at smaller inquiries it would be 'bad form' to go into too much detail.

The professional witness, or the chief lay witness, will read a summary of their proof, copies of which have been circulated to all parties at the inquiry. Whilst reading their summary they have the opportunity to interject remarks pertaining to issues discussed at the inquiry, positions taken by other parties and any relevant happenings outside the inquiry. The team leader will play 'midwife' to the most important points e.g. by asking the significance of certain statistics, or how a suggested alternative will overcome acknowledged drawbacks of the proposal. If the matter is complex, it is a good idea for the team leader to summarise the point succinctly so that its importance is not lost on the inspector, or anyone else. Clearly this double act means prior agreement, if not rehearsal. It may be, however, that the inspector will require that the full text of the proof be read out in the interests of clarity.

With regard to lay witnesses, they should have been encouraged to write down their objection, but copies can be produced shortly before the hearing begins that day, rather than weeks in advance. Preferably the evidence will be typed or written clearly on reasonable note paper, and the spelling checked for artistic licence: this is not an occasion for jotted notes in pencil on the back of an envelope. Each witness should introduce themselves with the personal information at the beginning of their proof. If their current or past employment is relevant to the case, they should give details

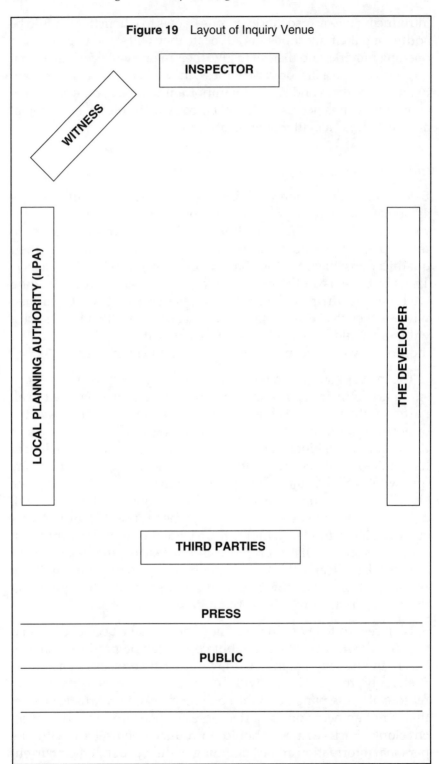

Figure 19   Layout of Inquiry Venue

e.g. the local doctor saying how long he has practised in the area and how many patients he has on his list. Other witnesses will have their special reason for wishing to give evidence at the inquiry e.g. HGV lorries are frequent visitors to their garden. The fact that such witnesses may lack professional qualifications in land-use planning does not mean that their evidence is not valuable. After all this is a *public* inquiry, and one of its functions is to ascertain the facts of the case. After the introduction, the witness is usually left to read through the evidence. If the team leader feels that a certain point hasn't been made as effectively as it might have been, he can ask a question of the witness, and hopefully, they will give the right reply.

(iv) Being Cross-Examined: Strategies and Tactics Deployed

Having psyched yourself up for cross-examination, it may not happen. There could be two reasons for this: either the evidence was too feeble to be worth challenging, or else it was incontrovertible, and opposing counsel decide not to give you the opportunity to re-state the case. You then have the problem of lowering your adrenalin levels without resorting to vandalism. Counsel mutter to the inspector that they will deal with your evidence by way of closing submissions. Too often this means that they will distort your case at that stage, and it is absolutely infuriating. One just has to hope that the inspector will note their cowardice in not cross-examining at the time, and discount the travesty of the facts presented to them later.

The character of cross-examination has been set out in (i). Many members of the public view cross-examination with some trepidation, and their fear is not wholly unfounded. On the other hand, if you know what to expect and how to counter attack, you will enjoy it: adrenalin rises, pulses race and instant slimming is not unknown! Keep your cool, and, if possible, your sense of humour. Do not allow yourself to be hurried. A pause before replying gives the impression of a considered opinion, even if the real reason was mental paralysis. If you need time to confer with colleagues, ask the inspector. Similarly, make sure you have adequate time to digest any documents sprung on you: ask for a short adjournment if necessary.

Opposing counsel may commence with a few preliminary rounds on matters of little consequence. By these means a nervous or suspicious witness may have his fears allayed and be lulled into a false sense of security. On the other hand, these initial rounds may be used to undermine the self-confident witness, and, indeed, those with less self confidence. The professional standing of the witness may be queried, although this can seriously backfire: an expert witness with an M.A.(Cantab) was asked what subjects he studied to obtain it... Another ploy is to point out inconsistencies in the group's stance over the years: minutes of meetings, and press cuttings can come back to haunt you. Similarly expert witnesses may be asked to square their current views with those they have expressed in past publications. If a witness is in need of protection from unfair cross questioning, then it is the job of the team leader to protest at such tactics.

Like performers in other fields, each cross-examiner has his own style. If you are a third party you will have the opportunity to take stock of opposing counsel whilst they are cross-examining LPA witnesses. There are those who coax and charm the required information out of the witnesses, making the whole business as painless as possible. Their reassuring manner, particularly when the objective is in sight, or achieved, saves time in dealing with the protestations of the witness or any post hoc retractions of evidence. Other cross-examiners adopt a more aggressive approach, which may be particularly upsetting to those unaccustomed to giving evidence at inquiries. Certain professional advocates habitually leap to their feet in fits of feigned indignation, protesting at the least infringement of their witness's integrity, so do feel free to defend your witness from offensive questioning.

The technique of cross-examination is varied according to the matter in hand. Sometimes the questions appear to relate to each other, and at other times they do not. Mostly they appear innocuous, requiring 'yes' or 'no' type responses, but beware! It is important that the witness be seen to concede at the end of the series, thus impressing the inspector. If the witness refuses, the cross examiner will circle again from a different angle, using every resource in the language of persuasion. Alternatively he will drop the subject and return to it later, when he has thought of a way to make the proposition more palatable to the witness.

Cross examination is not a debate as the questioner enjoys the prerogative of choosing the subject and asking the questions. He can therefore opt to break the witness's concentration by introducing some irrelevance, and then reverting to the original series of questions. He may appear to accept the witness's view wholeheartedly, or go part way with him. A variation is to ask a hypothetical question. If a witness is stubborn he may have to be impressed with the quality of evidence to the contrary, or the prestige of those endorsing it.

Further recalcitrance may lead to repeated discrediting of the witness, his organisation, his case, and/or his overall performance at the inquiry: all this in the good cause of undermining the witness's confidence and extracting a concession. In desperation the cross-examiner may try to get the witness to agree to a related issue instead. Such is the importance of agreement, that a daring cross-examiner may assert agreement where none exists. If a victory is achieved then the cross-examiner may celebrate with another, on a related but essentially extraneous issue.

The above exposes the strategies and tactics which *may* be used during cross examination. Yes, it looks horrendous, but 'the works' will only be deployed at big inquiries where highly professional witnesses are more than equal to the attack, and enjoy the challenge. It is unlikely that they will have lost any sleep before commencing battle. On the other hand, some of these techniques may be used during smaller inquiries but there is no need to feel daunted: there are techniques available for counter-attack.

> *'Never assume that a third party is a bumbling amateur who has nothing better to do than spend a day at a public inquiry objecting to a given development proposal. On rare occasions this may indeed be the case, but generally third parties present carefully studied and ordered cases that must always be scrutinized and, on occasions, cross examined.'*
> Butterworth's Planning Law Encyclopaedia

(v) Being Cross-Examined: Means of Counter-Attack

Witnesses need not fall over themselves to concede, thus diminishing the value of their evidence, or have their case partially or completely destroyed. The following are tactics which can be adopted, or adapted by the creative witness.

If he can divine the strategy of the cross-examiner, he can expose where the questioner is leading and deny the implications. Better still, he can use the question to air his own views and further his case. Alternatively, he can turn the question to his advantage by putting the other side of the coin. The expertise of the witness, be it in some technical subject, or knowledge of the locality, can transform the answer to a question away from what was intended by the cross-examiner, thus pointing up a gap in their knowledge.

Hypothetical questions are best dealt with by an answer which is obviously hypothetical. Lastly, there is no substitute for your full concentration on the question, for working out the extent to which they apparently agree with you, where you part company, and which of the above techniques you can use to deal with the remainder of the question.

When things are going badly, the witness may play for time by asking for questions to be repeated. If he is eloquent he may give a long speech which does not answer the question (just like a politician being interviewed), during the course of which he might:

(a) redefine the question and then retract the statement;

(b) purport to agree with the question and then retract the statement;

(c) isolate himself from the rest of the team by giving his 'personal' opinion.

If the going gets tough, he should seek help from fellow team mates. However, if a concession is extracted at last, he should diminish its value to lessen the damage to the case. A common way to do this is to enlarge the context, thus apparently reducing the size of the problem.

Here again, these means of counter-attack are much in evidence at big inquiries, but they are available for use by anyone, both you and your opponents. If the cross-examination has made inroads into your case, then there is an opportunity to repair them during re-examination.

(vi)   Re-examination

Re-examination usually follows straight after cross-examination, in which case there is no time for team leader and witness to confer, and, in any case, the witness and their advocate may well be at a distance from each other (see Fig.19). Given this situation it is essential that the witness understands the purpose of this move in the game: the team leader is not continuing the cross-examination – it is not a matter that with friends like that you don't need enemies – but rather seeking to redress the balance after cross examination.

The subject matter of re-examination is restricted, therefore, to the issues raised during the previous move, and there will be protests if other subjects are brought in at this stage. The team leader should keep a note of all the questions asked and the replies given by his witness during cross-examination. If something is irretrievable it is better to abandon it than the witness fail a second time, thus reinforcing the case of your opponents. In other words, only bother to re-examine points which are capable of being turned again to your advantage. A position may be retrieved by further explanation. A crucial argument may be reinforced by reaffirmation, to wedge it firmly in the inspector's mind. Finally, if a concession of some consequence was extracted during cross-examination, now is the opportunity to minimise its importance to the case. Re-examination is an extremely useful move, and single objectors or advocate/witnesses can find themselves denied it. However, with leave from the inspector, they may gather their wits, and sum up their position at the end of the cross-examination.

(vii)   Inspector's Questions

An inspector may ask questions at any time during the proceedings, but they are most likely after a witness has been cross-examined and re-examined. Whereas you may have been on the defensive vis a vis opposing counsel, do not transfer this attitude to the inspector. Offer your opinion in an open and honest manner, qualifying it only where necessary. Listen to the question because you will sense how his mind is working and this could be instructive.

(viii)   The Closing Statement

Only the major parties to an inquiry are bound to produce a closing statement. However, if given the opportunity by an inspector, third parties may make their mark with a punchy summary of their case. All concerned will be grateful for brevity and wit, but you can certainly make an impact with three or four key issues, culminating with a recommendation to the inspector to refuse or allow the application or appeal. If you are unable to be present, then send in a legible copy of a closing statement but it must reach the inspector before the formal close of the inquiry.

For all who make closing statements, the objective is to show that you case is as completely intact as when the case opened. Events of the hearing, particularly the stance of allies, cross examination and re-examination, are used to support the case, and inconvenient facts omitted, with major concessions made less damaging by disclaimers. There are times when one wonders if one's opponents actually heard the same evidence that everyone else has sat through for days, weeks, or months on end. If it is any comfort inspector's do not set much store by closing speeches, knowing that advocacy has little to do with truth by this stage.

Changing Positions

Sometimes those putting forward a proposal will alter it in some way during the course of an inquiry. You should ask for time to consider the new situation, and then make another appearance at the inquiry or submit a written representation to the inspector if you feel the proposal is not in your interests.

That said, as the inquiry progresses it is sometimes possible to work out a compromise acceptable to you and those putting forward the scheme. Indeed there could be some tactical advantage, from their point of view, in reaching some agreement, so that the rest of the scheme is left unscathed. If a compromise is reached, the inspector should be informed immediately, but it is up to him what notice he takes of it when making a decision.

Planning Conditions & Obligations

The main parties are encouraged to reach agreement on conditions and planning obligations before the end of the inquiry. Whether or not they are successful, any such proposals should meet the criteria set out in DoE Circular 11/96 and 1/97 respectively (see Appendix IX). If third parties have a particular view on the conditions they would like to see imposed, they should discuss the matter with the LPA, who are likely to be receptive. If they get no joy with them, then approach the inspector. It should be remembered that he, or the Secretary of State can impose their own conditions if they see fit.

 *Costs*

The last move within the inquiry itself is a set piece battle between counsel for the appellant and the LPA, over costs (see Fig.10). These do not usually involve third parties. However there are exceptions:

a) Sometimes inquiries or hearings are cancelled at the last minute. Inconvenient though this is, there can be good reasons for it e.g. the appellant has reached agreement with the LPA, or there has been a change in policy relevant to that application. If there are no good planning reasons, the developer may be liable for the costs, not only of the LPA but also third parties, provided the LPA knew of their intention to participate in the inquiry

b) With regard to the inquiry itself, awards of costs either in favour or against third parties will not be considered in relation to issues of substance, but if one of the main parties has caused procedural difficulties e.g. an unnecessary adjournment during the inquiry, then they may make an application.

It should be noted that although third parties are indeed eligible for costs from appellants in the run up to an inquiry, it is essential that the appellant and the LPA know of their intention to participate in the inquiry.

Making an application for costs is not the same thing as getting them: although applications are made at 66% of hearings and inquiries, awards are made in only 28% of these cases (1995/96). The actual amount depends on agreement between the parties. If that fails, the matter is referred to the Taxing Office of the Supreme Court for determination.

'The statutory provisions for the award of costs do *not* apply to the Crown, including Government Departments. If any party considers that they have incurred "wasted" or unnecessary costs directly as a result of unreasonable conduct by a Government Department, it is open to the party to approach them directly. Under the Citizen's Charter, all public bodies should have well publicised and easy to use complaints procedures'

DoE Circular 8/93 Awards of Costs Incurred in Planning and
Other Proceedings
Annex 4, para.3

Good Luck!

The Site Visit

An inspector is entitled to make an unaccompanied site visit before or during an inquiry, and will normally indicate that he has done so. In addition he will make a site visit accompanied by the appellant, the LPA and any statutory party i.e. representatives of the various levels of government plus owners and tenants of the land. If you are not eligible to attend, give instructions to a statutory party who you regard as an ally, and ask them to point out to the inspector, things you would like him to see. Should anyone fail to materialise, of those eligible to participate, the inspector may proceed without them

Such visits are often under-estimated in their importance, in terms of the inspector's final decision. It must be remembered that inspectors are never allocated to an inquiry with which they have personal or professional links. This helps them to be objective, but means that they need to familiarise themselves with the area in order to understand references made at the inquiry, and arrive at an informed judgement as to what should happen. It could be that the inspector will ask questions at the inquiry in order to elicit comment on something he noted on a pre-inquiry visit to the site.

If you are eligible to participate, do go along. However, it is important to appreciate the purpose of the visit. It is *not* to reiterate arguments at the inquiry, *nor* to raise issues you forgot to mention in your evidence. If you do, you will be silenced, and this can puzzle objectors who the inspector has encouraged to be forthcoming at the inquiry. The reason is that the site visit is just to enable the inspector to see for himself the features which would be affected by the development. Therefore your role is confined to pointing out anything which you would like him to bear in mind when taking his decision. So make a list of items to be incorporated into the itinerary. If you cannot attend, send a representative armed with the list: it is really a matter of drawing things to the attention of the inspector, so is not important who actually does it.

Our learned friends are never to be seen on site visits: they are hot-house plants. Those who will brave the elements should be suitably attired and shod: elegant footwear can be ruined by a short cut across a ploughed field or through the excretions of a collapsed sewer. There are some things beyond your control, however. If you are trying to save a beauty spot from development, it may sound less convincing in thick mist or an icy gale. The other problem is the personal interests of the inspector. Does that heap of moss grown masonry bring history to life for him, or will he view it as a pile of uninteresting old stones? Be comforted by the fact that, if it is a protected site, government policy will over-rule any personal antipathy.

ROADS: INQUIRY PROCEDURE

As with local plan inquiries, those into major road schemes may continue for months, so that objectors may have to make several appearances at the inquiry, and certainly keep track of what is happening in their absence. For minor local authority road improvements, a day could suffice. Inquiries nearly always go on longer than the Inspector, or the promoting authority, expects!

Procedure at Motorway/Trunk Road Inquiries

The Inquiry is conducted by a 'Panel Inspector', an 'Independent Inspector nominated by the Lord Chancellor' who is a member of the 'Panel' supervised by the Planning Inspectorate, whose costs are reimbursed by the DTp (see p.121). He may be assisted by an Assessor who is not usually a Panel Member, but rather a hired-in specialist. DoE Professional Inspectors do not conduct trunk road inquiries.

The Inspector is likely to hold a Pre-Inquiry Meeting if the Inquiry is likely to be at all complex.

The Inspector opens the Inquiry and explains the procedures. Procedural matters and other difficulties not handled at any Pre-Inquiry Meeting held can be raised by any party.

Figure 20

Opening Speech by DTp (HA) barrister

Evidence in chief by HA witnesses

Other parties put questions in elucidation to HA witnesses

Supporters of road scheme, and any local authorities taking part, make statements

Cross-examination of supporters and local authorities

Objectors introduce their cases

(Objectors may cross-examine HA witnesses before calling their own; if so, HA barrister may then re-examine his witnesses. They may prefer to cross-examine DTp evidence in chief along with rebuttal evidence: see below.)

Objectors present their own cases

Objectors can be cross-examined on their evidence by HA and any supporters, and by counter-objectors if the objector proposes an alternative route

---

Objectors can be re-examined by their own advocate. If the objector is doing a solo performance, he can ask to make a statement in lieu of re-examination to clarify anything raised in cross-examination.

HA gives its 'rebuttal evidence'.

Objectors cross-examine HA witnesses on their rebuttal evidence, and on the HA evidence in chief if this was not done earlier

HA Barrister can re-examine his witnesses

Counter-objectors (to any alternative route presented by objectors) present their case.

Objectors cross-examine counter objectors.

If there is new evidence at this stage or further matters, these have to be put in before closing statements as these must not introduce new evidence. (See below under 'Rebuttals')

Closing statements, from all sides, in reverse order, with HA speaking last.

Procedure at Local Authority Road Scheme Inquiries

The Procedures are in principle the same as at trunk road inquiries. But there are likely to be fewer parties, and the local authority may be represented by its own solicitor, not a barrister. In many cases there are no 'alternative routes' being promoted, so that the counter-objection element does not take place.

There are two features of road inquiries which stand out to members of the public as differing from town and country planning inquiries: 'Rebuttal' and 'Counter-objections'. The latter are sometimes used at Local Plan Inquiries to describe objections to 'Changes' to the Local Plan put on deposit before or during the Local Plan Inquiry; but this should not be confused with 'counter-objection to alternative routes' at road inquiries.

Rebuttals

These are proofs of evidence presented by the HA (or, at some local authority road scheme inquiries, by the authority) when it asserts a 'right of reply' to an objector's evidence, while appearing to deny the objector any further say. The 'rebuttal proof' can contain complex and quite new arguments, facts and figures. It can also repeat large chunks of text from earlier HA evidence or policy statements and seek to win the argument by sheer weight of paper. A long rebuttal will normally indicate that the objector has made an effective case.

Objectors are then asked to cross-examine this new evidence. This is something that barristers may well do effectively, but unrepresented objectors are then at a serious disadvantage. Firstly, you are entitled to have time to consider the new proof of evidence. Secondly, you can submit a further proof if you consider that this would more effectively deal with the rebuttal than trying to 'answer' it by cross-examination. The procedure announced by the Inspector does not provide for this, but it is not excluded by the Procedure Rules. If you insist on being permitted to do this, and the Inquiry runs for long enough, you should do so. If you do, the HA may produce a further rebuttal; but this is unlikely to add anything to the main one, so that there will be no real need to reply to that except in closing statement. A closing statement is not an opportunity to answer a main Rebuttal Proof, however, as closing statements cannot introduce any new evidence whereas the HA Rebuttal will normally do so.

You should also beware of local authorities who support the road putting in 'Rebuttal' to your objection. Their right to do this is questionable; if permitted, you should aim to answer them on paper.

Counter-Objections

Alternative routes submitted before the due date, usually 14 days before opening of the Inquiry, will be advertised in the press and often notified to affected landowners. Objections to alternative routes are termed 'counter-objections'. They are in a separate file available from the opening of the Inquiry. If you propose an alternative you should copy and study these. Any significant number can be fatal to your case for an alternative route. If you can, aim to answer these in your main case, or by a supplementary statement.

Yes! A monster 12-lane bypass will march across Britain!

There have been sensational developments at a public inquiry in the West Country, where a Department of Transport officer has let slip some of the real thinking behind the DoT's road-building programme. Here is part of his testimony at yesterday's session of the Nether Broughton Bypass Inquiry.

Counsel: Now, the main A1234 thunders through the tiny village high street of Nether Broughton, does it not?
DoT: No.
Counsel: No?
DoT: No. The road itself is totally silent and immobile. However, the lorries and cars that thunder along it do make a certain amount of noise.
Counsel: Bit of a clever clogs, are we?
DoT: You could say that. I prefer to think of myself as one of the fastest rising stars in the DoT.

Counsel: We'll see about that. Now, Nether Broughton is a typical English village, is it not?

DoT: In what way?

Counsel: The windows are all double-glazed. They have notices saying: 'Build the Bypass Now'. The place is covered in dust left by the lorries. The pavement is covered with wreaths and crosses left in tribute to those who attempted to cross the road alive but failed. There are many For Sale signs . . .

DoT: Yes, yes, it is a typical English village.

Counsel: One of those which have helped to make the British countryside what it is today?

DoT: If you mean a hell of a place to build roads in, then yes.

Counsel: You propose to build a bypass to relieve this pressure?

DoT: We do. It is our dearest wish to bring a measure of tranquillity back to this once charming spot.

Counsel: Now, would you describe the projected bypass?

DoT: Certainly. It will be a 12-lane highway . . .

Chairman: One moment, Mr Twistleton. Do you mean 12 lanes each side, or six on one side, six on the other?

DoT: It is all to do with reversible traffic flow.

Chairman: What is reversible traffic flow? Will car drivers be allowed to reverse down the slow lanes or something?

DoT: Not exactly. It's to do with the main commuter traffic which goes one way during the morning and another way at night.

Counsel: Or is this part of some more sinister programme? Is it possible that this nightmarish 12-lane highway, whose construction is likely to prove more of a headache to poor Nether Broughton than its present troubles, could be part of some Euroroute which will march across Britain, covering our glorious landscape in a ghastly web of concrete superhighways from which huge lorries can spit forth their miasma of pollution, shaking the road to bits as they pass?

DoT: No.

Counsel: No, what?

DoT: No, I don't think it will be particularly ghastly.

Counsel: Ah! So you *do* admit that there will be a web of monster highways laying a corset of constricting and choking concrete across Britain!

DoT: I don't know. What is a corset?

Chairman: I can't believe my ears. You've never seen a corset?

DoT: No, sir.

Chairman: Did you never dress up in mummy's underwear as a child?

DoT: No, sir.

Chairman: Good heavens. What a strange, deprived childhood . . .

Counsel: May I put it to you another way? Does the DoT plan to build huge highways for lorries across Britain?

DoT: Yes, sir.

Counsel: Ah ha! Of which the Nether Broughton bypass will form part?

DoT: No, sir.

Counsel: Then why in God's name is it a 12-lane carriageway?

DoT: Do I have to answer that question truthfully?

Counsel: Is there any reason why you cannot?

DoT: Yes. Because I have been told by the DoT that I shall lose my job if I do.

Chairman: You must answer it.

Counsel: Let me ask you once again, why are you building a 12-lane bypass for Nether Broughton? All the village needs is a dual-carriage bypass. To build a 12-lane highway will mean gashing the local hill-side, cutting down trees, destroying houses . . .

DoT: Yes. That is the point.

Counsel: The point is to destroy trees and houses?

DoT: No. The point is to create the maximum damage and distur-bance. To create a gash on the hillside visible from the moon. To cut a swath through woodland. To leave earthworks reminiscent of a First World War no man's land. To send the bulldozers in like tanks into battle. To uncover the rocks beneath, and let them shine through like the bones of a tortured skeleton. To . . .

Chairman: Never mind the cheap similies and metaphors. I thought you DoT chappies wanted to create the least mess possible, so as to get the public a bit on your side.

DoT: What I am about to tell you, sir, is for your ears only.

Chairman: Of course. Mum's the word, as Sigmund Freud always said.

DoT: Generally speaking, we do try to minimise mess and nuisance. But sometimes we try to create the worst possible eyesore.

Counsel: Why?

DoT: Well, we know that whatever we do, there will be protest. There will be ecologists, and rail enthusiasts, and Green Party people, and celebrities, and media stars . . . What we at the DoT call 'rent-a-mob'.

Chairman: I expect that's humorous. I'm not very good at under-standing jokes made by other people. Carry on.

DoT: So our policy is to try to make one bit of road-building so obvi-ously out of proportion and insensitive that it attracts all the protest – thus diverting everyone's anger from the projects we really want to build.

Counsel: You mean some road projects are created solely to draw the flak?

DoT: Oh, yes.

Counsel: Did Twyford Down come into that category?

DoT: Twyford Down wasn't one of mine, but I do remember col-leagues laughing and discussing how they could find the most at-risk spot on the downs and drive a motorway through it.

Counsel: And Batheaston?

DoT: That's different. That is genuinely part of a new Euro super-highway to be driven across England.

Counsel: Why?

DoT: So we can compete with the Continentals in the volume of traffic taken by road?

Counsel: But we already have more freight going by road than any other European country.

DoT: No, we don't.

Counsel: Yes, we do.

DoT: No, we don't.

Counsel: Yes, we do.

Chairman: I am afraid he is right, Twistleton. I have the figures here.

DoT: Gosh, I had no idea. How terrific!

Counsel: So the Nether Broughton Bypass plan is being made as deliberately hideous as possible in order to divert attention from other schemes?

DoT: Yes.

Counsel: How do you ensure that it does become a focus for people's anger?

DoT: Oh, we employ public relations people. We leak the relevant documents. We brief journalists. We infiltrate the protesters. . . .

Counsel: How?

DoT: Easy. We send DoT people on training courses and teach them to live rough, up trees, in tents, anywhere in the open, and then we get them to join the ranks of the protesters.

Counsel: And then what do your infiltrators do?

DoT: They push very hard for the protest to be moved to one of our pet projects like Nether Broughton, which we know is totally unimportant, and will probably never be built.

Chairman: Tell me one thing. If you are a DoT man, why are you telling us all this?

DoT: Because, sir, I am a roads protestor who infiltrated the DoT years ago in order to find out what was going on, and to tell the public when the time was ripe. And there is more to tell!

Miles Kington, Independent, 26/27th May 1995

After the Inquiry

Reports and Decision Letters

The amount of report writing done by the inspectorate has been dramatically reduced since they themselves have been empowered to make decisions. The decision letter is much shorter, being comprised of the main points at issue, plus the verdict. As over 95%

of decisions are taken by the inspector, much time is saved and the outcome known much sooner: an uncomplicated case may only take a few months. The decision letter will be sent to all parties which were entitled to appear at the inquiry, plus anyone else who, having appeared, asked to be notified of the decision. These parties are entitled to ask the Secretary of State if they may see any of the documents cited in the decision letter plus the assessor's report if any.

For the residue of appeals recovered by the Secretary of State, plus call-in cases, reports are still written. Very often only the conclusions are set out with the Minister's decision, but the whole report, including that of the assessor, is available if applied for within four weeks of the decision. Other documents may be made available for inspection, if requested within six weeks. On rare occasions the inspector may refrain from making a specific recommendation, but he has to explain why he has adopted this course.

By definition, cases decided by the Secretary of State tend to be the more complex and contentious. In his advice to the Minister, the inspector has to make sure that every fact has an obvious source within the the Report, is related to an issue argued at the inquiry, and that conclusions can be deduced from those facts. The inspector cannot just base the recommendations on something he saw on the site visit, but not included in the evidence before him at the inquiry. Thus inspector's reports tend to take longer to write than decision letters, and then they have to be approved or otherwise by the Minister.

> 'A park and ride car park would be a largely open use, and it might reasonably be sited in a Green Belt area, if its materials or design were suitable, and no other site was available. In this case the land to be used for car parking might not be particularly intrusive when not in use, provided its surface was designed with care. However, if it were covered with parked cars, I should not regard it as maintaining the open character of the area.
>
> Inspector's Report on Superstore/Park & Ride Site on periphery of Tunbridge Wells.

Re-opening the Inquiry

If the Secretary of State differs from the inspector on any matter of fact mentioned in the report, or contributing to the conclusions, or any new evidence (apart from government policy changes), he cannot issue a decision unless he notifies all parties who were entitled to appear at the inquiry. They then have three weeks in which to comment on the Minister's reasons for disagreeing the report, as asking for the inquiry to be re-opened. If the appellant or the LPA wish the inquiry to be re-opened, the Secretary of State is bound to do it, but otherwise it is at his discretion.

Should that happen, he will advise those who were entitled, and did appear at the previous inquiry, of the issues upon which further evidence is invited during the re-opened inquiry. The timescale adopted for the run up to this second inquiry is at the Minister's discretion: it could well be a case for the truncated version of events allowed for under Rule 10 (see Appendix VIII)

 Complaints About the Inspectorate

Following the publication of the Citizens Charter in 1991, the Inspectorate were expected to create a clear and well publicised procedure for handling grievances about the way in which a given inquiry was conducted. Any given complaint should be sent to the headquarters of the English Inspectorate in Bristol or the Welsh Inspectorate in Cardiff (see Appendix IV). There the Quality Assurance Unit will sift the wheat from the chaff, with serious accusations being forwarded to the line manager of the inspector concerned. Should the complaint turn out to be well-founded, then disciplinary action will be taken against the relevant inspector. In exceptional cases an *ex gratia* payment can be made to parties if a mistake led to them incurring costs which were wasted by their appearance at the inquiry.

An alternative is to lodge a complaint with the Parliamentary Ombudsman. He has to be approached via a Member of Parliament, but it does not have to be the MP for the area. He will investigate the matter and write a report which has to be taken on board by the inspectorate. Other than that he has no powers to change the decision.

It should be remembered, however, that any complaints about the decision letter itself, should not be directed to the Inspectorate or the Parliamentary Ombudsman, because that letter is written in the name of the Secretary of State, and the proper channel for challenging the decision is by an appeal to the High Court.

Planning Appeals: a Guide (The Planning Inspectorate) 1995

REDRESS

If you wish to question the validity of a decision by an inspector or the Secretary of State, in terms of the procedure by which it was reached, there is provision for this under the 1990 TCP Act s. 288. For further detail see Section VI on Redress.

DECISIONS ON ROAD SCHEMES

Trunk Roads and DTp Motorways

Until the setting up of the HA in 1994, the most disturbing aspect of decision-making on trunk road schemes was that the Inspector's report went not to the Secretary of State but to the Regional Office of the DTp which promoted the scheme. The DTp staff which promoted the road scheme and gave evidence at the Inquiry thus vetted the Report, sometimes sending a list of errors to the Inspector, via the Planning Inspectorate, which he had to correct! They then drafted the decision letter and sent copies to the Private Offices of the respective Ministers in DTp and DoE, with the intended decision letter as the 'advice'. It is hardly surprising that this procedure caused severe lack of public confidence in the decision-making process. The DTp road planners were able to push their own schemes through easily when they wrote the decision letters on them.

While there is an apparent similarity with the Local Planning Authority which considers the Inspector's Report on its own Local Plan and adopts its own Plan, there are basic differences. The Local Plan Inspector's Report is published before the LPA takes any view on its recommendations, elected members are involved and can be lobbied, and the whole process makes it difficult for the LPA to disagree with an Inspector; moreover there is a further *Modifications* stage which gives scope for further objections. In the case of road schemes, all decisions are in private. In the 1970s and 80s there were some alarming cases where Inspectors' recommendations were circumvented or overridden by this decision-making process.

Since 1994, the procedure for decisions has been changed in practice within the DTp, although there has been no legal change. This is a result of the setting up of the 'arms-length' HA. In Wales and Scotland there has been no change and the above procedure still applies.

The DTp's published policy statements do not give a complete picture of the new procedures for decision-making. The only known statement is contained in a letter from the then Secretary of State for Transport, John MacGregor, to Mark Sullivan of the CPRE in a letter of 4 July 1994:

> First of all let me emphasise that decisions following inquiries are taken jointly by the Secretaries of State for the Environment and Transport. They are not a matter for the Secretary of State for Transport alone.
>
> We have now established a central team of officials based in the headquarters of DTp, to receive inspector's reports from the Planning Inspectorate Executive Agency. Their role is to advise Ministers, after consultation with colleagues in the DoE, on the inspector's recommendations. These officials are not members of the HA, and play no part in the promotion of trunk road schemes. The team became fully functional on the 6th June and all new Inspector's Reports and related inquiry documents have been sent directly to them from that date....

How far this procedure is an improvement on the pre-HA arrangement remains to be seen. At present it appears that the DTp in London manages the decision letter production, but it is signed by the Regional Director in the the Government Office. A three-way debate between DTp London, Government Office, and the HA appears to take place before a decision is offered in draft to Ministers, and when agreed by them, announced.

Local Authority roads

Inspector's Reports on local authority road schemes go to the DoE section of the relevant Government Office, if they involve called-in planning applications or listed building consents. However, if they are confined to SROs and CPOs, Inspector's reports are considered by the DTp Local Authority Orders section in Newcastle-on-Tyne, from where the decision letter on these Orders comes (see Appendix IV). So there is an element of confusion here too, and two decision letters can sometimes be issued, one from Secretary of State for Environment, and one from Transport.

There are however no furtive 'stopovers' of an Inspector's report in the office of the local highway authority. The DoE and DTp rarely have any motive to disagree with an Inspector on a local authority road scheme. If he recommends refusal of planning consent or that Orders not be confirmed, this is likely to be accepted. Thus objectors stand a better chance of making an impact if they are opposing a local authority road scheme.

The Highways (Inquiries Procedure) Rules 1994 (S.I. 1994 No 3263) (E&W)
Campaigner's Guide to Road Proposals, CPRE, 1993

Section V

Redress

INTRODUCTION

Despite its apolitical image, planning is 'political' in that it is almost inevitable that decisions benefit some sections of the population and disbenefit others. Thus there are bound to be those who will be disappointed when planning permission is either granted or refused, whether by local or central government. This situation gives rise to another fiction: the means of redress outlined in the remainder of this section are geared to procedural matters, but people pursue them because they disagree with the substance of the decision, not primarily because they are concerned with procedural niceties. Why do they choose this route? The truth is that there is no alternative: unless there is an infringement of European law, policy is the prerogative of government and thus not open to question in terms of its application in an individual case.

This section is divided into three parts: the role of the Ombudsmen, both Parliamentary and Local Government; Court action, using the Town and Country Planning Act or judicial review; and the European law dimension, in terms of Article 169 proceedings, the Doctrine of Direct Effect etc.

OMBUDSMEN

'The Ombudsman' was introduced to British public life from Sweden, following the administrative debacle of the Crichel Down affair. In 1967 the Parliamentary Commissioner for Administration took office, and the 1974 Local Government Act created the Commission for Local Administration. Like every other conceivable branch of government, the ombudsmen have been caught up in the 1991 Citizens Charter, and required to produce a clear and well publicized complaints procedure. In fairness one should say that the Commissioners have always given the impression of being on the side of the public, but, along with the rest of the herd, they have to be seen to be such.

The Parliamentary Ombudsman

The Parliamentary Ombudsman oversees the operations of the departments of central government and an enormous range of other public bodies in England, Scotland and Wales. Complaints have to be sent via a Member of Parliament, although it does not have to be the MP for the area. Direct approaches will be returned, although the Ombudsman may tell the complainant's MP about the case and indicate his willingness to help. This cumbersome procedure is all in the good cause of preserving MPs' sense of responsibility for solving their constituent's problems. The MP then decides whether or not to refer the matter to the Parliamentary Ombudsman.

What can be investigated by the Parliamentary Ombudsman? Basically he is looking at bad or failed administration which has led to injustice: avoidable delay; bias; failure to give correct advice; discourtesy; failure to follow correct procedures; failure to take into account representations; mistakes in handling claims; and refusal of access to official information.

What falls beyond his remit? He will not usually look at complaints about events which happened more than 12 months before the MP was contacted, or matters which could be dealt with by an appeal to a tribunal or recourse to the courts. He cannot investigate complaints about matters pertaining to government policy or legislation; crime or national security; matters before the courts; contractual or commercial dealings of Government Departments or other listed bodies, *unless it concerns the compulsory purchase of land or its subsequent disposal*; public service personnel matters.

If the Ombudsman decides to investigate, an officer will examine the paperwork and may conduct interviews in order to collect the facts of the case: the Ombudsman is imbued with the same powers as a High Court judge in terms of calling for evidence and summoning witnesses, which may even include Ministers. The decision as to whether there has been maladministration leading to an injustice and whether to recommend a remedy, rests with the Ombudsman himself.

He aims to sort out a case within three months but more complex issues can take six months or more. If the body complained about offers to rectify the situation before the investigations are completed, you will be told via your MP. Otherwise the Ombudsman's report is sent to the MP with a copy for the person who registered the complaint.

If the Parliamentary Ombudsman upholds your complaint, what remedy can you expect? Basically he will endeavour to set things right in administrative terms, which may or may not affect the ultimate decision; he is concerned with procedure not substance per se. If appropriate, some financial recompense will be made. There are few occasions when the Parliamentary Commissioner has his findings rejected completely, but should that happen a special report is presented to Parliament, and the relevant Minister questioned in the House.

 The Local Government Ombudsman

There are three Local Government Ombudsmen based in various parts of England, and one in Wales. The bodies under their scrutiny include: district, county, city or borough councils but not parish, town or community councils; new town development corporations (housing only); urban development corporations (planning matters only); joint boards of local authorities, including national parks; the (Norfolk) Broads Authority; the Environment Agency (flood defence and drainage only). Complaints must relate to specific individuals or groups, rather than the population generally. They can be brought by individuals or companies, but not by employees or elected member of any of these bodies, or even local councils (parish, town and community councils in England and Wales), despite the fact that they are not potential candidates for investigation by the Local Government Ombudsmen.

Before rushing off to the ombudsman you are expected to try and sort out the matter with the offending body. You must take action within twelve months. Unlike the Parliamentary Ombudsman, those for local government can be approached directly by contacting the appropriate office (see Appendix IV). Complaints must be in writing on the official form, with or without a covering letter. If this presents difficulties, help may be obtained from your councillor or the Citizens Advice Bureau. If translation is required, the Ombudsman's office will arrange for it to be done.

The type of maladministration does not have to be defined by whoever is lodging the complaint, but what the Ombudsman is looking for is: undue delay; not following procedures laid down in law or practice; breaking promises; erroneous information; and not making decisions in the right way. If the complaint is not one which can be investigated, then you will be told as soon as possible. An example might be improper conduct when processing a planning application e.g. an 'unofficial' site visit with the planning committee to test the waters. If you are trying to take pre-emptive action before permission is given, then the Ombudsman will refuse to take the case on the grounds that the damage has not been done i.e. that ancient woodland has not yet been felled to make way for yet more executive housing in the London/Paris/Brussels triangle. Lobby your local councillors and contact your MP: a letter from counsel threatening judicial review might do wonders (see below).

If your complaint is taken on board, then a full investigation will be mounted: files sent for and people interviewed. Your name is unlikely to be divulged: this would only be done on rare occasions and with good reason, but raise the matter with your case officer if you are worried. The nature of an acceptable remedy is likely to be discussed with you: it might be an apology; a rerun of that decision using the correct procedure; reform of best practice in that authority; or a payment to cover expenses which should not have had to be incurred.

When the Ombudsman's report arrives in the offices of the local authority, a notice has to be placed in the local paper for two successive weeks, announcing the advent of the report, and saying where it can be inspected. If the local authority ignores the report, then another may be issued within three months. If he still gets no joy from the local authority, then he may require the council to publish an agreed statement in the local paper: if they wish, the council may put their side of the case in a statement. Beyond this the Ombudsman is powerless to act: unlike the Courts he cannot enforce his decision. However, this only happens on rare occasions.

Although the ombudsman may appear to be a toothless tiger, local authorities do not like being investigated because it is time consuming and embarrassing, and the bad publicity resulting from an adverse finding is a spur to action in these days when image is so important, not only amongst charge-payers, but also within the fraternity of local government itself. Perhaps it is reassuring to know that the old fashioned concept of 'bad form' can surface in the guise of corporate competitiveness.

REDRESS: POLLUTION CASES

If an *existing* development is causing a public nuisance because it generates noise, dust smell smoke fumes etc., or a *proposal*, with the potential to cause pollution, has been granted planning permission, do not despair. The 1990 Environmental Protection Act provides a valuable tool for the use of communities. They may persuade their local authority to serve an abatement notice under ss.80 & 81 which imposes all or any of the following requirements:

a) lessening, prohibiting or restricting the nuisance;

b) undertaking measures to ensure (a).

Those continuing to offend are liable to be fined.

If the local authority is reluctant to act, then, under s.82 EPA 1990, any individual may take the matter to a magistrates' court, and, if they agree that the alleged nuisance exists, they can serve an abatement notice as above, and fine those causing the nuisance if they continue to pollute the environment.

If in doubt, particularly in respect of a development which has yet to start operating, consult a solicitor knowledgeable in pollution law: there are many available through the ELF (see Appendix IV).

> *Learned counsel will meet in Taunton Somerset, this week, to argue over the fate of Corky, the cock who crowed too much. Corky was silenced last year by a noise abatement order and now a court action for nuisance is being brought against his owner. The first crow came at 5.07 a.m. ... increasing to greater intensity with 42 crows between 6 a.m. and 6.30 a.m. the noise in the bedroom (of the complainant) amounted to 39 decibels ... ten decibels above singing birds and bleating sheep. (The complainant) fears that if he loses his case, he could be almost encircled by cocks.*
>
> The Independent 1995

THE HIGH COURT

A decision may be challenged in the High Court under 1990 TCP Act, ss.287 & 288: the former is primarily aimed at questioning the validity of development plans, whereas the latter is concerned with individual development control decisions, whether taken by local government, or resulting from an appeal. These two sections also encompass a miscellaneous collection of orders from tree preservation to footpaths, highways, and simplified planning zones, not to mention the obligations of statutory undertakers. There is also provision for challenging a listed building enforcement notice under s.65 of 1990 LBCA Act.

Who is eligible to take the matter to the High Court? The phrase used is 'Any person aggrieved'. At one time this was interpreted as only those whose legal rights had been jeopardised by the decision, but since the 1960s there has been a gradual liberalisation of the system. An important landmark was the 1969 Inquiries Procedure rules which allowed the ordinary citizen to appear at an inquiry at the inspector's discretion: if they participated in the inquiry, why should they not be able to challenge that very procedure? Subsequent judgements have extended this right to anyone or any local authority which has a legitimate grievance as a result of the decision.

When an appeal decision arrives, for example, it is accompanied by a sheet informing one of the right to challenge the decision within six weeks. This time limit applies to all decisions. It is a short enough time to make such a potentially costly decision, and made the shorter by the fact that it dates from the issuing of the decision rather than its receipt by interested parties. Clearly one has to contemplate possible litigation before the decision is out so as to swing into action, peradventure the decision goes against one. However, the point of having such a time limit is not to impede the development rights of those affected: otherwise buildings may have been demolished and the foundations laid for the new building.

On what grounds may one challenge the decision? If one looks at ss.287 & 288 of the 1990 TCP Act, anyone repairing to the Courts must be able to show that the activity in question is not within the powers of the Act, or that relevant requirements pertaining to that activity have not been met. In practice there appear to be seven main grounds for a challenge in the courts:

a) A relevant factor has not been taken into account:

Clearly the definition of what is relevant varies with the case, but you are on safe ground if something is specified in the legislation. Even so there are vague terms in legislation, which keep the lawyers busy in Court, defining and redefining their meaning e.g. 'material consideration'. *It should be noted that so long as the matter is given a mention in the decision, it is deemed to have been taken into account: the fact that this item was not accorded the weight which other people would have given it, is not a grounds for challenge in the High Court.*

b) An irrelevant factor has been taken into account,

Here again it is a matter of judgement as to what is deemed to be irrelevant, and planning grounds are many and various. The fact that there may have been a political motive lurking behind a bona fide planning factor, does not make it actionable.

c) The decision is totally unreasonable:

This does not mean that the Court, or indeed any other group of people, faced with the same set of facts, could not have reached a different conclusion. It just means that the decision is arbitrary, illogical or perverse: the fashionable term is 'irrational'. In practice this is the most difficult ground on which to challenge a decision.

d) A decision is contrary to natural justice:

If one looks at the various inquiry Rules, they are embodiments of natural justice in terms of giving all parties a right to put their case. The rule against bias is designed to ensure that the decision maker is impartial, be it local councillors, the inspector or the Secretary of State. Thus anyone having a financial or personal interest in a scheme is debarred from partaking in the decision. This also manifests itself in the conduct of inspectors at inquiries: they are never seen to have private conversations with any one of the participants, and they should never give the impression that they have already made up their mind on the issue.

e) The decision must represent an effective exercise of any discretion given by the state:

Whilst the Courts acknowledge the major role played by policy in development control decisions, there is such a thing as being too inflexible: the adjudicator should also be seen to have exercised some discretion, by at least having heard the case to the contrary. The Court's task is to pinpoint when freedom of choice has been surrendered.

f) Mistaken facts:

Unfortunately mistaken facts are not unknown: in Scotland, the reporter (a tartan inspector) issues his findings of fact to participants to check for error, but this practice has always been deemed to be too expensive south of the Border, and is about to be discontinued north of it because it delays the decision, and therefore development. However, it is not enough for there to be a mistake. It is a matter of proving that it was germane to the decision: that had the adjudicator realised the true situation, the decision would have been different. If this is the case, it will vitiate the decision.

g) The requirements of the legislation must be observed:

The procedures laid down in the 1990 TCP Act, and subsidiary regulations, must be observed. If there is an oversight, it must also have adverse effects of a practical nature in order to cause the decision to be set aside. Decisions must also be seen to be fair i.e. backed up with clear reasoning: this applies to all decisions from refusing a planning application by a LPA, or the Secretary of State, to a local authority's verdict on the Secretary of State's decision. The Courts have insisted that reasons must be clear and intelligible, as well as dealing with the major points raised in the course of the arguments: this is echoed in DoE Circular 10/88 para.51.

Section 287 & 288 are very specific about the matters which are subject to challenge in the High Court under the 1990 TCP Act. In any given year less than 1% of appeals under s.78 TCP Act are challenged in the courts, but that could have more to do with the cost of failure than satisfaction with the outcome.

What about other potential abuses of power by public authorities? These may be dealt with by means of judicial review.

THIS IS A HEALTH SPA ...
MINERAL WATER IS PRECIOUS – CONSERVE IT
THE PUBLIC ARE ONLY ALLOWED TO SWIM IN BATHING COSTUMES
NO NUDE BATHING ALLOWED
NO BATHING IN CLOTHING ALLOWED
THE USE OF SOAP & SHAMPOO IS STRICTLY FORBIDDEN
NO SHAVING ALLOWED
NO WASHING OF CLOTHES ALLOWED
NO WASHING OF GROCERIES ALLOWED

YOU ARE ENTERING THIS POOL AT YOUR OWN RISK

Notice outside of Spa in Mbabane, Swaziland

JUDICIAL REVIEW

Judicial review is a remedy designed to control the activities of public authorities. A preliminary application has to be made to the Supreme Court for permission to proceed with an application for judicial review. This is in order to weed out frivolous or unfounded allegations of malpractice, and convince the Court to award a remedy.

SUPREME COURT

For those who are unaware of the existence of Britain's Supreme Court, it was created in 1873 and consists of the Court of Appeal, the High Court of Justice and the Crown Court (Supreme Court Act 1981)

There appear to be four main hurdles to be crossed by any applicant.

(a)   Sufficient Interest

Whether or not one is considered to have 'sufficient interest' to bring the case depends on a number of things: the terms of the legislation under which the action took place; the nature of the beast; and the merits of the case. It is difficult to predict whether or not a given applicant will be deemed to have sufficient interest. However, it is comforting to know that the House of Lords won't stand for any nonsense by public authorities who try to escape their responsibilities, by using 'insufficient interest' to cloak their nefarious activities.

(b)   No Delay

Whereas one has six weeks in which to appeal to the High Court under the 1990 Act, there are three months in which to make an application for judicial review. On the other hand it is as well to be prompt, as the court may take the view that, even if the application was made within three months, that was not soon enough in the circumstances. It should be noted that the three months run from when the problem should have become apparent, which may not be for some time after a decision was made.

(c)　Lawfulness of the Decision

As with applications to the High Court, it is a matter of showing that the public authority has exceeded the powers given to it, either by statute or some other source: the correct procedures may not have been fulfilled; the legislation may have been misinterpreted; the bounds of discretion may have been exceeded; or natural justice flouted. The difficulty for the Court is to tread the narrow line between ensuring a decision has been properly made, and substituting their own decision for that of the public authority.

(d)　Granting a Remedy

Even if an authority has exceeded its powers, if little damage has been done, the court may refuse to grant a remedy: in fact they have wide discretion *not to grant* a legal remedy. Alternatively the courts may consider that the individual should be forced to pursue an alternative means of redress e.g. a challenge based on the 1990 TCP Act or LBCA Act. The need for a speedy decision may be a relevant factor, as may the types of remedies available by means of judicial review: a positive or negative injunction; prohibition or spur to action by the body concerned; damages. It should be noted that the latter is never awarded by itself, but always as an adjunct to one of the other remedies.

Conclusion

Thus, the only way to query a decision is by questioning the manner in which it was made. However, there is an inbuilt penalty: if you are successful, the most you will achieve is a quashing of the decision, which has the effect of setting the procedure back to the stage when it went off-beam, and so the decision has to be taken again, using the correct mechanism. In 50% of cases, the unfavourable verdict will be arrived at the second time, so the complainant will have achieved nothing except the expenditure of time and money, whilst what they really wanted was a different decision altogether. If one looks at the tomes on planning law, it is 99% procedure, and the function of the courts is to make sure that everyone, from the Secretary of State downwards, abides by what is laid down in primary and secondary legislation. Thus what is on offer is a *review* of a procedure rather than an *appeal* which would allow the court to substitute its own decision.

If you are contemplating action through the courts, clearly you need expert advice from a lawyer competent to give advice on the pitfalls and your likelihood of success. If you don't know where to turn, contact ELF (see Appendix IV)

Peter Morgan & Susan Nott, Development control: Law, Policy & Practice, (London, Butterworths, Second Edition) 1995

EUROPEAN DIMENSION

As can be seen from Fig.13, European law brings a new dimension to the protection of the environment, and the regulation of activities which could have an adverse effect on it. If one is trying to utilize its provisions, however, two sets of problems may arise:

a) the national law has not caught up with the relevant European Directive despite the fact that the time limit for implementation has been exceeded;

b) or, more usually, that the transposition into national law is partial or incorrect.

With regard to (a), two courses of are open to the citizen: a complaint to the European Commission under Article 169 proceedings and/or court action invoking the doctrine of Direct Effect. The rest of this Section looks at these issues.

Article 169 Proceedings

The failure to transpose European law into national law, is a matter between the Commission and the Member State. However the Commission is happy to receive complaints from the general public, and readers will perhaps not be surprised to know that the British lodge twice as many complaints as any other nationality....

Unlike issues concerned with free trade and competition, the Commission does not employ Community inspectors, working within Member States, to check possible breaches of environmental law: moves to establish such an inspectorate were firmly rejected by Member States. This is why complaints from the public are so important. If the Commission is satisfied that there has been a breach of Community Law, Article 169 of the Treaty of Rome sets up procedures which could lead to the Member State appearing before the European Court of Justice in Luxembourg.

There is no specific procedure for lodging complaints. Given that the purpose is to alert the Commission, rather than resolving matters in a private dispute, the complainant may be an individual, an association or any sort of corporate animal, and the subject of their grievance need not be in their country of residence. It costs nothing to lodge a complaint. All that is necessary is that you make a representation, in any of the Community languages (e.g. English but not Welsh), to the Environment Commissioner at the Brussels office of the European Commission (see Appendix IV). Bear in mind the following points:

a) Make your letter concise, and append any supporting evidence such as reports or correspondence;

b) Visual material such as photographs and even videos can accompany the formal letter;

c) It is not essential to identify precisely which aspect of Community Law has been transgressed, but clearly it is helpful if you can point those examining your case in the right direction: it might be helpful to enlist the support of a national NGO which has the staff to focus your case. Obversely, if the matter is not dealt with under Community Law, the Commission cannot deal with it;

d) Once the complaint has been lodged, don't hold your breath: matters proceed slowly because officers are overworked on the enforcement side. On the other hand if there are important new developments in your case, and the matter is urgent, the Commission may be contacted by telephone/fax, but remember to quote the reference number of your complaint.

Article 169 proceedings tend to fall into three groups: cases where the Member State has failed to transpose, say, a directive, into national legislation within the requisite time; cases where some progress towards implementation has been made but the transposition is incomplete; and cases where the legal niceties have been finalized, but there is failure to apply the law in practice. It is likely that the former two categories will be picked up by the officers of the Environment Directorate, or consultants working for them, in their official capacity of monitoring the implementation of a Directive. However, they are very reliant on the public to report whether the legislation is being observed in practice.

On receiving a complaint, it will be scrutinized by lawyers in the Environment Directorate (otherwise known as DG XI). They will let you know immediately if there is nothing that can be done e.g. the proposed development falls in Annex II of the Environmental Assessment legislation, so calling for an Environmental Statement is only a matter of discretion. If it is a matter they can deal with, you will be assigned a file number, which you must use in any subsequent contact with the Commission. They will then begin their own investigations, usually commencing with a letter to the relevant Member State asking for their side of the story. Certain Member States, not usually Britain, have a propensity to delay their response at this stage.

The lawyers may also involve the technical unit, within DG XI, dealing with that type of case e.g. water pollution. These units can also act as a brake on proceedings because they are working with the Member States on implementation, and may advise that a more conciliatory tone will get the best results in the long run. Liaison with the technical units also promotes an even-handed approach so that proceedings are not instituted against one Member State, whilst another, committing the same misdemeanour gets off Scot-free: apart from being unjust, this would be a political gaff, and fodder for the tabloid press in the 'victimized' country.

If, from the evidence, there appears to be grounds for saying that the Member State is in breach of Community Law, a one page summary is prepared proposing that a letter of Formal Notice (known in Euro-Speak as a 169 letter) be sent to the Member State. This is considered jointly by the lawyers of DG XI, and the Commission's Legal Service, and the decision taken whether the case should be raised at the twice yearly meeting of the Commission, attended by all members of the Commission's staff (the cabinet). If there is no satisfactory response, within two months, to a Formal Notice, then the same procedure is gone through again with the preparation of a Reasoned Opinion, setting out the arguments concerning the alleged infringement. By this stage only an unequivocal admission of guilt on the part of the errant Member State, plus the steps they propose to take to rectify the situation, will satisfy the Commission. If there is still no response then the Commission *may* refer the matter to the European Court of Justice (ECJ) in Luxembourg. This may take years, and over 90% of cases never reach this stage: they are sorted out at the Formal Notice or Reasoned Opinion stage. It may be quicker, if you can muster the resources, to go through the British Courts and thence to the ECJ.

The procedures, from the initial complaint to the Reasoned Opinion, are supposed to take about a year but it is not unknown for Member States to drag out the proceedings. Although it would not be politic for a Commissioner to veto a decision against his own country, mysterious alliances seem to be forged between Commissioners, and requests are frequently made for further reports to be made by the technical units, or suspension of proceedings whilst the relevant Member States looks into the matter and attempts to resolve the issue. Such requests, if agreed, will delay things for at least six months, before the the matter can be considered again at a Commission meeting. A little ingenuity coupled with political dexterity, can result in considerable delay. The other problem is the shortage of staff in the legal department of DG XI, but there is a sense in which this could be seen to be deliberate policy: as they police the implementation of Community Law, they are not 'top of the pops' with any Member State, who thus see it as being in their best interest to keep them on a shoestring. Given these constraints, the Commission will only seriously consider complaints from individual citizens where there is a general problem of implementation, rather than a one-off incident.

Doctrine of Direct Effect

Absence of National Provision

Over the years, the ECJ has developed a set of principles known as the *Doctrine of Direct Effect*. This means that individuals and bodies within a given State should not suffer because their government has failed to transpose a Directive, into their national legislation, or set up an appropriate administration to deliver the goods. The importance of this Doctrine is that, under certain circumstances, it is possible for an individual citizen, involved in an environmental dispute to take issue against a government body.

Under what circumstances can the Doctrine of Direct Effect be invoked? According to the European Court of Justice, the obligation in the Directive, in question, must be clear and unconditional. If a large amount of discretion is allowed, then it may be impossible to apply the doctrine. Secondly the Doctrine only applies when one of the parties is an 'emanation of the state' i.e. one of the protagonists is a public body, at central, regional or local level, or controlled by such a body i.e. the new privatized utilities. Thirdly, the time limit must have lapsed for transposing the legislation into national law.

> *A body, whatever its legal form, which has been made responsible.*
> *... for providing a public service under the control of the State,*
> *and has for that purpose special powers beyond those which result*
> *from the normal rules applicable in relations between individuals,*
> *is included among bodies against which the provisions of a*
> *Directive, capable of having Direct Effect, may be relied upon.*
> European Court of Justice

Imperfect National Implementation

Looking at British environmental legislation and policy documents
in the areas such as pollution, nature conservation, and
environmental information, it is easy to see that most of the statutes
have European pedigree. Nevertheless, problems do arise with the
practical implementation of this European law. The ECJ has held
that national courts are under an obligation to interpret national law
in the light of the wording and purpose of European Law. This
obligation is quite distinct from the doctrine of direct effect,
outlined above.

Applying European Environmental Law in the UK

Typically, cases involving the interpretation of national law in the
light of European law, or attempts to invoke the doctrine of direct
effect, surface in the High Court in actions brought under judicial
review. Many of the cases have been brought by the major
environmental NGOs such as Greenpeace, Friends of the Earth or
the RSPB. If there are difficulties in the interpretation of European
law when confronted with a British case, then the national courts
may repair to the European Court in Luxembourg for a ruling on
the interpretation of European law. They then have to apply it to the
facts of the given case. The problem is that it can take two years to
get a case through the European Court and this is a major deterrent.
What tends to happen is that British judges will 'have a go', and the
results are not always welcomed by either the litigants or those
concerned with the environment. The problem is that the British
legal system is geared to the protection of property, and concepts of
injury and damages: the approach is narrow but precise.

European lawyers adopt a much wider interpretation of law, a
'teleological' view of the matter: the preamble setting out the
intention of the legislation is of as much interest as the wording of
specific articles. Whenever European legislation is to be interpreted,

it is necessary to look at wider considerations such as rights and obligations under the Treaty and other European legislation, as well as underlying policy principles. Hopefully the passage of time will resolve the difficulties, as younger barristers nurtured on European Law, move upward into the judiciary.

European law deals primarily with rights and obligations, rather than remedies, which tend to remain the province of the national courts. That said, the discretion granted to Member States is not unlimited. The ECJ has developed a principle of effectiveness. The conditions set down in national law by which an individual may obtain a remedy for the breach of a directly effective right should be:

a) no less favourable than remedies available for similar claims under national law;

b) not be so framed as to render it virtually impossible to exercise the right.

The Future

It is a matter of concern that the progressive enlargement of the Community will bring subsidiarity in its train, and thus the wording of Directives become so vague that it will become impossible to implement either Article 169 proceedings, or the Doctrine of Direct Effect. If so the high standards set in the field of environmental law by the Commission will falter in the closing years of the twentieth century, when the need will be more acute than ever.

The Official Journal of the European Communities: the 'L' series contains the text of EC legislation: the 'C' series contains draft Directives and Regulations.
Encyclopaedia of European Law, Sweet & Maxwell
Control of Pollution Legislation, Sweet & Maxwell
Garner's Environmental Law, Butterworth's
Manual of Environmental Policy, Nigel Haigh ed. (Longmans)
DIY. Guides to Using European Law
Richard Macrory, A Campaigner's Guide to Using EC Environmental Law, (London, CPRE) 1992 Appendix 1 & 2.
Philip Mead & Alex Christians, European Issues in Environmental Litigation (London, the Environmental Law Foundation) 1996

For a basic understanding on how the EU works and the place of environmental law within it, see:

Publications produced by the EU and available from the Commission offices in the UK (see Appendix IV);

Ludwig Kramer, The EEC Treaty and Environmental Protection, (London, Sweet & Maxwell) 1990

Ludwig Kramer, Focus on European Environmental Law, (London, Sweet & Maxwell) 1992

Ludwig Kramer, EC Treaty and Environmental Law, (London, Sweet & Maxwell) 1995

Section VI

Procedures for Survival

INTRODUCTION

The foregoing Sections attempt to show how the procedural jigsaw fits together, and how to use it to best effect when involved in disputes over land use. This Section is different: it is borne of the frustration of trying to reconcile the character of much of contemporary development with 'sustainability', however defined.

The first part of this Section examines the rationale underlying the current land use system, and the procedures used to administer it. From the viewpoint of sustainability, there are two important points. First of all, the land-use planning system is geared to facilitating economic growth. Land use professionals find themselves trying to ameliorate the worst excesses of developments which are unsustainable both in character and mode of operation. So often, the question which crosses one's mind is not 'Where should it go?', but 'Should it be built at all?' The reason this matters is that, within the next twenty to thirty years, the Western World could be obliged to change its way of life so that it no longer consumes the lion's share of the world's resources. In the UK we will be compelled to become much more self-sufficient: this should mean making better, and more creative use of what we have, rather than going without.

This brings one to the second conclusion to be drawn from the previous Sections: the procedures militate against real public participation in decision making. If our society is to make a peaceful transition from the status quo to a de-materialised culture, then a number of conditions have to be fulfilled. A necessary prerequisite is a population which has been so educated that it can take a full part in debating vital issues, and which is aware of the downside of the free market so that it is supportive of the necessary changes to the system. It will be essential for government to be sensitive to public opinion if the supply of a given resource in a given location falls short of demand at national level. It will also be imperative that local government, and all other agencies concerned with the environment, have the legal and financial powers appropriate to the task. Given that investment decisions are a product of a broad raft of political, legal, fiscal and institutional structures, operating at home and abroad, it is vital that these be changed by central government and the EU, so that only sustainable projects come forward, from either the private or public sector.

However, as will be shown, there is a formidable obstacle in the way of achieving all this, at least in the short run. It is the financial and political power of free-market capitalism, which is dependent for its profits on exploiting the world's resources and its peoples. Either because they are ignorant, or because they are blinded by the myths of private enterprise and afraid to offend the wealth generators, the politicians fail to attribute familiar problems, at home and abroad, to the dysfunctional aspects of the free market.

Given the seriousness of the situation, what can be done? The last part of this Section looks at some suggestions. Yes, it will be a David and Goliath struggle, but this time it is really the case that 'There is no alternative.'

UNSUSTAINABLE DEVELOPMENT

The Investment Framework

Despite all the talk about the greening of government and the business community, the fact is that most of the development proposals with which we are faced are flagrantly unsustainable in character, and give rise to further deleterious side effects now and in the future:

> the road 'improvement' which will generate yet more traffic;

> the superstore which will destroy jobs in the town centre and amongst local suppliers, whilst generating road traffic over a wide area;

> the new housing estate, of 'vernacular' appearance constructed from materials supplied from all over the world, providing shelter for people whose lifestyle imposes excessive demands on the world's resources;

> and the quarry, which first supplies the voracious need for materials and then provides a depository for our household waste, and which generates traffic and pollution over a long period.

Yet Government policy, since the early nineties has espoused the rhetoric of 'sustainability'. By this it means minimizing negative impacts rather than querying the character of the development. The PPGs dutifully cater for all these manifestly unsustainable uses, because the economy is said to require it, yet discriminate against those who wish to opt for life in a tepee or bender. The irony is that the functional and financial test required of new agricultural units by PPG7 effectively precludes the genuine sustainable development because it is preoccupied with preventing speculative development for profit.

At present the environment is traded off against the demands made on it, and it is up to those regulating land use to minimise the adverse impacts. Thus they find themselves trying to apply policy advice on sustainability, contained in, say, the PPGs, to a development which is inherently unsustainable in terms of its purpose and mode of operation. In such circumstances, whatever the good intentions of civil servants (and even the odd politician), 'Sustainability' is usually no more than a fashionable bolt on extra, rather than an exercise in lateral thinking as to the most eco-friendly way to achieve a given objective e.g. the distribution of food.

Investment decisions are made in the light of the current political, institutional, legal and fiscal structures relevant to the proposal: if you change any of those variables, then the character of development proposals will change. For example, those responsible for an application for waste disposal by means of land-raising, will have taken into account: government policy that individual counties should be self sufficient in waste disposal; the possibility of importing waste from abroad; the shortage of void space in the waste local plan; the economics of transport as determined by government accounting structures and fiscal measures; the protection, or otherwise, afforded to agricultural land by government policy; national and international wildlife obligations pertaining to sites in the vicinity; the demand for recycled products encouraged by government policy; the accountancy conventions which determine the economies of scale in the waste disposal industry etc. etc.

Market forces provide the context for applications: the exploitation of natural resources, and the deployment of people, in the pursuit of profits for individuals and companies, and, hopefully, the prosperity of society in general. The paradigm of market capitalism provides the 'acceptable' definition of the problem, the 'correct' yardstick for measuring the success of the solution, and the 'right' balance between the means of achieving the chosen objective. This is why, as we saw in Section III, the scope for discussion over a given proposal is fairly narrow, and, furthermore, has to be conducted in terms of 'the public interest'. Thus, a potential developer has, given the bias in favour of development, the initial advantage of working with the grain of the system.

Procedural Bias

The procedures, too, are orientated in favour of development. It was ever thus: landowners and factory owners in the nineteenth century, who were amongst the few who were enfranchised, would not have voted for public health and pollution legislation had it been seen to inhibit their legitimate right, as they saw it, to do what they liked with their own. Hence the creation of the appeals system.

The desire not to inhibit development has underlain anxieties about keeping development plans up to date, ever since their introduction in the post war years. The speeding up of the appeals system began in 1962 when written representations made their debut, followed by the informal hearing in 1981. However, the whole tenor of the planning system was challenged by the 1985 White Paper, characteristically entitled 'Lifting the Burden':

> *It is an established principle of planning law that the developer is entitled to his permission unless there are sound, relevant and clear cut reasons for refusal ... Nor is the developer required to prove the case for the development he proposes to carry out: if the planning authority consider it necessary to refuse permission, the onus is on them to demonstrate clearly why the development cannot be permitted, and the reasons must be precise, specific, and relevant to the application.*

> *The town and country planning system ... imposes costs on the economy and constraints on enterprise that are not always justified by any real public benefit. Too often the very wide discretionary power that the system affords is used to apply excessively detailed and onerous controls of a kind that would not be tolerated in general legislation. If the system is to be effective, it must be used in a way that does not impose an unnecessary degree of regulation on firms and on individuals ... An efficient and simple system can speed the planning process and facilitate much needed development which helps to create jobs – in construction, in commerce and industry and in small firms.*

Cmnd 9571, paras. 3.1, 3.2, 3.4

In 1923 a Circular was issued from the Ministry of Health which emphasised that:

> the presumption should always be in favour of the person who wishes to undertake the development. ... (it is) particularly desirable that no obstacles should be placed in the way of proposed development unless it is clearly detrimental to important local needs or interests.
>
> Circular 368, January 29th, 1923

Although the phrase *presumption in favour of development* disappeared in the second version of PPG1 in 1992, the sentiment is still to be found in the 1997 version of PPG1, albeit given the fashionable gloss of sustainability. In the preceding Sections we have seen how, in a multiplicity of ways, the planning system has been speeded up in the good cause of facilitating economic development:

a) the expansion of 'permitted development' rights;

b) the ratchet mechanism operating within the Use Classes Order;

c) minimisation of the number of Environmental Assessments;

d) the sheer difficulty in getting cases called in by the Secretary of State, even if they are *Departures* from the development plan, local authority scheme or if the application is accompanied by an ES which deserves the scrutiny of an inquiry;

e) no third party right of appeal against a grant of planning permission by an LPA or the Secretary of State.

Secondly, some animals are more equal than others when it comes to influencing the process:

i) developers have the resources to employ planning specialists, conversant with policy-speak and the language of the market, to influence the policy process at the right level via the procedural mechanism. They may also benefit from government and/or commercial secrecy;

ii) as we have seen it is a 'top down' process, and many of the decisions on key variables e.g. the number of houses needed, are taken at a national and regional level. The quantity of minerals required or the amount of household rubbish likely to be generated in the plan period, are just built into the system. Until recently, the DTp simply inserted motorways into development plans and giant supermarkets still argue the need for more shopping at the EIP, making sure that the right policy gets inserted into the structure plan. By the time the issue reaches development control level, and the public has woken up to what is happening, there is a well established policy in favour of the development and the only question is location.

iii) ESs are commissioned by the applicants and can be economical with the truth. LPAs may be too desperate for jobs to want to query the ES, so unless the matter is called-in, which is unlikely, the ES is never questioned.

iv) budgetary constraints, in the public sector, make LPAs reluctant to devote staff time inquiries, and make them prey to threats of costs, or even the surcharging of members;

v) newly elected members are not always as well acquainted with law and policy as they might be;

vi) local people who, for the most part, are ignorant of the structure of government at all levels, unacquainted with the various strands of policy which might have a bearing on the issue, untutored in using procedure to best advantage, and devoid of funds to pay for professional advice. 'Public Participation' is a matter of fighting a rearguard action.

vii) the Courts and the Ombudsmen are there to see fair play over procedural matters rather than getting involved in substantive issues. In any case the courts are beyond the pocket of most people.

Thus, the procedures are also biased in the direction of development, in terms of having the resources and skills to operate the system to best advantage.

The Town & Country Planning Councillor's Summer School proved enlightening for at least one elected member, although her chief officer may have to revise his approach to recommendations. Following a session on PPGs, a member stood up and asked a question which had obviously been puzzling her for some time. 'Tell me about PPG 37,' she insisted. When assured by the seminar leaders that there was no such thing, she appeared even more confused. 'But my chief officer constantly quotes it', she complained.

PPG37, Planning Week, 6th October 1994

Capitalism versus the Planet

Whether we like it or not, we are caught up in free market capitalism, and unsustainability is the nature of the beast. When the debate started about 'world population and resources', in the late 1950s, the concern about the latter focused on the non renewable assets like fossil fuels and minerals. Thirty years on we are equally concerned about the despoliation of renewable resources: the erosion of agricultural land; the pollution of air and water; the destruction of biodiversity. The relentless plundering of the planet's resources is accompanied by the exploitation of her peoples. This has long been a problem in the Third World, but now it is hitting the developed world: the late Conservative Government's opposition to the EU's Social Chapter, and, indeed much other EU legislation, was based on fear of the Asian 'tigers'. Much of the world's population have become *Proles* in the service of the so called free market. What is shocking is seeing how many Chapters in Agenda 21, primarily aimed at Third World countries, apply to Britain in the nineties. Environmental and human degradation are the external costs of short term profitability. The multiplicity of effects, of such greed, will be experienced by children now in primary school, not just abstract 'future generations'.

> *The* love *of money is the root of all evil.*
>
> *1 Tim. 6 v.10*

However the misery is not equally shared. With just 20% of the world's people, the industrialised nations consume: three quarters of the world's energy, producing two thirds of all green house gases; 80% of its iron and steel; 93% of global industrial effluents and 95% of its hazardous wastes. Put more graphically, it is said that when the average American couple stops spawning at two children, it is the same as the average East Indian couple stopping at 66, or an Ethiopian couple drawing the line at 1,000. Each of us in the developed world make demands upon land use which do not just impact upon each other, in terms of pollution, waste and urban jungle, but also on what have been called 'ghost acres' abroad which produce the goods we need to maintain our standard of living.

Devon County Council have been researching the global footprint of communities. This involves drawing up a balance sheet of goods and services produced, consumed, imported and exported by a community. These calculations are conducted in terms of acres rather than money. It would seem that provisional data for Greater Manchester, shows that this large community requires what they call an *acquired carrying capacity* of ten times its own area, and London draws on resources from an area equivalent to the whole of the U.K. Other calculations have shown that every acre farmed in Britain requires two abroad. Obviously the same arguments apply to timber, minerals etc. Now this is not to say that trade should be abolished, but this excessive dependence on resources elsewhere, does much to explain environmental despoliation at home and abroad, and the pollution generated by mass transportation. The responsibility is ours.

With the world's population doubling in the next forty years, the situation is highly unstable, both in terms of environmental damage and international security. Whether we like it or not, we will be forced to 'de-materialise' our economy, to de-couple economic growth from the consumption of scarce resources. The Wuppertal Institute has calculated the approximate environmental space available for various resources and waste assimilation capacities. Present European levels of consumption will have to fall drastically, if some 'headroom' is to be allowed for the burgeoning populations of the South e.g. 77% reduction in CO_2 emissions, 85% reduction in cement consumption, 90% reduction in aluminium. To make it bearable, they give interim targets, of around 25% reductions, for the year 2010. It would seem that we have between twenty and forty years to get it right. All this has implications for land use planning *now*.

'When you've spent the whole of your political life dealing with humdrum issues like the environment, isn't it exciting to have a real crisis on your hands?'

Margaret Thatcher on the Falklands War.

Simon Fairlie, Low Impact Development, Jon Carpenter Publishing (Charlbury, Oxfordshire) 1996
Devon County Council & Devon Community Council, Developing Sustainable Communities, Devon Community Council, (1995)
Joy Williams, 'Baby Sham', The Independent Magazine, 19/10/96
Michael Jacobs, The Politics of the Real World, Earthscan (London 1996).
Friends of the Earth Europe, Towards Sustainable Europe, (1996)
Full text of Agenda 21 from Regency Press Corporation (see Appendix IV)

SHIFTING THE PARADIGM

Building-in Sustainability

As 'Sustainability' is one of the great issues of our time, it has generated a vast literature. Unfortunately, this discussion has to be limited to the aspects of the subject which impinge on what one might call the *realpolitik* of the situation: discussion of the factors require to affect change both in the way we take decisions, and the type of development proposals coming forward.

Environmental Education

Given the urgency of coming to terms with the demands on the environment and the limits to its capacity, it is essential that the message be conveyed to as wide an audience as possible. It is worrying how many young people have become tired of 'the Environment', either because they just feel impotent in the face of impossible odds or because they just hope that the predictions are untrue. Furthermore the signals are confused by misinformation put out by those with a vested interest in the status quo. It is imperative that an accurate picture, neither alarmist nor too optimistic, be presented to the population as a whole.

Environmental education is an enormous subject, but there are three neglected aspects. Either as children or as adults we are not made familiar with the mechanics of policy making. The vast majority of the population do not know how the EU, Parliament, or even local government, work, let alone the dynamics of the system in terms of the play-off between conflicting interests in the formulation of policies which, directly or indirectly affect the environment. Ministers are able to wriggle out of responsibilities, particularly with regard to matters European, because most of the population do not realise precisely who plays what role in the creation of policy. The result, all too frequently, is Travesty by Tabloid.

The second aspect of the subject is 'knowing the ropes' in terms of the procedures which govern individual land-use decisions. People can find themselves on a steep learning curve when some proposal for an undesirable development lands on their doorstep, or they find that their own home has been built on contaminated land. They know nothing of who takes which decision, the timescales involved, the information to which they have a statutory right, and the likely strategy of the opposition. For many people a planning dispute is their entry point into the wider environmental debate. We need to educate citizens in the skills necessary to play an active play in deciding the future of their environment, both in terms of having an input into policies which result in land-use proposals, and getting involved early enough in the planning system to make an impact. It is a matter of counter-balancing the influence of the developers.

> 'In a democratic age you might expect contemporary architecture to express democratic ideals and egalitarian values. But recent transformations of cities reflect the workings of businesses committed to short-term profit, where the pursuit of wealth has become an end in itself rather than a means to achieve broader goals. City planning world-wide is dominated by market forces and short-term financial imperatives – an approach most spectacularly illustrated by the chaotic, office dominated development on the Isle of Dogs, London. Not only have such developments eliminated variety of function in our city centres, but in this single minded search for profit, we have ignored the needs of the wider community.
>
> What is needed is greater emphasis on citizens' participation in city design and planning. We must put communal objectives centre stage. Educating our children is a necessary first step towards the participation of communities in decision-making. It is on this that we must focus our National Curriculum. Teaching children about biology and history, but not about their actual environment – the built one – leaves them ill-equipped to participate in the process of improving the city that so critically affects their lives. We must teach citizenship, and listen to citizens. So much of our future, and our 'quality of life' depends on getting this right.'
>
> Lord Rogers, Reith Lecture 1, 1995
> Published by Faber & Faber Ltd, 1997

The third subject is what used to be called political economy: the study of economics from different ideological perspectives, such as Capitalism and Marxism. To this we should add ecological economics, seen from the viewpoint of global sustainable development. People need to be made aware that, according to how the economy is organised, there are different outcomes in terms of the distribution of private wealth, the availability of public goods and the effects on the environment.

Although people are all too familiar with *environmental* issues like pollution, global warming, traffic, diminishing countryside and loss of biodiversity etc., they do not necessarily see them as dysfunctional effects of the economic system, let alone linking the latter with humanitarian and social issues such as the poverty, the arms trade, drugs trafficking, refugees, desertification, international aid, the debt crisis and the demands for a *Fortress Europe* policy. It is essential that the man in the street understands the interrelationship between all these issues, in order to build is popular support for a higher quality of life for everyone on the planet. Although it is easy to blame blinkered politicians, they reflect the selfishness and indifference of the rest of us. If the population at large took the view that their best interest lay in the solution of the problems besetting the wider world, then their elected representatives would follow them even if less than convinced: there would be votes in it.

Richard Douthwaite, The Growth Illusion, (Devon, Green Books, 1992)
Michael Jacobs, the Politics of the Real World, Earthscan (London 1996).

Supply & Demands

It is clear that, in the not too distant future, a given locality will have to limit its demands on 'ghost acres' within its region, within this country, and abroad. This will require a re-orientation of the planning system away from automatically trying to accommodate demands, many of which emanate from outside, to being instrumental in determining the capacity of an area to supply goods and services to its inhabitants and the wider world. In any given locality, the environment is not just a provider of resources and a sink for wastes, but is the life support system for humanity and the natural world alike. We damage it at our peril.

It would seem inevitable that we will be forced by events, such as resource shortages, global warming, or international instability, to become much more self sufficient in the future. To throw a cordon around each region, town and village, and look at the relationship between the different tiers in terms of imports and and exports, would be quite revealing. If one wanted to minimize unnecessary transport of goods and travel by people, and make each unit of the hierarchy as self-sufficient as possible, in meeting their material needs, the definition of what one considers to a be a 'resource' would both broaden and become more detailed. It would have to include every acre of agricultural land, and stand of timber, local biodiversity, existing building stock, the store of domestic, industrial and agricultural goods viewed with their potential to be re-used or recycled, the skills of all the people, and their financial resources. Anyone who lived in Europe before 1950, or has experience of the Third World, will not be unfamiliar with such concepts.

Now, in the nineties, there are those who are grappling with these issues and working from the ground-level upwards on the issues of sustainable communities. The BT/RSNC *Environment City* initiative aims to show how people are tackling the practical difficulties of translating sustainability into action. At the district and county level, LPAs and the people in their area are endeavouring to create a sustainable future under the auspices of Local Agenda 21. (see Fig.21) These efforts may be low key and unglamourous, but they are the stuff of which our future is made, no matter how sophisticated the rest of us fancy ourselves to be.

Figure 21   Local Agenda 21

The Earth Summit in Rio in 1992 placed the concept of 'sustainability' at the heart of economic and social development, and world leaders signed up to it. Apart from the international conventions on Biodiversity, Climate Change etc., there appeared another remarkable document, Agenda 21. This attested to the need to integrate policies on the environment, the economy, trade, social equity and development. In Chapter 28, it sets out the role to be played by local government world wide in achieving these objectives.

In fact an analysis of the specific actions contained in Agenda 21, show that more than half can be undertaken at local level, mostly in partnership with local people. A timetable was set: by 1996 local authorities should produce a 'Local Agenda 21' (LA21) in consultation with all sectors of the local community: the business sector, trade unions, parish councils, women's groups, voluntary organisations, and academic institutions at all levels.

At the Rio summit, Britain was one of the few countries to take a strong local government delegation, and a remarkable degree of cooperation has existed between the DoE and local government on this issue, if nothing else, in recent years. In the UK, the efforts on LA21 have been spearheaded by the Local Government Management Board (LGMB), which has produced a whole range of material to guide local authorities in their attempts to implement LA21 at ground level.

They are advised to put their own house in order, with regard to environmental practices, before going out to preach to the populace, or other public bodies. Indeed local authorities have found that they achieve the best results with rethinking and, if necessary re-organising the delivery of the services over which they have direct control. That said, in February 1997, of 472 local authorities, only a handful of local authorities have had their EMAS scheme [the Eco-Management and Audit Scheme for local government] externally accredited. However, there are another 30 seriously considering external validation, and 120 with environmental management systems in place which comply with EMAS. With the requirement to produce publicly available reports and its more stringent requirements, EMAS has the advantage over BS7750 (now superseded by ISO 14,001).

Within the local authority the next task is to incorporate environmental considerations into all policies, not just the obvious ones like planning and transport e.g. compulsory competitive tendering, health and anti-poverty strategies, tourism, investment, housing, and social services. A survey in 1996 has shown that although the greatest application has been made to the cohort of environmental services, that the rest are coming along: not surprisingly staff, in other areas, are having to become conversant with the implications.

Beyond the walls of the town hall, there is the challenge of involving the wider community. LGMB has produced literature on various topics e.g. 'Greening the Local Economy', or 'Sustainability in Rural Areas', and gives the local authorities tips on how to involve the local community in its objectives. It is as well to start with the individuals, groups and organisations already in contact with the different departments of the local authority, and build on these.

In order to make LA21 more user friendly, many local authorities have adopted more user friendly titles for their activities, so don't be surprised if some whacky, visionary title is given to LA21 is your area. Under the auspices of, say, 'Gobbleswick Going Greener', you may hear about awareness raising event, visits and talks, round-table discussions, educational initiatives, attempts to green the local economy, public access to computer databases on environmental information. Other projects may include choosing and developing indictors, and establishing targets for environmental improvement.

There are those who dismiss LA21 as no more than a series of talking shops. No doubt it is difficult to really bring about fundamental change, and no doubt there will be failures. However, the task is urgent and worthwhile. At the end of the day, 'the Environment' is about what happens on the ground near you, and local government tends to attract people who get satisfaction out of achieving something concrete – if that's the right term!

In terms of the land-use regulation system, which is the main subject of this book, LA21, in years to come, should do much to break down the barriers between 'us' and 'them': it should become a partnership. With regard to the environmental challenge, which has been outlined in this Section, LA21 could serve as a forum for discussing the resource base of an area, and, as new needs arise, and finding imaginative ways of handling 'excess demand' as we are forced to move in the direction of greater self-sufficiency.

Agenda 21: a Guide for Local Authorities in the UK, LGMB, 1995
Full text of Agenda 21 from Regency Press Corporation (see Appendix IV)

Clearly, what constitutes the resource base of a locality will evolve in the years to come. 'State of the Environment Reports', based on a snapshot of the critical variables at the moment, their current trends, and reasons underlying their health or otherwise, are now part of the scene in development planning. We are becoming increasingly conscious of reaching limits on key issues: air quality in urban areas, the acceptability of trunk-road building; the availability of potable water in southern Britain; or the tolerability of quarrying minerals in scenic areas. The key factor is what our society considers to be permissible. Science may inform our decisions, but it is rare that we 'run out' of a resource. Rather, each additional unit becomes more 'expensive', not just financially, but also in terms of the built or natural environment, or what is aesthetically acceptable. This is not to say that for a community to agree on an objective will necessarily be easy: scientific criteria, on, say, critical loads of pollutants, may be more persuasive than the integrity of some obscure aspect of the natural environment. Nevertheless difficult decisions will have to be taken.

In the future, it is likely that much of the ground work will be done by means of discussions between the LPA and local interests via the LA21 network in that area. However, the procedures outlined elsewhere in this book could be utilised to thrash out the supply side of the equation. The development plan system presents an opportunity for a community to determine its objectives, both quantitative and qualitative: options could be presented to the public, the issues debated, and yardsticks incorporated into the development plan. As we all know, arguments do not stop there, and it will be necessary to defend, or indeed update objectives at the development control level.

Given the need for communities to be increasingly self sufficient, it will be essential for central government to listen carefully to the views of its people. This has certain implications for the procedural mechanism. Central government could find itself:

a) considering the contribution of local people to development planning at all levels, to be of key importance, and thus they would no longer be the 'also rans' of the system;

b) being more liberal in the use of its discretion over EA for Schedule 2 projects, taking into account the *Dutch Dykes* case, and other ECJ judgements;

c) creating an independent body to undertake high quality ESs, which are presented as working documents not PR exercises;

d) making much greater use of its powers to call-in applications, especially where a complex ES had been prepared, or where the LPA was party to the development;

e) granting third party rights of appeal against approval, as in the Isle of Man;

f) awarding costs to third parties, for procedural reasons, outside the inquiry;

g) and facilitating debate by passing a proper Freedom of Information Act. (see Appendix VII)

It is not commonly known that, within the U.K., third party rights of appeal do exist. In the Isle of Man such rights are limited to public bodies, including the relevant LPA, owners and occupiers of the land, and others having 'sufficient interest', usually those owning or occupying neighbouring land. It has been shown that there is a 16% success rate. This may not seem very high, but then only a third of appellants actually win on appeal on the mainland.

Clearly there would be occasions when the message from the grassroots to the Government would be 'No more'. If localities are not to be overruled, this would require a government which is prepared to listen to grassroots opinion and withdraw a proposal. This would be subsidiarity in practice, which has been an anathema to the centralizers in charge of Whitehall.

Given that, in the foreseeable future, the demands upon our environment will much exceed the resources of our locality, the $64,000 question will be how to cope with the deficit. This is going to require some lateral thinking on the part of the community, and all tiers of government. In some cases it will be possible to make more efficient use of resources or switch to substitutes, but for many others it will necessitate re-defining the issue e.g. the mobility of people and goods instead of road transport, or a means of exchange instead of money.

To tackle these issues will necessitate our having an educated and inventive population: school children, students and adults will be encouraged to use their initiative to solve practical problems. The lateral thinking required to meet our needs by a less environmentally damaging route will need both 'blue sky' research, and the development of those ideas by means of a plethora of pilot projects, which are monitored, and the results fed back into the trials: it is likely that there will be disbenefits accompanying apparently more eco-friendly techniques, so it will be a matter of weighing up the pros and cons of proposed 'solutions'. It would be essential for funding bodies to be open-minded in their approach to assessing candidates for research money.

A future central government will have to be prepared to reform the broad canvass of legal, fiscal, institutional and political factors which form the backdrop to proposals for development in terms of defining the problems to be solved, the yardsticks of success, and the mix of measures to achieve a solution. Such reforms would pay dividends particularly with regard to major inquiries, where government is inevitably judge and jury in its own cause. Projects emanating from the private sector would also change: if Government had the courage to take a definite lead in the direction of sustainability. Business would follow and pick up the new opportunities presented. If land-use proposals kept within the parameters of sustainability, the issue would be where to put it, and that would be a big step forward.

With regard to the backdrop of policies which have a bearing on sustainability, some idea of their sheer variety can be gauged from a report, called *A Framework for Local Sustainability*, produced by the Local Government Management Board: natural resources, energy, transport, the quality of land air and water, solid waste management, biodiversity and rural land, economic development, and the urban environment. For each topic there is a section headed 'Actions required by central government to support local government', which calls on government to remove restrictions or to play a greater part in supporting sustainability. This report came out in 1993. Obviously, the detail, if not the topics, have changed by now and will continue to do so.

A measure which could be introduced now is a betterment tax, which would remove the incentive to sell green land for development just to recoup millions of pounds in undeserved capital gains, thus diminishing the stock of unspoiled land. It would also enable LPAs to provide facilities, and make up for deficits in provision e.g. public open space. It would also obviate the need for wide ranging s.106 planning obligations (see Appendix IX) which could be called in question either by the developer or the community.

Given that the built environment is said to have a turnover rate of 1% per annum, imaginative ways need to be found to deal with the existing and outstanding planning permissions (see Fig.22), which, in the light of sustainable development would now be viewed as 'mistakes', such as the current backlog of out of town retail permissions. If necessary compensation will have to be paid in order to prevent mistakes being perpetuated.

Figure 22   Action Against Current Unsustainable Uses

A comment frequently made about the planning system is that its powers are only relevant in a very small proportion of cases. This, so the argument goes, is because planning control is only about regulating new development proposals. Therefore it can do nothing about past mistakes. This is an inaccurate view of the legislation: a cursory knowledge of the provisions in the planning legislation (Town and Country Planning Act 1990) reveals why. Planning authorities are empowered to deal with existing problems on land by way of, for example, compulsory purchase and discontinuance orders. Where the public interest arguments justify such action it is therefore possible to deal with inappropriate uses (or uses inappropriately-located) by current planning mechanisms. Such powers can therefore be used in order to require modification of existing patterns in the use and development of land that conflict with the aims of sustainable development.

Naturally the legislation (as currently constituted) provides that compensation be paid to the landowner whose economic interests are thus harmed. However, this does not mean that this option should be overlooked. First, if sustainable development is taken seriously there might be a case for modifying the compensation rules in respect of such land uses etc. that are clearly damaging to the interests protected by sustainable development. Amortisation procedures could also be introduced – whereby a use is given 10 years to be 'wound down' so allowing the loss to be spread over that period and taken into account by the landowner etc. Such mechanisms could then be used to reduce the compensation liability. Such approaches are found in other jurisdictions were 'non-conforming uses' need to be eliminated on the grounds of the wider public interest.

A second option (working within the current legal framework) is also available to make discontinuance etc. a practicable tool. A strategic approach to dealing with unsustainable uses linked to past development activity could involve 'compensating' planning permissions for sustainable development: this approach would be perhaps initially set out by way of the plan-making process under the legislation. Thus the statutory development plan system can have a part to play in deciding appropriate use of the discontinuance powers: this would make the process transparent, it would remedy past mistakes and encourage changes to sustainable patterns of development. The element that would make such action more practicable would be to ensure that the 'carrot' of a compensatory permission were granted. In effect an unsustainable use/location would be swopped for a sustainable use/location. This would dramatically reduce the compensation to be paid since the 'carrot' of a compensating planning permission would offset the economic loss of the existing (but unsustainable) use. (The discontinuance order provisions under s.102 of the Town and Country Planning Act 1990 already provides for planning permission to be

granted in tandem with such orders as a way of reducing the compensation liability and so making such orders a practical tool.)

An important mechanism in any such strategy would be the contractual powers to conclude 'planning obligations' under s.106. This provides for a very flexible mechanism by which an unsustainable use can be discontinued in return
for a planning permission. In this situation the compensating planning permission can relate to another site: with discontinuance orders (as currently conceived under the legislation) the power to grant permission is tied to the land to
which the order relates. By using planning obligations the private and public
sectors could co-operate in working out the best solutions. This technique
would thus involve 'trading' the unsustainable use of one site for the sustainable development of another.

Evidence of United Kingdom Environmental Law Association
House of Lords Select Committee on Sustainable Development 1994/5

Over the years the issues to be tackled by central government will
change as mistakes, and negative side effects emerge, and new
challenges gain acceptance, such as the deleterious effects of
international trade and the effects on the Third World. There would
be much to be said for an independent Standing Commission to
take a long term look at the various policies affecting the
environment, and put various scenarios into the public domain for
discussion. Policies themselves should be subject to EA.

All the public bodies charged with making 'sustainability' a
reality, whether at central or local government level, will require
resources, in terms of manpower and money, to do the job properly.
This could mean: supervising the workings of other departments
across the board, in terms of educating staff and elected members;
auditing an increasing range of resources; public consultation at
every level; cleaning up dereliction; compensating those with
'unsustainable' permissions; and, most importantly, being able to
afford to take enforcement action.

Although the prospect of having to cut down our consumption of
resources smacks of the *hairshirt*, there are all manner of destructive
elements which currently contribute to the National GNP e.g. the
journey to work, pollution, litter and waste in general, fear and lack of
security. If one is very rich one may be able to fund all one's personal
or family needs, but no one can purchase a clean environment or a
personal ozone layer. The move towards a sustainable society would
mean the release of resources and energies to improve both the
quality of our lives and our environment e.g. high quality goods built
to last, meaningful jobs, public provision for old age, education,
health, clean air and a clean sea.

Why does all this sound like *Pie in the Sky*? The reason is the nature of the business culture dominates every aspect of life in Britain in the 1990s. Its all pervading influence, epitomised perhaps by BBC1's programme title 'Business Breakfast', is what makes suggestions, which otherwise might accord with commonsense, sound so *off the wall*. Let us take a closer look at the dominant culture of our age.

A. Blowers, Planning for a Sustainable Environment, Earthscan (1993)

House of Lords, Select Committee on Sustainable Development, 1994/5

LGMB, A Framework for Local Sustainability, (1993)

CPRE, Sense & Sustainability, (1993)

D. Korten, When Corporations Rule the World, Earthscan (1995)

R. Attfield & K. Bell, ed. Values, Conflict & Environment (Avebury Publishing, 1996)

BT/RSNC, Stepping Stones II: The Inside Story (BT Environment City) (RSNC, 1995)

BT/RSNC, Trading Futures: the Role of Business in Sustainability (BT Environment City), (RSNC 1995)

Know Your Enemy

Although the global market is not the only way to distribute goods and services, there is no time to invent a better system. The only option is strict regulation so that it serves mankind and the planet rather than the bank balances of the financial controllers. It is essential to redefine 'growth' and de-couple it from the unacceptable exploitation of resources and people. To achieve this within the next twenty years will take nothing short of a miracle, but if the planet is to remain fit for human habitation, we have to try. Given that the West takes the lion's share of the resources available, to reform our way of life would make a sizable contribution to solving the problem. However, to make any progress we have to be clear about how exactly the system operates, to whose advantage, and the mechanisms which keep it in place.

But surely, the British Government and the EU have become very environmentally conscious? What about the prodigious quantity of regulations and potential fiscal deterrents against environmental damage? Superficially this may seem to be the answer to dealing with externalities, but it cannot be the complete solution for several reasons. An upturn in trade can wipe out any reduction in, say, emission levels, for example. Industrial and commercial lobbies in both Brussels and London are active in reducing the pain of sustainability targets, and in delaying and minimising regulatory and fiscal measures, preferring that the costs be borne by the host population rather than themselves. They are backed up, in the UK, by the Treasury which is against hypothecated taxes e.g. a tax on motoring subsidising an improvement in public transport, because it would reduce *their control* over the nations's purse-strings, and *their priorities* for public expenditure. At the end of the day, it is a matter of keeping controls down to a minimum in order not to inhibit competition, and thus, trade.

Problems, be they on a global or local scale, will continue to surface because of the cumulative effect of a multiplicity of small decisions. Within the EU, they will escape regulation through ignorance, skilled manipulation of the policy process, evasion of the law, or because, in any given case, it fell below the threshold considered to be the economic cut-off point for action. Trans-national companies, be they involved in gun running, agricultural produce, industrial production or finance, will minimise the impact of such controls by transferring the major part of their operation to Eastern Europe of the Third World, where they can get on with the important business of making money at the expense of people and the environment.

> *When applying ethical criteria, it does limit the number of companies available for investment. This is because the UK has a significant historical association with arms manufacture, with its peripheral activates such as crowd control and torture equipment. On top of this is the institutional abuse of animals in the food industry, companies profiting from from environmental degradation, and other activities such as tobacco, alcohol and pornography production. Having said all this, there are still very large numbers of companies which are involved in none of the above, and which still make substantial profits. When looking long term, it is these companies which are likely to be least affected by changes in legislation or public opinion.*
>
> Lee Coates, Ethical Investor's Group

The beneficiaries are, firstly, the financial institutions which are the major shareholders in national and international companies. In Britain this process has been assisted greatly by privatisation of services hitherto run by the state, and the sale of assets in the ownership of the Crown. What remains under state control is also forced into bed with the private sector or obliged to operate in a competitive market regardless of whether that is the best way of achieving the objective e.g. education or health. Thus the private sector, at all levels, has grown and flourished. In order to keep up the momentum, and the supply of profits, the Big Fish do all in their power to keep such a government in place. The new Labour Government will antagonise them at their peril.

Such companies also promote an environmentally responsible image by anything from token green gestures like recycled polythene bags, and certain green product lines in supermarkets, to funding environmental education and community ventures, and under-writing research in academic institutions. There are times when expensive projects amount to money laundering: no one amongst the recipients dare ask what environmental damage was done in order to create the money which will fund that desirable green programme. Thus unsustainable operations win public, and therefore, political support. It's 'Business as Usual' with fashionable green trimmings.

If the private sector reaps profits and considerable political leverage, the government benefits from increased power. This may seem paradoxical but the truth is that we live in a managed not a market economy: as can be seen in Fig.23, the government is a major player in the economy because it determines the rules of competition and is the biggest customer in the economy. Thus although in Britain there has been a transfer of ownership to the private sector, the state is the client for 75% of the business, so it remains in control without the disbenefits of being held to account when things go wrong. Official secrecy cloaks much activity of critical importance in environmental disputes: as 'Client in Chief' government is able to shield the activities of the private sector, and where they cannot benefit from state secrecy, they can hide behind commercial secrecy (see Appendix VII).

The status quo is maintained by yet another aspect of this system. The apparent shortage of funds in the public sector is not a financial necessity but a political choice: it has the great advantage of keeping those who might query the system e.g. the BBC and Channel 4, academe, the civil service at all levels, and professionals in state employment, on a short rein. They are too busy competing for resources to campaign against the underlying rationale of the system. The workforce, as a whole, are putting in long hours, trying to hang on to their jobs, and save for their old age: they don't have too much surplus energy to challenge the system.

Figure 23   Myths of the 'Free Market'

Rolling back the frontiers of the State

In Western Europe, in all the so-called market economies, central government controls 45% of the GNP (including expenditure via EU or local authorities), local government, quangos and authorities under state regulation account for 15% of GNP, and another 15% of expenditure is determined directly by the state. Thus, whether they admit it or not, the British Government is responsible for about 75% of GNP.

The Private Sector shows initiative

The very existence and character of many goods and services available are determined by legislation which is the responsibility of government: an Act of Parliament can create a whole new industry e.g. personal pensions, or demand for a range of products e.g. to control pollution.

The Private Sector is more efficient than the Public Sector

'Private Sector, Good. Public Sector, Bad' is an Orwellian mantra which has controlled government policy for the past seventeen years. That people should believe that private sector provision is more efficient than that of the public sector, is not surprising, because the latter has lacked investment, the willingness to innovate, or proper management in the interests of the consumer.

On the other hand, there is no objective evidence to support the efficiency claims of the private sector. It is not more innovative because it cannot afford to bear the cost of 'blue sky' research: much that is privately funded is really the development of existing ideas, rather than the funding the generation of new ones. As the aim of the private sector is to maximise consumption, rather than deliver a service, and firms are able to control their own budgets, more jobs are created. That firms compete with each other to sell variants on the same thing, does not, necessarily, add to the common weal. In fact two thirds of the cost of goods and services go on distribution and advertising. Other costs are kept down by employing cheap labour here or in the Third World, and/or externalising environmental costs so that the rest of society pays for them now or in the future.

Level Playing Field

The idea that prices find their own level through the invisible hand of the market is just nor true. For that to work, everyone would have to have perfect information, which manifestly they don't, and their choices would be based on price, thus excluding other factors like quality, kudos, loyalty etc. Furthermore government is a major determinant of prices e.g. does the 'producer pay' for environment cost or its it spread over the whole community in taxation? Then there are accountancy conventions; subsidies, grants and levies. Thus the 'competitive environment' is carefully managed behind the scenes.

The Public Sector is Unproductive

In a modern economy there is a symbiotic relationship between the public and private sectors: there has to be. The private sector is reliant on the State to keep law and order, provide infrastructure for distribution, educate the workforce, keep it healthy, fund research, and organise communications. You may say that many of these services are being undertaken by the private sector, but it is the State which has to organise it: it wouldn't happen otherwise. Obversely, chaos can ensue if a service, which benefits from a unified approach, is totally deregulated. Through the emasculation of the public sector in the last seventeen years, Britain is now a candidate for Galbraith's famous maxim 'Private affluence and public squalor.'

> *'We want a bus service which looks more like a spider's web and less like a loo brush'*
>
> Mancunian

Wealth = Money

In any society, but especially one where the basic necessities are met for most people, the quantity of goods possessed is not the main determinant of the quality of life. Time for relationships, fulfilling activity, freedom from fear or financial insecurity, a pleasant environment etc. are the things which people value. As the Beatles sang 'Money can't buy you love'. As such factors cannot readily be priced, they get left out of the frame in the free market. Discounting such intangibles accounts for much unhappiness in Britain today. Sustainability is about the wholeness of people, as well as the preservation of the planet. Untrammelled market forces reduced the quality of life. True wealth is generated by organising society to function in the long term interests of its inhabitants, rather than short term gain. This has to be done by means of public services rather than the private sector whose first responsibility is to produce profits for shareholders: in Britain, unlike Germany or Japan, the situation is exacerbated by shareholders wanting a high return in a very short time.

Money = Goods

The amount of money in circulation equals thirty times the value of world production! How come? Within national boundaries, banks can lend up to nine times their assets. If you take out a loan, the necessary money is 'created' by making ledger entries. The reason they are so keen for you to take out a loan is that they can instantly lend out nine times that amount. It follows that a 15% interest rate represents a true rate of 135%, and the credit card rate of 30–35% reaps 270–415%. If lending to another country, there are no ratios to be observed. Thus Third world countries have been talked into loans, the money for which is conjured out of the air, and then they are charged exorbitant rates of interest which grind down the lives of their people, and force them to exploit their natural resources and plant cash crops, in order to pay back the loan, and supply materials for the Western world. Loans are about profits for shareholders, not about investment in long term development. The international banking community has by far the greatest claim on the wealth of nations: this situation could turn critical if, as is more than possible, there is war over resources in 21st century. Money represents power not goods.

Thus next time you are told 'There is no money', realise that it is not money which is in limited supply, but the political will to use all our resources to achieve a sustainable society. Under the leadership of those with vision, the public sector is best placed to direct the operation, and, where possible, harness the energies of the private sector in this endeavour. It is said that without vision, the people perish. They will.

J.Raven, The New Wealth of Nations, Bloomfield Books,(Sudbury, 1996)
W.Hutton, The State We're In, Jonathan Cape, (1995)

As the Work Ethic is still alive and well after several centuries, those out of work are blamed for their lack of effort. Meanwhile, school children and students are led to believe that 'education = training' for a job: anything beyond that is a waste of time. It is not unknown to be greeted by university postgraduates saying, 'Do we have to read that?'. They have been nurtured on the idea that education is about ticking boxes, that they are fazed by being expected to read more widely, and collate ideas for themselves. Thus, it would be understandable if most of the coming generation do not query the dominant culture. The myths of the market place (see Fig.23) are all pervading, and provide a smokescreen for the alliance between Government, Big Business and the the more affluent members of the population who fear any threat to their living standards.

How does all this impinge on the political, legal and financial requirements set out above in 'Building-in Sustainability'? Basically, the social and economic priorities of any government, in the 1990s, mean that they are unlikely to break their alliance with those who generate wealth under the current system. It is said that information is power. It remains to be seen whether the Labour Government's definition of 'Education' extends beyond training, let alone to making the population conversant with political economy. Academics can only live in hope of resources for fundamental research. Maybe the Government will see fit to introduce a Freedom of Information Act, but hitherto official secrecy has proved too convenient to those in power, whatever their political complexion (see Appendix VII).

Money is also power. To allow lower tiers of government adequate funding to carry out their responsibilities under the heading of sustainable development may be seen as a threat to the hegemony of Whitehall. With regard to using their own power and influence, one can only hope that the Labour Government will re-draw the canvass of national and international controls which give rise to environmentally damaging development proposals, at home or abroad. For central government to devolve power downwards, or use its own power to alter the financial or legal status quo, will upset key players amongst those who put them in charge of Britain PLC. Politically it could prove to be both courageous and suicidal.

WHY MINERALS WEEK? – THE COMMERCIAL ARGUMENT

Powerful environmental lobbies have not only succeeded in increasing society's awareness of environmental issues, but are going further to persuade society that resource utilisation itself is undesirable and unsustainable. All too often the media focus on negative aspects of our industry. It is in our interest as an industry to try to restore the balance to the debate by reminding society of the essential link between minerals, the maintenance of our standard of living and the enhancement of the the standards of living of others wherever they may live in the world.

These are not arguments of narrow self-interest. As business leaders we have a wider responsibility to take an active role in the development of public policy … If we do so effectively, our short term prospects will be improved and we will have contributed to the long term improvement of international economic growth.

Minerals Week *will provide a high profile national focus through which we will communicate primary messages together. It will provide a myriad of opportunities for individual companies to talk with audiences critical to the prosperity of their own organisations. . . . .*

Thursday will be Education Professionals Day. A key Strategic platform behind Minerals Week 1988 *is to seek to influence tomorrow's adults. This means securing the support of today's teachers.*

Friday and Saturday … will seek to build on this by taking the message into the communities which have an existing or proposed minerals extraction operation in their area.

An application has been made for Government funding for part of the total cost of the project. Based on initial indications of support from key government departments, the application to the 'sector challenge' funds may open a door to government financial support. … It may be possible to achieve funding to match that committed by the industry as well as the industry's already extensive 'in kind' contribution of time and resources.

Extract from 'Celebrating the Nation's Mineral Wealth'

WHERE DO WE GO FROM HERE?

The above is a sobering appraisal of the situation we are in, as indeed, is the rest of world. How does one break the strangle-hold of the big corporations and financial institutions over all governments and most politicians?

Well no matter how large a business, it needs customers and if these are not forthcoming it will founder. Green consumerism is fraught with difficulties: there are the inherent problems in comparing 'greeness' coupled with the misinformation put out by those more interested in image and profits than the environment. However, in the UK, it is possible to contact the Women's Environmental Network – WENDi which has set up a national telephone hot-line on green consumerism. If you wish to know about the ethical and environmental practices of the companies producing consumer goods, contact The Ethical Consumer (see Appendix IV for both addresses).

Secondly, business requires investment. For example, it is not unknown for the mainstream supermarket chains to lease back their existing stores to fund new ones. Their financiers can be banks, insurance companies and pension funds. Which bank do you use? Where do you invest your savings? Who is in charge of your pension? Even if none of these things are relevant to your circumstances, what about your workplace, sports club, favourite charity, or religious organisation? That money makes the world go round is as true as it ever was, and by being scrupulous where you put your funds, or those of an organisation you care about, you can make a difference to what might land up on your doorstep, or on someone else's. If you want advice on ethical banking or investment, contact the UK Social Investment Forum.(see Appendix IV)

Thirdly, although environmentally damaging business interests have too much sway in certain political quarters, at the end of the day, politicians are voted in by the population. As has been shown, it is essential that *Middle England*, or whichever section of the population is being wooed by the politicians, are both concerned about these issues and link them to a defective economic machine. Only then will the politicians have the courage to challenge the system at a national and international level. What is the attitude of your MP to the issues discussed in this Section: are they for 'Business as Usual with Green Trimmings', or do they have any cognisance of the massive changes which lie ahead in the next twenty years? Are they prepared to exercise the sort of statesmanship which will be required to solve difficult problems? Given the need for Government and the EU to be sensitive to public opinion in years to come, what are their views on electoral reform? If your MP or MEP, is fully appraised of all these issues, vote for them, whatever their political affiliation!

The three approaches listed above are ways of tapping into the heart of the problem, but do not neglect the war of attrition via policy-making. Having said that the current government is not interested in policy changes which might interfere with their conception of economic growth, it would be untrue to say that progress hasn't been made over the last few years, particularly since Rio, and that progress won't be made in future. It is just that, as is illustrated above, it is difficult: the trick is to prove that the eco-friendly way of doing things which achieves, or at least does not interfere with their own agenda. NGOs and professional groups are past masters at the art of doing this. If you have expertise to offer on a given subject, make your own contribution to the debate. But, in any case, support those who do espouse your views.

Then there are the environmental practices of your workplace, if any. Does your firm or organisation have an environmental management system? Does it conform to BS 7750 or ISO 14,001. Does your firm aspire to EMAS and see the benefits of full accreditation? (see Fig.21). If not, why not contact the United Kingdom Accreditation Service (see Appendix IV)

Lastly, how about your own lifestyle? Even the most eco-conscious have their blind spots: to 'save the whale' is easier than saving the ozone layer. It is arguable that growing some of your own food, or habitually cycling to the shops, is more important in real terms than appearing as an expert witness at a major inquiry, or before a Parliamentary Select Committee. If you don't know where to start, or wish to extend your green activities, the New Economics Foundation (see Appendix IV) has produced just the booklet for you. It gives examples of viable schemes for the provision of food, money, energy, transport, housing, land etc., and invites you to to get in touch with those running these schemes. At the end of the day, what matters is what happens on the ground.

No man made a greater mistake than the man who did nothing, because he could only do a little.

Edmund Burke

This Common Inheritance: UK Annual Report 1996, HMSO (1996)
Russell Sparkes, The Ethical Investor, Harper Collins, (London, 1995)
J. Raven, the New Wealth of Nations, Bloomfield Books (1996)
'The Ethical Consumer' (published by The Ethical Consumer Research Association – see Appendix IV)
D.Korten, When Corporations Rule the World, Earthscan (1995)
A.Rowell, Green Backlash, Routledge,(1996)
Community Works! – a Guide to Community Economic Action (New Economics Foundation, 1997)

CONCLUSION

This Section may appear to be a radical departure from the rest of this book, but it is a commentary on the wider economic and social context in which so may disputes over land use take place. Many of those participating have an uneasy feeling that they are looking through the wrong end of the telescope: that there are deeper issues which ought to be addressed first. Unfortunately that seems unlikely. Given the gravity of the situation, the lack of urgency is striking. One cannot help but feel that if Planet Earth were to be invaded by Martians, that strategies would be formulated at international and national level and well resourced plans of action would gather pace at ground level.

The destruction of our habitat is less dramatic. The decision makers are not afforded the luxury of feeling macho when the temperature of the sea rises or a species becomes extinct. People are, and increasingly will be, adversely affected by the results rather than the immediate causes of the problem. The prime causes, however, are the dysfunctional aspects of the economic system. Until these are recognised for what they are by those who control the system, we are left with the feeble substitute of each of us doing our bit, according to our means. It is true that, the regulation of land use in this country is only one aspect of the debate about sustainability here, let alone in the Third World, but it does give a perspective on the problem. What is certain, however, is that development proposals which are truly sustainable in character, will not be the stock-in-trade of the planning system until these broader issues are faced and dealt with satisfactorily.

There is nothing new in Man's inhumanity to Man, and, by definition, the ruling elite in any culture dominates the language, but the difference between the current situation, and anything which has happened before, is that the untrammelled power of the free market could literally cost us the Earth.

'The power of the private sector in the last years of the 20th century is unprecedented in the history of the world. ... 49 out of the 100 top economies today are companies, not countries. ... Since the private sector is the key to providing living standards, it will have to change direction if we are not to suck the planet dry of its ability to support all life including our own. In business terms, we are living off our capital and, as any manager know, living on borrowed time. Unless we find a way of living off of renewable revenue, The World PLC *will go out of business.'*

Dr. Simon Lyster, Director General, RSNC
in 'Trading Futures'

Appendix I

INFORMATION FROM OFFICIAL SOURCES

PARLIAMENTARY PUBLICATIONS

Command Papers: the name arises from the preamble formerly carried on all these papers, 'Presented to Parliament . . . by command of Her (or His) Majesty'. These are government papers appearing at the instigation of Ministers of the Crown. Nowadays they say 'Presented to Parliament by the Secretary of State for . . . by command of her Majesty.'

They include:

(a) State Papers e.g. Treaties

(b) Consultative Documents. Some of these are called Green Papers. These invite comment on proposed legislation.

(c) White Papers. These indicate the intention of government to legislate but modification is still possible.

(d) Reports of some major Committees and Commissions of Inquiry and of Royal Commissions.

(e) Government replies to the Reports of Select Committees.

(f) Annual Reports, statistics etc.

The Papers are numbered consecutively, but over the years the prefixes have changed so you must cite the correct one: unprefixed 1868–69, C1870-99, Cd 1900–18, Cmd 1919–56, Cmnd 1956 to 1986. The current series is prefixed CM.

House of Commons Paper:

these arise out of the deliberations of the House and its Committees.

(a) Papers and Reports of Select Committees

(b) Minutes of Proceedings of Standing Committees

(c) Annual and other Reports, Accounts etc.

House of Commons Bill:

a proposed Act of Parliament, emanating from the Government or a Private Member i.e. a Backbench MP, at any stage after its introduction and prior to the Royal Assent.

N.B. There are also House of Lords Bills and Papers.

Acts of Parliament:	the legislative decree of the Queen in Parliament i.e. a statute. There are Public, General, Local, Personal and Private Acts. They are divided into Sections and appended by Schedules.
Statutory Instruments:	detailed legislation in the spirit of an Act, which enables a Minister to cover all eventualities and keep up to date with developments.
Hansard:	a verbatim report of the proceedings of Parliament.

PUBLICATIONS BY DEPARMENTS OF CENTRAL GOVERNMENT
PPGs, MPGs & RPGs
User friendly planning guidance of key importance to most disputes. It comes in three demoninations: Planning, Minerals and Regional Policy Guidance. [see Annex to this Appendix]

Circulars: Issued by government Departments with the intention of explaining new legislation and policy. Numbered consecutively and by year: DoE 22/80 means the 22nd Circular issued by the DoE in 1980.

Policy Notes: current Ministerial policy on contemporary problems in development control e.g. disabled access and Derelict Land Grant. Issued as guidance to planning officers. Revised in the light of changes. List of Current Notes available from DoE.

Design Bulletins: information and general advice on best practice with regard to design of the built environment. Prepared by Departmental Research Units.

Occasional Papers: Research Papers prepared by Departmental Research Units on specific topics.

Departmental Advice Notes and Standards: issued by the Department of Transport on technical aspects of traffic engineering and control.

Departmental Publications: Multifarious reports on issues of the day, statistical records, annual reports etc. See 'Sectional List' provided for each government Department by The Stationery Office.

PUBLICATIONS BY LOCAL PLANNING AUTHORITIES

Structure Plans: set out the county's policy for the development of its area, plus diagrammatic maps.
Local Plans: *Subject Plans,* usually produced by the county council on issues which cross the boundaries of district councils e.g. minerals and waste disposal.
Action Area Plans can be prepared by either county or district councils and are designed to cope with comprehensive redevelopment. They are few in number as they carry no financial assistance from central government so other means are sought by local authorities.
District Plans are by far the most common variety of Local Plan. In England and Wales they are only prepared for areas where there is likely to be change. They have to conform to Structure Plans.
The local authority will have maps and details concerning any statutory designations in the area e.g. conservation areas, ancient monuments, TPOs, SSSIs, listed buildings etc.

Possible publications may include:

Development Briefs for certain key sites in the area, outlining the type of development which would be favourably considered by the local planning authority.

Design Guides for sensitive areas such as conservation areas.

Policy Documents on local problems such as caravans, lorry parking, advertisements.

Policy Proposals and consultation documents e.g. on a possible Housing Action Area or General Improvement Area.

Reports commissioned by the local authority from private consultants or public bodies such as the Landscape Advisory Committee.

ANNEX

Planning Policy Guidance Notes

PPG1   General Policy & Principals
PPG2   Green Belts
PPG3   Housing
PPG4   Industrial and Commercial Development and Small Firms
PPG5   Simplified Planning Zones
PPG6   Town Centres and Retail Developments
PPG7   The Countryside – Environmental Quality and Economic and Social Development
PPG8   Telecommunications
PPG9   Nature Conservation
PPG12   Development Plans and Regional Planning Guidance
PPG13   Transport
PPG14   Development on Unstable Land
PPG15   Planning and the Historic Environment
PPG16   Archaeology and Planning
PPG17   Sport and Recreation
PPG18   Enforcing Planning Control
PPG19   Outdoor Advertisement Control
PPG20   Coastal Planning
PPG21   Tourism
PPG22   Renewable Energy
PPG23   Planning and Pollution Control
PPG24   Planning and Noise

Planning Guidance (Wales): Planning Policy

This comprises planning policy guidance for Wales, was published in May 1996 and presents, in the words of the Welsh Office 'integrated planning policy guidance in a concise and accessible forum'.

Planning Guidance (Wales): Unitary Development Plans

Published in April 1996 and provides the newly established Unitary Authorities with guidance on the preparation of Unitary Development Plans.

Planning Guidance (Wales): Technical Advice Notes (Wales)

PG(W) will be supplemented by technical advice in a series of topic based Technical Advice Notes (Wales), procedural advice in Circulars and by an Index of extant planning guidance.

The following TAN(W)s were published in final form on 5 December 1996:

TAN(W)1	Joint Housing Land Availability Studies
TAN(W)2	Planning and Affordable Housing
TAN(W)3	Simplified Planning Zones
TAN(W)4	Retailing and Town Centres
TAN(W)5	Nature Conservation and Planning
TAN(W)6	Development Involving Agricultural Land
TAN(W)7	Outdoor Advertisement Control
TAN(W)8	Renewable Energy.

The second batch of consultation draft TAN(W)s were issued on 10 December 1996. This group comprises:

TAN(W)9	Planning, Pollution Control and Waste Management
TAN(W)10	Transport
TAN(W)11	Noise
TAN(W)12	Design
TAN(W)13	Coastal Planning
TAN(W)14	Environmental Assessment
TAN(W)15	Enforcement of Planning Control
TAN(W)16	Tree Preservation Orders
TAN(W)17	Rural Development
TAN(W)18	Telecommunications
TAN(W)19	Development on Unstable Land
TAN(W)20	Development of Contaminated Land
TAN(W)21	Development and Flood Risk
TAN(W)22	Sport and Recreation
TAN(W)23	Tourism

Minerals Planning Guidance Notes

MPG1	General Considerations and the Development Plan System
MPG2	Applications, Permissions and Conditions
MPG3	Coal Mining and Colliery Spoil Disposal
MPG4	The Review of Mineral Working Sites
MPG5	Minerals Planning and the General Development Order
MPG6	Guidelines For Aggregates Provision in England
MPG7	The Reclamation of Mineral Workings
MPG8	Planning and Compensation Act 1991: Interim Development Order Permissions (IDOS) – Statutory Provisions and Procedures
MPG9	Planning and Compensation Act 1991: Interim Development Order Permissions (IDOs) – Conditions
MPG10	Provision of Raw Material for the Cement Industry
MPG11	The Control of Noise at Surface Mineral Workings
MPG12	Treatment of Disused Mine Openings and Availability of Information on Mined Ground

Wales: Minerals Planning Guidance

The Welsh Office is currently working to replace the MPG series in Wales with a single compendium of mineral planning policy in Wales supplemented by a series of Technical Advice Notes.

Regional Planning Guidance Notes

RPG1   Strategic Guidance for Tyne and Wear
RPG2   Strategic Guidance for West Yorkshire
RPG3   Strategic Guidance for London
RPG4   Strategic Guidance for Manchester
RPG5   Strategic Guidance for South Yorkshire
RPG6   Regional Planning Guidance for East Anglia
RPG7   Regional Planning Guidance for Northern Region
RPG8   Regional Planning Guidance for the East Midlands
RPG9   Regional Planning Guidance for the South East
RPG10   Regional Planning Guidance for the South West

Note: The following regional guidance documents, currently in PPG series, will be revised and re-issued as RPGs:

PPG10   Strategic Guidance for the West Midlands
PPG11   Strategic Guidance for Merseyside

Wales: Regional Planning Guidance: Currently (Feb 1997) non-existent.

Appendix II

1987 No. 764

TOWN AND COUNTRY PLANNING, ENGLAND AND WALES

The Town and Country Planning (Use Classes) Order 1987

SCHEDULE

PART A

Class A1. Shops

Use for all or any of the following purposes–

    (a) for the retail sale of goods other than hot food,

    (b) as a post office,

    (c) for the sale of tickets or as a travel agency,

    (d) for the sale of sandwiches or other cold food for consumption off the premises,

    (e) for hairdressing,

    (f) for the direction of funerals,

    (g) for the display of goods for sale,

    (h) for the hiring out of domestic or personal goods or articles,

    (i) for the reception of goods to be washed, cleaned or repaired,

where the sale, display or service is to visiting members of the public.

Class A2. Financial and professional services

Use for the provision of–

    (a) financial services, or

    (b) professional services (other than health or medical services), or

    (c) any other services (including use as a betting office) which it is appropriate to provide in a shopping area,

where the services are provided principally to visiting members of the public.

Class A3. Food and drink

Use for the sale of food or drink for consumption on the premises or of hot food for consumption off the premises.

PART B

Class B1. Business

Use for all or any of the following purposes–

    (a) as an office other than a use within class A2 (financial and professional services),

    (b) for research and development of products or processes, or

    (c) for any industrial process,

being a use which can be carried out in any residential area without detriment to the amenity of that area by reason of noise, vibration, smell, fumes, smoke, soot, ash, dust or grit.

Class B2. General industrial

Use for the carrying on of an industrial process other than one falling within class B1 above or within classes B3 to B7 below.

Class B3. Special Industrial Group A

Use for the work registrable under the Alkali, etc. Works Regulation Act 1906(**a**) and which is not included in any of classes B4 to B7 below.

Class B4. Special Industrial Group B

Use for any of the following processes, except where the process is ancillary to the getting, dressing or treatment of minerals and is carried on in or adjacent to a quarry or mine:–

    (a) smelting, calcining, sintering or reducing ores, minerals, concentrates or mattes;

    (b) converting, refining, re-heating, annealing, hardening, melting, carburising, forging or casting metals or alloys other than pressure die-casting;

    (c) recovering metal from scrap or drosses or ashes;

    (d) galvanizing;

    (e) pickling or treating metal in acid;

    (f) chromium plating.

Class B5. Special Industrial Group C

Use for any of the following processes, except where the process is ancillary to the getting, dressing or treatment of minerals and is carried on in or adjacent to a quarry or mine:–

    (a) burning bricks or pipes;

    (b) burning lime or dolomite;

    (c) producing zinc oxide, cement or alumina;

    (d) foaming, crushing, screening or heating minerals or slag;

    (e) processing pulverized fuel ash by heat;

    (f) producing carbonate of lime or hydrated lime;

    (g) producing inorganic pigments by calcining, roasting or grinding.

Class B6. Special Industrial Group D

Use for any of the following processes:–

(a) distilling, refining or blending oils (other than petroleum or petroleum products);
(b) producing or using cellulose or using other pressure sprayed metal finishes (other than in vehicle repair workshops in connection with minor repairs, or the application of plastic powder by the use of fluidised bed and electrostatic spray techniques);
(c) boiling linseed oil or running gum;
(d) processes involving the use of hot pitch or bitumen (except the use of bitumen in the manufacture of roofing felt at temperatures not exceeding 220°C and also the manufacture of coated roadstone);
(e) stoving enamelled ware;
(f) producing aliphatic esters of the lower fatty acids, butyric acid, caramel, hexamine, idoform, napthols, resin products (excluding plastic moulding or extrusion operations and producing plastic sheets, rods, tubes, filaments, fibres or optical components produced by casting, calendering, moulding, shaping or extrusion), salicyclic acid or sulphonated organic compounds;
(g) producing rubber from scrap;
(h) chemical processes in which chlorphenols or chlorcresols are used as intermediates;
(i) manufacturing acetylene from calcium carbide;
(j) manufacturing, recovering or using pyridine or picolines, any methyl or ethyl amnie or acrylates.

Class B7. Special Industrial Group E

Use for carrying on any of the following industries, businesses or trades:–

Boiling blood, chitterlings, nettlings or soap.
Boiling, burning, grinding or steaming bones.
Boiling or cleaning tripe.
Breeding maggots from putrescible animal matter.
Cleaning, adapting or treating animal hair.
Curing fish.
Dealing in rags and bones (including receiving, storing, sorting or manipulating rags in, or likely to become in, an offensive condition, or any bones, rabbit skins, fat or putrescible animal products of a similar nature).
Dressing or scraping fish skins.
Drying skins.
Making manure from bones, fish, offal, blood, spent hops, beans or other putrescible animal or vegetable matter.
Making or scraping guts.
Manufacturing animal charcoal, blood albumen, candles, catgut, glue, fish oil, size or feeding stuff for animals or poultry from meat, fish, blood, bone, feathers, fat or animal offal either in an offensive condition or subjected to any process causing noxious or injurious effluvia.
Melting, refining or extracting fat or tallow.
Preparing skins for working.

Class B8. Storage or distribution

Use for storage or as a distribution centre.

PART C

Class C1. Hotels and hostels

Use as a hotel, boarding or guest house or as a hostel where, in each case, no significant element of care is provided.

Class C2. Residential institutions

Use for the provision of residential accommodation and care to people in need of care (other than a use within class C3 (dwelling houses)).
Use as a hospital or nursing home.
Use as a residential school, college or training centre.

Class C3. Dwellinghouses

Use as a dwellinghouse (whether or not as a sole or main residence)–

- (a) by a single person or by people living together as a family, or
- (b) by not more than 6 residents living together as a single household (including a household where care is provided for residents).

PART D

Class D1. Non-residential institutions

Any use not including a residential use–

- (a) for the provision of any medical or health services except the use of premises attached to the residence of the consultant or practitioner,
- (b) as a crêche, day nursery or day centre,
- (c) for the provision of education,
- (d) for the display of works of art (otherwise than for sale or hire),
- (e) as a museum,
- (f) as a public library or public reading room,
- (g) as a public hall or exhibition hall,
- (h) for, or in connection with, public worship or religious instruction.

Class D2. Assembly and leisure

Use as–

- (a) a cinema,
- (b) a concert hall,
- (c) a bingo hall or casino,
- (d) a dance hall,
- (e) a swimming bath, skating rink, gymnasium or area for other indoor or outdoor sports or recreations, not involving motorised vehicles or firearms.

Nicholas Ridley

28th April 1987

Secretary of State for the Environment

DoE Circular 9/95
General Development Order Consolidation

TABLE 1

Class in Part 3 of Schedule 2 to the Permitted Development Order	From UCO Class (if any)	To UCO Class (if any)
A	A3 (food and drink)	A1 (shops)
A	Sale or display for sale of motor vehicles[1]	A1 (shops)
B(a)	B2 (general industrial)	B1 (business)
B(a)	B8 (storage and distribution)[2]	B1 (business)
B(b)	B1 (business)	B8 (storage and distribution)[2]
B(b)	B2 (general industrial)	B8 (storage and distribution)[2]
C	A3 (food and drink)	A2 (financial and professional services)
D	Premises within A2 (financial and professional services) with display window at ground floor level	A1 (shops)
F(a)	A1 (shops)	Mixed A1 (shops) and single flat uses, other than a flat at ground floor level[1]
F(b)	A2 (financial and professional services)	Mixed A2 (financial and professional services) and single flat uses, other than a flat at ground floor level[1]
F(c)	Premises within A2 (financial and professional services) with display window at ground floor level	Mixed A1 (shops) and single flat uses, other than a flat at ground floor level[1]
G(a)	Mixed A1 (shops) and single flat uses[1]	A1 (shops)
G(b)	Mixed A2 (financial and professional services) and single flat uses[1]	A2 (financial and professional services)
G(c)	Premises of mixed A2 (financial and professional services) and single flat uses with display window at ground floor level[1]	A1 (shops)

[1] No use class is specified in the Schedule to the UCO for the sale or display for sale of motor vehicles, nor for mixed uses.
[2] Not permitted by the Permitted Development Order where change of use relates to more than 235 square metres of floor space in the building.

Appendix III

Final Text of Council Directive 97/11/EC Amending Directive 85/337/EEC On The Assessment Of The Effects Of Certain Public And Private Projects On The Environment

Adopted by Council on 3 March 1997

ANNEX I

PROJECTS SUBJECT TO ARTICLE 4(1)

1. Crude-oil refineries (excluding undertakings manufacturing only lubricants from crude oil) and installations for the gasification and liquefaction of 500 tonnes or more of coal or bituminous shale per day.

2. — Thermal power stations and other combustion installations with a heat output of 300 megawatts or more, and
   — nuclear power stations and other nuclear reactors including the dismantling or decommissioning of such power stations or reactors(*) (except research installations for the production and conversion of fissionable and fertile materials, whose maximum power does not exceed 1 kilowatt continuous thermal load).

3. (a) Installations for the reprocessing of irradiated nuclear fuel.
   (b) Installations designed:
      — for the production or enrichment of nuclear fuel,
      — for the processing of irradiated nuclear fuel or high-level radioactive waste,
      — for the final disposal of irradiated nuclear fuel,
      — solely for the final disposal of radioactive waste,
      — solely for the storage (planned for more than 10 years) of irradiated nuclear fuels or radioactive waste in a different site than the production site.

4. — Integrated works for the initial smelting of cast-iron and steel;
   — Installations for the production of non-ferrous crude metals from ore, concentrates or secondary raw materials by metallurgical, chemical or electrolytic processes.

(*) Nuclear power stations and other nuclear reactors cease to be such an installation when all nuclear fuel and other radioactively contaminated elements have been removed permanently from the installation site.

5. Installations for the extraction of asbestos and for the processing and trans-
    formation of asbestos and products containing asbestos: for asbestos-cement
    products, with an annual production of more than 20 000 tonnes of finished
    products, for friction material, with an annual production of more than 50
    tonnes of finished products, and for other uses of asbestos, utilization of more
    than 200 tonnes per year.

6. Integrated chemical installations, i.e. those installations for the manufacture
    on an industrial scale of substances using chemical conversion processes, in
    which several units are juxtaposed and are functionally linked to one another
    and which are:
    (i)   for the production of basic organic chemicals;
    (ii) for the production of basic inorganic chemicals;
    (iii) for the production of phosphorous-, or nitrogen- or potassium-based fer-
          tilizers (simple or compound fertilizers);
    (iv) for the production of basic plant health products and of biocides;
    (v)   for the production of basic pharmaceutical products using a chemical or
          biological process;
    (vi) for the production of explosives.

7. (a) Construction of lines for long-distance railway traffic and of airports([1])
        with a basic runway length of 2100m or more;
    (b) Construction of motorways and express roads([2]);
    (c) Construction of a new road of four or more lanes, or realignment and/or
        widening of an existing road of two lanes or less so as to provide four or
        more lanes, where such new road, or realigned and/or widened section
        of road would be 10 km or more in a continuous length.

8. (a) Inland waterways and ports for inland-waterway traffic which permit
        the passage of vessels of over 1350 tonnes;
    (b) Trading ports, piers for loading and unloading connected to land and
        outside ports (excluding ferry piers) which can take vessels of over 1350
        tonnes.

9. Waste disposal installations for the incineration, chemical treatment as
    defined in Annex IIA to Directive 75/442/EEC([3]) under heading D9, or land-
    fill of hazardous waste (i.e. waste to which Directive 91/689/EEC([4]) applies).

10. Waste disposal installations for the incineration or chemical treatment as
    defined in Annex IIA to Directive 74/442/EEC under heading D9 of non-haz-
    ardous waste with a capacity exceeding 100 tonnes per day.

11. Groundwater abstraction or artificial groundwater recharge schemes where
    the annual volume of water abstracted or recharged is equivalent to or
    exceeds 10 million cubic metres.

([1]) For the purposes of this Directive, 'airport' means airports which comply with the defin-
    ition in the 1944 Chicago Convention setting up the International Civil Aviation
    Organization (Annex 14).
([2]) For the purposes of the Directive, 'express road' means a road which complies with the
    definition in the European Agreement on Main International Traffic Arteries of 15
    November 1975.
([3]) OJ No L 194, 25.7.1975, p. 39. Directive as last amended by Commission Decision
    94/3/EC (OJ No L 5, 7.1.1994, p. 15).
([4]) OJ No L 377, 31.12.1991, p. 20. Directive as last amended by Directive 94/31/EC (OJ No L
    168, 2.7.1994, p. 28).

12. (a) Works for the transfer of water resources between river basins where this transfer aims at preventing possible shortages of water and where the amount of water transferred exceeds 100 million cubic metres/year;

    (b) In all other cases, works for the transfer of water resources between river basins where the multi-annual average flow of the basin of abstraction exceeds 2000 million cubic metres/year and where the amount of water transferred exceeds 5% of this flow.

    In both cases transfers of piped drinking water are excluded.

13. Waste water treatment plants with a capacity exceeding 150 000 population equivalent as defined in Article 2 point (6) of Directive 91/271/EEC (^{1}).

14. Extraction of petroleum and natural gas for commercial purposes where the amount extracted exceeds 500 tonnes/day in the case of petroleum and 500 000 m^3/day in the case of gas.

15. Dams and other installations designed for the holding back or permanent storage of water, where a new or additional amount of water held back or stored exceeds 10 million cubic metres.

16. Pipelines for the transport of gas, oil or chemicals which a diameter of more than 800 mm and a length of more than 40 km.

17. Installations for the intensive rearing of poultry or pigs with more than:

    (a) 85 000 places for broilers, 60 000 places for hens;
    (b) 3 000 places for production pigs (over 30 kg); or
    (c) 900 places for sows.

18. Industrial plants for the

    (a) production of pulp from timber or similar fibrous materials;
    (b) production of paper and board with a production capacity exceeding 200 tonnes per day.

19. Quarries and open-cast mining where the surface of the site exceeds 25 hectares, or peat extraction, where the surface of the site exceeds 150 hectares.

20. Construction of overhead electrical power lines with a voltage of 220 kV or more and a length of more than 15 km.

21. Installations for storage of petroleum, petrochemical, or chemical products with a capacity of 200 000 tonnes or more.

ANNEX II

PROJECTS SUBJECT TO ARTICLE 4(2)

1. Agriculture, silviculture and aquaculture

    (a) Projects for the restructuring of rural land holdings;
    (b) Projects for the use of uncultivated land or semi-natural areas for intensive agricultural purposes;

(^{1}) OJ No L 135, 30.5.1991, p. 40. Directive as last amended by the 1994 Act of Accession.

    (c) Water management projects for agriculture, including irrigation and land drainage projects;

    (d) Initial afforestation and deforestation for the purposes of conversion to another type of land use;

    (e) Intensive livestock installations (projects not included in Annex I);

    (f) Intensive fish farming;

    (g) Reclamation of land from the sea.

2. Extractive industry

    (a) Quarries, open-cast mining and peat extraction (projects not included in Annex I);

    (b) Underground mining;

    (c) Extraction of minerals by marine or fluvial dredging;

    (d) Deep drillings, in particular;
- geothermal drilling,
- drilling for the storage of nuclear waste material,
- drilling for water supplies,

    with the exception of drillings for investigating the stability of the soil;

    (e) Surface industrial installations for the extraction of coal, petroleum, natural gas and ores, as well as bituminous shale.

3. Energy industry

    (a) Industrial installations for the production of electricity, steam and hot water (projects not included in Annex I);

    (b) Industrial installations for carrying gas, steam and hot water; transmission of electrical energy by overhead cables (projects not included in Annex I);

    (c) Surface storage of natural gas;

    (d) Underground storage of combustible gases;

    (e) Surface storage of fossil fuels;

    (f) Industrial briquetting of coal and lignite;

    (g) Installations for the processing and storage of radioactive waste (unless included in Annex I);

    (h) Installations for hydroelectric energy production;

    (i) Installations for the harnessing of wind power for energy production (wind farms).

4. Production and processing of metals

    (a) Installations for the production of pig iron or steel (primary or secondary fusion) including continuous casting;

    (b) Installations for the processing of ferrous metals:
      (i) hot-rolling mills;
      (ii) smitheries with hammers;
      (iii) application of protective fused metal coats;

    (c) Ferrous metal foundries;

    (d) Installations for the smelting, including the alloyage, of non-ferrous metals, excluding precious metals, including recovered products (refining, foundry casting, etc.);

    (e) Installations for surface treatment of metals and plastic materials using an electrolytic or chemical process;

    (f) Manufacture and assembly of motor vehicles and manufacture of motor-vehicle engines;

(g) Shipyards;
(h) Installations for the construction and repair of aircraft;
(i) Manufacture of railway equipment;
(j) Swaging by explosives;
(k) Installations for the roasting and sintering of metallic ores.

5. Mineral industry

    (a) Coke ovens (dry coal distillation);
    (b) Installations for the manufacture of cement;
    (c) Installations for the production of asbestos and the manufacture of asbestos-products (projects not included in Annex I);
    (d) Installations for the manufacture of glass including glass fibre;
    (e) Installations for smelting mineral substances including the production of mineral fibres;
    (f) Manufacture of ceramic products by burning, in particular roofing tiles, bricks, refractory bricks, tiles, stoneware or porcelain.

6. Chemical industry (Projects not included in Annex I)

    (a) Treatment of intermediate products and production of chemicals;
    (b) Production of pesticides and pharmaceutical products, paint and varnishes, elastomers and peroxides;
    (c) Storage facilities for petroleum, petrochemical and chemical products.

7. Food industry

    (a) Manufacture of vegetable and animal oils and fats;
    (b) Packing and canning of animal and vegetable products;
    (c) Manufacture of dairy products;
    (d) Brewing and malting;
    (e) Confectionery and syrup manufacture;
    (f) Installations for the slaughter of animals;
    (g) Industrial starch manufacturing installations;
    (h) Fish-meal and fish-oil factories;
    (i) Sugar factories.

8. Textile, leather, wood and paper industries

    (a) Industrial plants for the production of paper and board (projects not included in Annex I);
    (b) Plants for the pretreatment (operations such as washing, bleaching, mercerization) or dyeing of fibres or textiles;
    (c) Plants for the tanning of hides and skins;
    (d) Cellulose-processing and production installations.

9. Rubber industry

    Manufacture and treatment of elastomer-based products.

10. Infrastructure projects

    (a) Industrial estate development projects;
    (b) Urban development projects, including the construction of shopping centres and car parks;
    (c) Construction of railways and intermodal transshipment facilities, and of intermodal terminals (projects not included in Annex I);

(d) Construction of airfields (projects not included in Annex I);

(e) Construction of roads, harbours and port installations, including fishing harbours (projects not included in Annex I);

(f) Inland-waterway construction not included in Annex I, canalization and flood-relief works;

(g) Dams and other installations designed to hold water or store it on a long-term basis (projects not included in Annex I);

(h) Tramways, elevated and underground railways, suspended lines or similar lines of a particular type, used exclusively or mainly for passenger transport;

(i) Oil and gas pipeline installations (projects not included in Annex I);

(j) Installation of long-distance aqueducts;

(k) Coastal work to combat erosion and maritime works capable of altering the coast through the construction, for example, of dykes, moles, jetties and other sea defence works, excluding the maintenance and reconstruction of such works;

(l) Groundwater abstraction and artificial groundwater recharge schemes not included in Annex I;

(m) Works for the transfer of water resources between river basins not included in Annex I.

11. Other projects

(a) Permanent racing and test tracks for motorized vehicles;

(b) Installations for the disposal of waste (projects not included in Annex I);

(c) Waste-water treatment plants (projects not included in Annex I);

(d) Sludge-deposition sites;

(e) Storage of scrap iron, including scrap vehicles;

(f) Test benches for engines, turbines or reactors;

(g) Installations for the manufacture of artificial mineral fibres;

(h) Installations for the recovery or destruction of explosive substances;

(i) Knackers' yards.

12. Tourism and leisure

(a) Ski-runs, ski-lifts and cable-cars and associated developments;

(b) Marinas;

(c) Holiday villages and hotel complexes outside urban areas and associated developments;

(d) Permanent camp sites and caravan sites;

(e) Theme parks.

13. — Any change or extension of projects listed in Annex I or Annex II, already authorized, executed or in the process of being executed, which may have significant adverse effects on the environment;

— Projects in Annex I, undertaken exclusively or mainly for the development and testing of new methods or products and not used for more than two years.

ANNEX III

SELECTION CRITERIA REFERRED TO IN ARTICLE 4(3)

1. Characteristics of projects

The characteristics of projects must be considered having regard, in particular, to:
— the size of the project;
— the cumulation with other projects;
— the use of natural resources;
— the production of waste;
— pollution and nuisances;
— the risk of accidents, having regard in particular to substances or technologies used.

2. Location of projects

The environmental sensitivity of geographical areas likely to be affected by projects must be considered, having regard, in particular, to:
— the existing land use;
— the relative abundance, quality and regenerative capacity of natural resources in the area;
— the absorption capacity of the natural environment, paying particular attention to the following areas;
  (a) wetlands;
  (b) coastal zones;
  (c) mountain and forest areas;
  (d) nature reserves and parks;
  (e) areas classified or protected under Member States' legislation; special protection areas designated by Member States pursuant to Directive 79/409/EEC and 92/43/EEC;
  (f) areas in which the environmental quality standards laid down in Community legislation have already been exceeded;
  (g) densely populated areas;
  (h) landscapes of historical, cultural or archaeological significance.

3. Characteristics of the potential impact

The potential significant effects of projects must be considered in relation to criteria set out under 1 and 2 above, and having regard in particular to:
— the extent of the impact (geographical area and size of the affected population);
— the transfrontier nature of the impact;
— the magnitude and complexity of the impact;
— the probability of the impact;
— the duration, frequency and reversibility of the impact.

ANNEX IV

INFORMATION REFERRED TO IN ARTICLE 5(1)

1. Description of the project, including in particular:

   — a description of the physical characteristics of the whole project and the land-use requirements during the construction and operational phases;
   — a description of the main characteristics of the production processes, for instance, nature and quantity of the materials used;
   — an estimate, by type and quantity, of expected residues and emissions (water, air and soil pollution, noise, vibration, light, heat, radiation, etc.) resulting from the operation of the proposed project.

2. An outline of the main alternatives studied by the developer and an indication of the main reasons for his choice, taking into account the environmental effects.

3. A description of the aspects of the environment likely to be significantly affected by the proposed project, including, in particular, population, fauna, flora, soil, water, air, climatic factors, material assets, including the architectural and archaeological heritage, landscape and the inter-relationship between the above factors.

4. A description(¹) of the likely significant effects of the proposed project on the environment resulting from:

   — the existence of the project;
   — the use of natural resources;
   — the emission of pollutants, the creation of nuisances and the elimination of waste,

   and the description by the developer of the forecasting methods used to assess the effects on the environment.

5. A description of the measures envisaged to prevent, reduce and where possible offset any significant adverse effects on the environment.

6. A non-technical summary of the information provided under the above headings.

7. An indication of any difficulties (technical deficiencies or lack of know-how) encountered by the developer in compiling the required information.

(¹) This description should cover the direct effects and any indirect, secondary, cumulative, short, medium and long-term, permanent and temporary, positive and negative effects of the project.'

Appendix IV

LIST OF USEFUL ADDRESSES

Advisory Board for Redundant Churches
Fielden House, Little College Street, London SW1P 3SH Tel: 0171 222 9603

Ancient Monuments Society
St. Ann's Vestry Hall, 2 Church Entry, London EC4V 5AB Tel: 0171 236 3934

Architectural Heritage Fund
27 John Adam Street, London WC2N 6HX Tel: 0171 925 0199

Association of London Government
36, Old Queen Street, London SW1H 9JF Tel: 0171 222 7799

The British Archaeologists' and Developers' Liaison Group
British Property Federation, 35 Catherine Place, London SW1E 6DY
Tel: 0171 828 0111

British Tourist Authority
Thames Tower, Black's Road, Hammersmith, London W6 9EL
Tel: 0181 846 9000

CADW: Welsh Historic Monuments Executive Agency
Brunel House, 9th Floor, 2 Fitzalan Road, Cardiff CF2 1UY Tel: 01222 465511

Campaign for Freedom of Information
Suite 102, 66 Baldwin's Gdns., London EC1N 7RJ Tel: 0171 831 7477

The Central Council for Physical Recreation
Francis House, Francis Street, London SW1P 1DE Tel: 0171 828 3163/4

Charity Commission
57/60 Haymarket, London SW1Y 4QX Tel: 0171 210 4450

Civic Trust
17 Carlton House Terrace, London SW1Y 5AW Tel: 0171 930 0914

Commission of the European Communities
Jean Monnet House, 8 Storey's Gate, London SW1P 3AT Tel: 0171 973 1992

Commission of the European Communities
Rue de la Loi, 200, B1040 Brussels, Belgium Tel: 00 32 2 299 1111

Council for British Archaeology
Bowes Morrell House, 111 Walmgate, York YO1 2UA Tel: 01904 671417

Council for the Care of Churches
83 London Wall, London EC2M 5NA Tel: 0171 638 0971

Council for National Parks
246 Lavender Hill, London SW11 1LJ Tel: 0171 924 4077

Council for the Protection of Rural England (CPRE)
Warwick House, 25 Buckingham Palace Road, London SW1 OPP
Tel: 0171 976 6433

Countryside Commission
John Dower House, Crescent Place, Cheltenham, Glos GL50 3RA Tel: 01242 340345

The Countryside Council for Wales
Plas Penrhos, Ffordd Penrhos, Bangor, Gwynedd LL57 2LQ Tel: 01248 370444

Crown Estate Commissioners
Marine Estates, 16 Carlton House Terrace, London SW1Y 5AH Tel: 0171 210 3000

DoE (Inspectorate)
Tollgate Houses, Houlton Street, Bristol BS2 9DJ Tel: 0117 987 8743

Department of the Environment (Public Enquiry Office)
2 Marsham Street, London SW1P 3EB Tel: 0171 276 0900

Department of National Heritage
2–4 Cockspur Street, London SW1Y 5DH Tel: 0171 211 6000

DTp
2 Marsham Street, London SW1P 3EB Tel: 0171 271 5000

DTp
Welbar House, Gallowgate, Newcastle, NE1 4TX Tel: 0191 201 3300

English Heritage
Fortress House, 23 Savile Row, London W1X 1AB Tel: 0171 973 3000

English Historic Towns Forum
The Huntingdon Centre, The Vineyards, The Paragon, Bath BA1 5NA
Tel: 01225 469157

English Nature
Northminster House, Peterborough PE1 1UA Tel: 01733 455000

English Tourist Board
Thames Tower, Black's Road, Hammersmith, London W6 9EL Tel: 0181 846 9000

Environment Agency
Rivers House, Waterside Drive, Aztec West, Almondsbury, Bristol BS12 4UD
Tel: 01454 624400

The Environment Council
21 Elizabeth Street, London SW1W 9RP Tel: 0171 824 8411

Environmental Law Foundation (ELF)
Lincoln's Inn House, 42 Kingsway, London WC2B 6EX Tel: 0171 404 1030

Ethical Consumer Research Association
ECRA Publishing Ltd., Unit 21, 41 Old Birley Street, Manchester M15 5RF
Tel: 0161 226 2929

Ethical Investors Group U.K. Ltd
Milestone, Greet Road, Greet, Cheltenham GL54 5BG Tel: 01242 604550

Foundation for International Environmental Law & Development (FIELD), SOAS
University of London, 46/47 Russell Square, London WC1B 4JP
Tel: 0171 637 7950

Friends of the Earth
26-28 Underwood Street, London N1 7JQ Tel: 0171 490 1555

Garden History Society
Station House, Church Lane, Wickwar, Wotton-under-Edge Tel: 01454 294888

Georgian Group
37 Spital Square, London E1 6DY Tel: 0171 377 1722

Goad, Chas Ltd
Salisbury Square, Old Hatfield, Hants AL9 5BJ Tel: 01707 274641

Greenpeace
Canonbury Villas, London N1 2PN Tel: 0171 865 8100

HM Land Registry
32 Lincoln's Inn Field, London WC2A 3PH Tel: 0171 917 8888

HMSO Publications (Orders)
P.O. Box 276, London SW8 5DT Tel: 0171 873 9090

House of Commons
Public Information Office, London SW1A OAA Tel: 0171 219 4272

Institute of Environmental Assessment
Welton House, Limekiln Way, Lincoln LN2 4US Tel: 01522 540069

Institute of Environmental Health Officers
Chadwick Court, 15 Hatfields, London SE1 8DJ Tel: 0171 928 6006

The Institute of Field Archaeologists
The Minerals Engineering Building, University of Birmingham, P.O. Box 363,
Birmingham B15 2TT Tel: 0121 4712788

Oxford Institute of Retail Management
Templeton College, Kennington, Oxford OX1 5NY Tel: 01865 735422

Joint Nature Conservation Committee
Monkstone House, City Road, Peterborough PE1 1JY Tel: 01733 62626

The Law Society
50/52 Chancery Lane, London WC2A 1SX Tel: 0171 320 5810

Local Government Association
26 Chapter Street, London SW1P 4ND Tel: 0171 834 2222

Local Government Management Board
Layden House, 76–86 Turnmill Street, London EC1M 5QU Tel: 0171 296 6600

**Local Government Ombudsman (Greater London, Kent, Surrey, East Sussex &
West Sussex)**
21 Queen Anne's Gate, London SW1H 9BU Tel: 0171 915 3210

Local Government Ombudsman (East Anglia, the South-West, the West, the South and most of Central England)
The Oaks No 2, Westwood Way, Westwood Business Park, Coventry CV4 8JB
Tel: 01203 695999

Local Government Ombudsman (Cheshire, Derbyshire, Nottinghamshire, Lincolnshire and the North of England)
Beverley House, 17 Shipton Road, York YO3 6FZ Tel: 01904 663200

Manchester University – Environmental Assessment Unit
Oxford Road, Manchester M13 9PL Tel: 0161 275 2000

The National Association of Local Councils (NALC)
109 Great Russell Street, London WC1B 3LD Tel: 0171 637 1865

National Rivers Authority (now The Environment Agency)
Rivers House, Waterside Drive Aztec West, Almondsbury, Bristol BS12 4AU Tel: 01454 624409

National Society for Clean Air and Environmental Protection
136 North Street, Brighton, BN1 1RG Tel: 01273 326 313

National Council for Voluntary Organisations (NVCO)
Regents Wharf, 8 All Saints Street, London N1 9RL Tel: 0171 713 6161

New Economics Foundation (NEF)
Vine Court, 1st Floor, 112/116 Whitechapel Road, London E1 1JE
Tel: 0171 377 5696

Ombudsman (Office of the Parliamentary Commissioner for Administration or Parliamentary Ombudsman)
Church House, Great Smith Street, London SW1P 3BW Tel: 0171 276 2130

Ombudsman (access to Official Information)
Millbank Tower, Millbank, London SW1P 4QP Tel: 0171 217 4003

Open Spaces Society
25a Bell Street, Henley-on-Thames, Oxfordshire RG9 2BA Tel: 01491 573 535

Oxford Brookes University
Gypsy Lane, Headington, Oxford OX3 OPB Tel: 01865 741 111

Pedestrians Association
126 Aldersgate Street, London EC1A 4JQ Tel: 0171 490 0750

The Planning Inspectorate, Department of Environment
Tollgate House, Houlton Street, Bristol BS2 9DJ Tel: 0117 9878000

The Planning Inspectorate (Wales)
Cathays Park, Cardiff, CF1 3NQ Tel: 01222 823892

Ramblers Association
1/5 Wandsworth Road, London SW8 2DJ Tel: 0171 582 6878

The Regency Press Corporation
Gordon House, 6 Lissendon Gardens, London NW5 1LX Tel: 0171 284 4858

Royal College of Veterinary Surgeons
Belgravia House, 62/64 Horseferry Road, London SW1P 2AF Tel: 0171 222 2001

Royal Commission on the Historical Monuments of England
Fortress House, 23 Savile Row, London W1X 1AB Tel: 0171 973 3500

Royal Institute of British Architects (RIBA)
66 Portland Place, London W1N 4AD Tel: 0171 580 5533

Royal Institute of Chartered Surveyors (RICS)
12 Great George Street, London SW1P 3AD Tel: 0171 222 7000

Royal Society for Nature Conservation (RSNC)
The Green, Waterside South, Witham Park, Lincoln LN5 7JR Tel: 01522 544400

Royal Town Planning Institute (RTPI)
26 Portland Square, London W1N 4BE Tel: 0171 636 9107

Rural Development Commission
11 Cowley Street, London SW1P 3EB Tel: 0171 276 6969

Society for the Protection of Ancient Buildings
37 Spital Square, London E1 6DY Tel: 0171 377 1644

The Sports Council
16 Upper Woburn Place, London WC1H OQP Tel: 0171 388 1277

The Sports Council for Wales
National Sports Centre for Wales, Sophia Gardens, Cardiff CF1 9SW Tel: 01222 397571

Theatres Trust
Doric House, 22 Charing Cross Road, London WC2H Tel: 0171 836 8591

Town & Country Planning Association (TCPA)
17 Carlton House Terrace, London SW1Y 5AS Tel: 0171 930 8903

Transport 2000
Walkden House, 10 Melton Street, London NW1 2EJ Tel: 0171 388 8386

Twentieth Century Society
58 Crescent Lane, London SW4 9PU Tel: 0171 793 9898

UK Social Investment Forum
1st Floor, Vine Court, 112 Whitechapel Road, London E1 1JE
Tel: 0171 377 5907

UKELA (UK Environmental Law Association)
Honeycroft House, Pangbourne Road, Upper Basildon, RG8 8LR Tel: 01491 671631

UNA (United Nations Association)
3 Whitehall Court, London SW1A 2EL Tel: 0171 930 2931

United Kingdom Accreditation Service
Audley House, 13 Palace Street, London SW1E 5HS Tel: 0171 233 7111

United Kingdom Association of Building Preservation Trusts
c/- The Architectural Heritage Fund, 27 John Adam Street, London WC2N 6HX
Tel: 0171 930 1629

Urban Villages Forum
8 Stratton Street, London W1X 5FD Tel: 0171 629 1600

Victorian Society
1 Priory Gardens, Bedford Park, London W4 1TT Tel: 0181 994 1019

Wales Tourist Board
Davis Street, Cardiff, South Glamorgan CF12 2FU Tel: 01222 475214

Welsh Office
Crown Building, Cathays Park, Cardiff CF1 3NQ Tel: 01222 825111

Women's Environmental Network
87 Worship Street, London EC2A 4BE Tel: 0171 247 5227

World Wildlife Fund
Panda House, Weyside Park, Godalming, Surrey GU7 1XR Tel: 01483 426444

The Wildlife Trusts
The Green, Waterside South, Witham Park, Lincoln LN5 7JR Tel: 01522 544400

Appendix V

STATUTORY CONSULTEES

According to Article 10 of the 1995 GDPO, LPAs are obliged to consult the following bodies, if in their opinion the proposal falls within certain categories, set out below, unless:

TABLE

Para	Description of Development	Consultee
(a)	Development likely to affect land in Greater London or in a metropolitan county	The local planning authority concerned
(b)	Development likely to affect land in a non-metropolitan county, other than land in a National Park	The district planning authority concerned (**a**)
(c)	Development likely to affect land in a National Park	The county planning authority concerned
(d)	Development within an area which has been notified to the local planning authority by the Health and Safety Executive for the purpose of this provision because of the presence within the vicinity of toxic, highly reactive, explosive or inflammable substances and which involves the provision of– (i) residential accommodation; (ii) more than 250 square metres of retail floor space; (iii) more than 500 square metres of office floor space; or (iv) more than 750 square metres of floor space to be used for an industrial process, or which is otherwise likely to result in a material increase in the number of persons working within or visiting the notified area	The Health and Safety Executive

(**a**) For cases where functions have been transferred from the county council to the district council or vice versa see regulation 5 of the Local Government Changes for England Regulations 1994 (S.I. 1994/867) and section 1 of the Act.

(e)	Development likely to result in a material increase in the volume or a material change in the character of traffic–	
	(i) entering or leaving a trunk road; or	In England, the Secretary of State for Transport and, in Wales, the Secretary of State for Wales.
	(ii) using a level crossing over a railway	The operator of the network which includes or consists of the railway in question, and in England, the Secretary of State for Transport and, in Wales, the Secretary of State for Wales
(f)	Development likely to result in a material increase in the volume or a material change in the character of traffic entering or leaving a classified road or proposed highway	The local highway authority concerned
(g)	Development likely to prejudice the improvement or construction of a classified road or proposed highway	The local highway authority concerned
(h)	Development involving–	
	(i) the formation, laying out or alteration of any of access to a highway (other than a trunk road); or	The local highway authority concerned
	(ii) the construction of a highway or private means of access to premises affording access to a road in relation to which a toll order is in force	The local highway authority concerned, and in the case of a road subject to a concession, the concessionaire
(i)	Development which consists of or includes the laying out or construction of a new street	The local highway authority
(j)	Development which involves the provision of a building or pipe-line in an area of coal working notified by the Coal Authority to the local planning authority	The Coal Authority
(k)	Development involving or including mining operations	The National Rivers Authority

(l)	Development within three kilometres of Windsor Castle, Windsor Great Park, or Windsor Home Park, or within 800 metres of any other royal palace or park, which might affect the amenities (including security) of that palace or park	The Secretary of State for National Heritage
(m)	Development of land in Greater London involving the demolition, in whole or part, or the material alteration of a listed building	The Historic Buildings and Monuments Commission for England
(n)	Development likely to affect the site of a scheduled monument	In England, the Historic Buildings and Monuments Commission for England, and, in Wales, the Secretary of State for Wales
(o)	Development likely to affect any garden or park of special historic interest which is registered in accordance with section 8C of the Historic Buildings and Ancient Monuments Act 1953(**a**) (register of gardens) and which is classified as Grade I or Grade II*.	The Historic Buildings and Monuments Commission for England
(p)	Development involving the carrying out of works or operations in the bed of or on the banks of a river or stream	The National Rivers Authority
(q)	Development for the purpose of refining or storing mineral oils and their derivatives	The National Rivers Authority
(r)	Development involving the use of land for the deposit of refuse or waste	The National Rivers Authority
(s)	Development relating to the retention, treatment or disposal of sewage, trade-waste, slurry or sludge (other than the laying of sewers, the construction of pumphouses in a line of sewers, the construction of septic tanks and cesspools serving single dwellinghouses or single caravans or single buildings in which not more than ten people will normally reside, work or congregate, and works ancillary thereto)	The National Rivers Authority
(t)	Development relating to the use of land as a cemetery	The National Rivers Authority

(**a**) 1953 c.49 (1 & 2 Eliz. 2); section 8C was inserted by section 33 of, and paragraph 10 of Schedule 4 to, the National Heritage Act 1983 (c.47).

(u)	Development– (i) in or likely to affect a site of special scientific interest of which notification has been given, or has effect as if given, to the local planning authority by the Nature Conservancy Council for England or the Countryside Council for Wales, in accordance with section 28 of the Wildlife and Countryside Act 1981(**a**) (areas of special scientific interest); or (ii) within an area which has been notified to the local planning authority by the Nature Conservancy Council for England or the Countryside Council for Wales, and which is within two kilometres of a site of special scientific interest of which notification has been given or has effect as if given as aforesaid	The Council which gave, or is to be regarded as having given, the notice
(v)	Development involving any land on which there is a theatre	The Theatres Trust
(w)	Development which is not for agricultural purposes and is not in accordance with the provisions of a development plan and involves– (i) the loss of not less than 20 hecatres of grades 1, 2 or 3a agricultural land which is for the time being used (or was last used) for agricultural purposes; or (ii) the loss of less than 20 hectares of grades 1, 2 or 3a agricultural land which is for the time being used (or was last used) for agricultural purposes, in circumstances in which the development is likely to lead to a further loss of agricultural land amounting cumulatively to 20 hectares or more	In England, the Minister of Agriculture, Fisheries and Food and, in Wales, the Secretary of State for Wales
(x)	Development within 250 metres of land which– (i) is or has, at any time in the 30 years before the relevant application, been used for the deposit of refuse or waste; and (ii) has been notified to the local planning authority by the waste regulation authority for the purposes of this provision	The waste regulation authority concerned
(y)	Development for the purposes of fish farming	The National Rivers Authority

With regard to non-statutory consultees, the situation is even more complicated, and readers would be advised to consult DoE Circular 9/95, Appendix for details.

(**a**) 1981 c. 69.

Appendix VI

INFORMATION ON STATUS QUO

Existing Situation

Before embarking on the wider trawl of official information in relation to a given application, what information is available on the existing site and the surrounding area?

1. The Land Registry (see Appendix IV) holds details of land ownership, claims by adverse possession, mortgages etc. This begs the question of whether the property has been registered. Often land which has not been built on remains unregistered, so you may be unlucky if you are trying to find the owner of that unused ground behind your house, which you covet as an extension to your garden.

2. Information relating to the local authority decision making process is available under the Local Government (Access to Information) Act 1985: this includes committee reports, agendas, reports, minutes and background papers. With regard to planning, this includes permissions, conditions, s.106 agreements, enforcement and stop notices etc. So you can discover the thinking behind what have turned out to be 'mistakes'.

3. The Land Charges Dept. of the LPA will hold details of property, registered under the Land Charges Act 1972, such as: various extant planning permissions: is the existing permission subject to the s.106 obligation; is it a listed building or in a conservation area; is it in a smoke control zone; is it near an adopted road; has it got trees protected by Tree Preservation Orders; has it been been subject to environmental health notices etc.?

4 District councils and metropolitan boroughs keep lists which are publicly available on various subjects: housing action areas, housing renewal areas, and general improvement areas; conservation areas; unused or under used local authority land; common land; reservoirs; tree preservation orders; and caravan sites.

5. Various information is accessible which pertains to individual buildings: whether they are listed, and applications of building regulations.

6. Information relating to forward planning: development plans, enterprise and simplified planning zones; Register of planning applications and ESs; current minerals permissions and applications; applications for

certificates of lawful use; planning permissions, stop notices and enforcement notices etc.

7.   Local authorities have to make available their statements and documents prior to a public inquiry into highways, and electricity generating stations or overhead power lines: all of which are often regarded with suspicion by local people.

8.   Last, but not least, there is information available on a motley collection of subjects, ranging from maps of sewers to registers of stray dogs, not to mention taxi drivers and persons licensed to exhibit or train performing animals!

ROADS

Thanks to a provision, made curiously under the Wildlife and Countryside Act 1981, there are maps available showing highways, footpaths and bridleways. Also highways authorities have to make available statements on their position and other documents prior to a public inquiry.

POLLUTION

With regard to pollutants of all denominations, registers are now publicly available for you to inspect. Where are these to be found and what do they contain?

1.   Water Quality

The keeping of registers by the Environment Agency was begun under the 1989 Registers Regulations (1989 S.I.1160). When the water industry was privatised, the National Rivers Authority (NRA) was created to be its watchdog, and a new system of regulation was introduced under a series of Acts: under the 1995 Environment Act, the powers vested in the NRA were passed to the new Environment Agency. Information, included in the registers, comprises details of applications and consents to discharge into controlled waters; the conditions imposed; monitoring samples of effluent and water; information derived from the analysis of such samples; and any action taken. Consents from as far back as August 1985 have been included on the Register. Under the Water Resources Act 1989 (WRA), s.85, it is an offence to 'cause or permit poisonous, noxious or polluting matter or solid waste' to enter controlled waters. Usually entries are made within 28 days of such an event.

Registers also contain statutory water quality objectives (WRA s.83), which the Environment Agency and Secretary of State have a duty to do their utmost to achieve. The objectives should not be confused with river classifications which are not legally binding. Quality objectives depends on the category of use e.g. fisheries (6 sub-classes), abstraction for possible supply (3 classes), abstraction for industrial or agricultural use (2 classes), water sports, commercial harvest of fish and shell fish, and special ecosystems. Where they apply, European Community standards are also placed on the Register. These may only pertain to certain designated stretches of water, and may vary according to its hardness.

Registers are held at Environment Agency Regional Head Office, but some copies or parts may find their way to divisional offices. Under WRA s.190(2), Registers have to be freely available to the public at all reasonable hours and copying facilities available at a modest charge. Obtaining copies costs 10p a sheet and, if the request is made by phone, an hourly fee may be levied. Computers can select information by National Grid references from an Ordnance Survey map. It is advisable to phone ahead for an appointment to ensure that someone will be there to help you find your way around the Register. They should have a list of all consents and all sampling points, river by river, grouped by name. It might be advisable to ask for assistance just to ensure that you have all the information available e.g. any amendments to consents.

It has to be admitted that Registers may be incomplete if it is considered to be contrary to the public interest, liable to divulge a trade secret, or contrary to the interests of national security: the latter may well include MOD property, or outfalls from plants in the nuclear field.

In addition there are Registers, maintained by sewerage undertakers, containing all consents given to those discharging trade effluent of either an industrial or agricultural nature, into the sewers. Details include name of the consent-holder, the date of consent, the date of any subsequent conditions, the type of consent, the grid reference of the discharge point, any variations in the conditions, details of the consent giver if other than Environment Agency, and details of any notices in relation to consents.

2.   Air Quality & Polluting Industries

Under the Environmental Protection Act (EPA) 1990, the local authority (district councils in the shires) has to keep and make publicly available Registers both on air polluters, and on industries using, what are known in statutory lingo, 'prescribed processes' and 'prescribed substances'. Part I of EPA introduces Integrated Pollution Control (IPC) by which HMIP, but now the Environment Agency, and the relevant district council, London Borough, or metropolitan district council will authorise and regulate over 200 of the most seriously polluting categories of industrial process, covering around 5000 chemical plants, refineries etc. at over 8000 premises.

EPA s.20 provides for the setting up of Registers, to be held by the Environment Agency and the local authority in the area where the prescribed process is being carried out. Air pollution registers are held by the local authority by the environmental health department. The Registers give details on: applications for consent; the authorisations granted; any variation, enforcement, or prohibition notices; any appeal under EPA s.15; convictions for offences under EPA s.23(1); directions given to the authority by the Secretary of State; and other matters relating to polluting activities.

Part II of the EPA 1990 deals with solid waste: its collection, recycling, deposit and other forms of disposal. Under s.30, waste regulation authorities include the county councils in England, the respective waste regulation bodies of the metropolitan areas, and the district councils in Wales and Scotland. The Environment Agency has now become responsible for waste regulation.

Each area office of the Environment Agency is now a Waste Regulation Authority. Each one has the duty, under EPA s.67, to prepare and publish an annual report on licence holders: current or recently current licences granted by the authority; current or recently current applications; applications to modify licences; notices to modify licences; notices to suspend or revoke licences; notices with respect to conditions; convictions of license holders under the EPA 1990; activities of the Waste Regulation Authorities in respect of existing licensees or closed landfills; any directions given by the Secretary of State; such matters relating to the keeping, treatment or disposal of waste as may be prescribed. In contrast to the IPC Registers, all material, published or otherwise, is likely to be included.

Many of the items to be listed in the EPA Registers could be regarded as 'sensitive', not to say embarrassing, to holders of authorisations, and the Environment Agency will have to sell them the idea that it is good PR to be seen to be responsible. On the other hand, there are the usual exemptions for trade secrets and national security relating to air quality, IPC and Waste Regulation (ss.21,22,65, & 66).

3. *Contaminated Land*

The Environmental Protection Act 1990 caused a furore amongst those concerned with development by trying to introduce registers for contaminated land: overnight such land would become a financial liability, impossible to mortgage or insure. However, it is a case of out of the frying pan and into the fire. The Environment Act 1995 has given local authorities rights to inspect dubious ground and serve clean up notices on the owner, or do it themselves and send in the bill to the owner. The problem will arise should the owners have vanished in the mists of time, or be otherwise untraceable, leaving the LPA or private householders to pick up the tab.

4.   *Radioactivity*

Information is available from the Environment Agency on the use of radioactive material and the use of mobile radioactive apparatus with regard to: all applications and authorizations; documents issued by the Environment Agency; documents sent by the Secretary of State; notices and relevant convictions. Also on accumulations of radioactive waste.

5.   *Public Safety*

For those worried about public health and/or an exciting environment, there is a variety of information:

a) registers of premises used for the storage of explosives;

b) registers of notices served by local authorities on factories, shops, railway stations, cinemas, and other public places, for breaches of the Health and Safety at Work Act, Fire Precautions Act, Safety of Sports Grounds Act, Food and Environmental Protection Act, and the Environment and Safety Information Act 1988;

c) applications for Hazardous Substances consent which includes information on the site, a map, the planning history, the hazardous substance, a substance location plan, and the manner of keeping it under control. It also contains details of all proceedings on it, such as revocations, modifications, claims for deemed consent, and directions.

6.   *Litter*

After the above litany of murder and mayhem, mere litter comes as something of an anticlimax. Nevertheless, it is an all too present feature of our wasteful society, careless of public open space, hedgerow or street. However, the EPA 1990 devotes Section IV to this problem. The local authority, usually the district or borough, is obliged to keep registers showing litter control areas, street litter notices, and any variation or additions to notices resulting from appeals by suspected litter-bugs.

7.   *Noise*

John Cage's exercises in silent music, are an attempt to draw to our attention the rising crescendo of ambient noise in our environment. Local authorities keep registers of Noise Abatement Zones: NAZs can be used reduce noise from commercial and industrial premises in areas of mixed development. The local authority also keeps maps or lists of buildings eligible for insulation works. The latter is also covered by Building Regulations. If you are troubled by excessive noise, s.79 1990 EPA may provide a remedy (see p.192).

Appendix VII

OPEN GOVERNMENT

For many years now there has been a war of attrition between those wanting a Freedom of Information Act and 'Open Government', and those who prefer the comfortable life behind a veil of secrecy. Secrecy has been described as a British Disease. Its origins lie with the nineteenth century civil service and it succeeded in incorporating its intentions into the statute book in the shape of the 1911 Official Secrets Act: the excuse was suspected German espionage in naval dockyards, and the Bill went through in half an hour flat, one hot afternoon just before the summer adjournment. Section 1 deals with national security, the world of John Le Carre. It was the blanket coverage of Section 2 which brought the original Act into disrepute: it imposed penal sanctions on anyone imparting or receiving official information, with no distinction between security and other information.

In 1989 Section 2 was repealed and its replacement narrowed the field of possible prosecution to security and intelligence, defence, international relations, and law enforcement. This may sound far removed from environmental concerns but nuclear energy and the disposal of nuclear waste could come under 'Defence', and pollution under international relations. The Act should not be taken to mean that information outside these categories is therefore open to public view: there are still secret files. A civil servant disclosing embarrassing information would just be sacked rather than prosecuted. In July 1993 the 'Open Government' White Paper listed some 251 statutory provisions, identified by the British Government, prohibiting disclosure.

During the last few years there have been ministerial mutterings about opening up government, and there have been moves in the right direction, but these have to be seen within the context of the legacy of official secrecy. On 4th April 1994 the Government launched its Code of Practice over Open Government, yet little or nothing was done to tell the public how to extract information from Departments of State: the determined citizen might find a folded piece of A4 card in Citizen's Advice Bureaux, regional Government Offices and law advice centres. The bodies covered by the code are listed on the card: they are the same as those subject to the Parliamentary Ombudsman. It seems that the first step is to write to the

Department, agency or body, explaining what information you are looking for, and be as precise as possible. They are supposed to respond within twenty days.

Given the lack of media coverage it is not surprising that few people have made use of the new code. Those coping with motorway cones are clearly more deserving of a helpline than a beleaguered citizen dealing with a recalcitrant Department. Official responses have proved less than satisfactory: some never arrive, some are late and others less than fulsome. The British public is still not allowed to join the grown ups in terms of being allowed to *see* the actual documents. The public has to rely on officials producing the highlights - no doubt heavily edited, if the document is embarrassing to the official body concerned. Some information is free, but the rest is chargeable to reduce the burden on the taxpayer.

Such bodies are allowed to reject a request for information if it impinges on internal decision making, commercial confidence, or the enforcement of law or defence. Taken at face value such exemptions are entirely reasonable, but the culture of secrecy means they are liable to be stretched to cover a multitude of facts which would be made available by a less paranoic national executive, such as those enjoyed by many of our EU partners, USA, Canada, and Australia. Any complaints about the British system have to be made via an MP to the Parliamentary Ombudsman, who has no powers to 'punish' an erring department. Clearly the Code of Practice is no substitute for a Freedom of Information Act.

Meanwhile the EU directive of Freedom of Access to Information on the Environment, passed by the Council of Ministers in 1990 [90/313/EC], constitutes the most extensive piece of legislation applicable in the UK on access to information. At the end of 1992 this was transposed into the UK Regulations (S.I.1992 No.3240). The definition of the environment bears an uncanny resemblance to that used in the environmental assessment legislation [see Appendix III]. Information covers any available information in written, visual, aural or data-base form on the state of the environment, activities or measures which do or could affect it, whether positively or negatively. Who has to provide such information?

a) Ministers of the Crown, Government Departments, local authorities and other persons carrying out functions of public administration at a national, regional or local level and...have responsibilities in relation to the environment.

b) any body with public responsibilities for the environment which does not fall within (a) but is under the control of a person falling within that sub-paragraph.

The draft regulations listed the 211 potential bodies to be affected by the legislation, but the statutory instrument fought shy of being so specific because 'circumstances vary and change'. At the time when the Regulations were first introduced, concern was expressed about possible exemption of the newly privatised industries, often major contributors to the state of the environment. However, these fears seem to be subsiding because the judiciary, in the few cases brought before the courts, seem to be impatient with excuses on grounds of eligibility or commercial confidentiality.

The information must be held by the relevant body, retained in an accessible form, and not be available under any other statutory provision e.g. Local Government (Access to Information Act) 1985 and the 1990 Environmental Protection Act. It is however, important to realise that Registers contain only such information as the provider is prepared to divulge to public view: it can be a sanitized version of the truth. There are now a number of these which are products of legislation pertaining to the environment and the DoE has produced a guide to them. However, the information referred to in the Regulations is in addition to that on the Registers, but it is difficult to know what is available as public bodies do not publish lists of information, let alone that which they consider beyond reach because of the exemptions.

CDL publishes details of the expenditure committed by different government departments in publicising their respective 'open government' codes. The DoE spent £170 on such publicity, compared with £1,602 by the DTI, and £22,981 by the highest departmental spender, the Department of Education and Employment.

Environment Business, 17.1.96

The Directive lists sixteen exceptions to the right to know, some mandatory and some discretionary, Needless to say the British Government has opted for maximum secrecy. In addition there is subtle but important changes in the wording. In the U.K. Regulations, Articles 4.1 and 4.2 allow exemptions:

a) where the disclosure of any such information can be claimed to be confidential: this gives great scope to private sector suppliers to government;

b) where it *affects* national security whereas the Regulations talk of 'information *relating to*' and clearly the former is narrower in scope than the latter;

c) where the information 'is sub judice' but in the Regulations this has been broadened to include any actual or prospective other proceedings including public or other inquiries;

d) for internal communications, but the Regulations have widened it so that commercial organisations can shelter under it without have to show any commercial confidentiality whatever;

e) for information contained in a document or other record which is incomplete. That gives plenty of scope for non-disclosure;

f) for information relating to matters of commercial or industrial confidentiality or affecting intellectual property rights. Here again the potential for abuse is rife.

The Regulations can also be found wanting in respect of the practical arrangements for the provision of information, and charging for it: both are open to narrow and mean interpretation, given the existing wording. There could also be problems in getting the information in reasonable time: up to two months is allowed, whereas one may have to respond to a planning proposal within 21 days.

Much more serious, however, is the absence of a means of appeal, despite express provision in the Directive. Although, as we shall see, the appeal is a time honoured means of settling environmental disputes, it does not extend to getting the information to fight your case. Instead aggrieved parties have to go through time-consuming and expensive judicial review, which is inappropriate to the purpose because it is designed to investigate breaches of statutory duty. The real problem is the transposition from the Directive to the Regulations themselves: only a trip to the European Court can sort that out. There are imperfections in the Directive too: it has been reviewed during 1996 by the House of Lords Select Committee on European Affairs. Thus the image of openness which the current Government would wish to create is handicapped by the legacy of secrecy bequeathed by past generations of policy makers, at Cabinet level and the 'Sir Humphrey's of SW1'. In addition, that legacy is just too comfortable for the current incumbents of government and their confederates in the private sector.

> *Genuinely sensitive information makes up a small part of our official secrets. Truth is suppressed, not to protect the country from enemy agents, but to protect the Government of the day against the people.*
>
> Roy Hattersley MP

The Environmental Information Regulations S.I.1992 No.3240

Gisele Bakkenist, Environmental Information, [London, Cameron May, 1994]

Delivering the Right to Know, [London, Friends of the Earth, 2nd April 1993]

William Birtles, 'A Right to Know: the Environmental Information Regulations 1992', [1993] Journal of Planning and Environment Law p.p.615 - 626

Peter Roderick, 'Implementation of the EC Directive of Freedom of Access to Environmental Information', [1995].

Appendix VIII

1992 No. 2039

TRIBUNALS AND INQUIRIES

The Town and Country Planning Appeals (Determination by Inspectors) (Inquiries Procedure) Rules 1992

Made   *24th August 1992*
Laid before Parliament   *7th September 1992*
Coming into force   *30th September 1992*

The Lord Chancellor, in exercise of the powers conferred on him by section 11 of the Tribunals and Inquiries Act 1971, and all other powers enabling him in that behalf, and after consultation with the Council on Tribunals, hereby makes the following Rules:

Citation and commencement

1. These Rules may be cited as the Town and Country Planning Appeals (Determination by Inspectors) (Inquiries Procedure) Rules 1992 and shall come into force on 30th September 1992.

Interpretation

2. In these Rules, unless the context otherwise requires–
"assessor" means a person appointed by the Secretary of State to sit with an inspector at an inquiry or re-opened inquiry to advise the inspector on such matters arising as the Secretary of State may specify;
"the Commission" means the Historic Buildings and Monuments Commission for England;
"conservation area consent" has the meaning given in section 74(1) of the Listed Buildings Act;
"development order" has the meaning given in section 59 of the Planning Act;
"document" includes a photograph, map or plan;
"inquiry" means a local inquiry in relation to which these Rules apply;
"inspector" means a person appointed by the Secretary of State under Schedule 6 to the Planning Act or, as the case may be, Schedule 3 to the Listed Buildings Act to determine an appeal;
"land" means the land or building to which an inquiry relates;
"the Listed Buildings Act" means the Planning (Listed Buildings and Conservation Areas) Act 1990;

"listed building consent" has the meaning given in section 8(7) of the Listed Buildings Act;

"local planning authority" means the body who were responsible for dealing with the application occasioning the appeal;

"the Planning Act" means the Town and Country Planning Act 1990;

"pre-inquiry meeting" means a meeting held before an inquiry to consider what may be done with a view to securing that the inquiry is conducted efficiently and expeditiously;

"relevant date" means the date of the written notice informing the appellant and the local planning authority that an inquiry is to be held, and "relevant notice" means that notice;

"the 1988 Rules" means the Town and Country Planning Appeals (Determination by Inspectors) (Inquiries Procedure) Rules 1988;

"statement of case" means, and is comprised of, a written statement which contains full particulars of the case which a person proposes to put forward at an inquiry, and a list of any documents which that person intends to refer to or put in evidence.

"statutory party" means–

(a) a person mentioned in paragraph (1)(b)(i) of article 22A of the Town and Country Planning General Development Order 1988 whose representations the inspector is required by paragraph (3) of that article to take into account in determining the appeal to which an inquiry relates, and such a person whose representations the local planning authority were required by paragraph (1) of that article to take into account in determining the application occasioning the appeal; and

(b) a person whose representations the inspector is required by paragraphs (3)(b) and (5) of regulation 6 of the Planning (Listed Buildings and Conversation Areas) Regulations 1990 to take into account in determining the appeal to which an inquiry relates, and a person whose representations the local planning authority were required by paragraph (3)(b) of that regulation to take into account in determining the application occasioning the appeal.

Application of Rules

3.—(1) These Rules apply in relation to any local inquiry held in England or Wales by an inspector before he determines–

(a) an appeal to the Secretary of State in relation to planning permission under section 78 of the Planning Act;

(b) an appeal to the Secretary of State in relation to listed building consent under section 20 of the Listed Buildings Act, or in relation to conservation area consent under that section as applied by virtue of section 74(3) of that Act,

but do not apply to any local inquiry by reason of the application of any provision mentioned in this paragraph by any other enactment.

(2) Where these Rules apply in relation to an appeal which at some time fell to be disposed of in accordnce with the Town and Country Planning (Inquiries Procedure) Rules 1992 or Rules superseded by those Rules, any step taken or thing done under those Rules which could have been done under any corresponding provision of these Rules shall have effect as if it had been taken or done under that corresponding provision.

Preliminary information to be supplied by local planning authority

4.—(1) The local planning authority shall, on receipt of a notice informing them that an inquiry is to be held ("the relevant notice"), forthwith inform the Secretary of State and the appellant in writing of the name and address of any statutory party who has made representations to them; and the Secretary of State shall as soon as practicable thereafter inform the appellant and the local planning authority of the name and address of any statutory party who has made representations to him.

(2) This paragraph applies where–
- (a) the Secretary of State has given to the local planning authority a direction restricting the grant of planning permission for which application was made; or
- (b) in a case relating to listed building consent, the Commission has given a direction to the local planning authority pursuant to section 14(2) of the Listed Buildings Act as to how the application is to be determined; or
- (c) the Secretary of State or any other Minister of the Crown or any government department, or any body falling within rule 11(1)(c), has expressed in writing to the local planning authority the view that the application should not be granted either wholly or in part, or should be granted only subject to conditions; or
- (d) any authority or person consulted in pursuance of a development order has made representations to the local planning authority about the application.

(3) Where paragraph (2) applies, the local planning authority shall forthwith after the date of the relevant notice ("the relevant date") inform the person or body concerned of the inquiry and, unless they have already done so, that person or body shall thereupon give the local planning authority a written statement of the reasons for making the direction, expressing the view or making the representations, as the case may be.

Notification of identity of inspector

5.—(1) Subject to paragraph (2), the Secretary of State shall notify the name of the inspector to every person entitled to appear at the inquiry.

(2) Where the Secretary of State appoints another inspector instead of the person previously appointed and it is not practicable to notify the new appointment before the inquiry is held, the inspector holding the inquiry shall, at its commencement, announce his name and the fact of his appointment.

Service of statements of case etc.

6.—(1) Subject to paragraph (4), the local planning authority shall, not later than 6 weeks after the relevant date, serve a statement of case on the Secretary of State, the appellant and any statutory party.

(2) Where rule 4(2) applies, the local planning authority shall–
- (a) include in their statement of case the terms of–
  - (i) any direction given together with a statement of the reasons therefor; and
  - (ii) any view expressed or representation made on which they intend to rely in their submissions at the inquiry; and

(b) within the period mentioned in paragraph (1) supply a copy of their statement to the person or body concerned.

(3) Subject to paragraph (4), the appellant shall, not later than 9 weeks after the relevant date, serve a statement of case on the Secretary of State, the local planning authority and any statutory party.

(4) The statement of case mentioned in paragraph (1) or, as the case may be, paragraph (3) shall be served no later than the day which is 4 weeks before the date fixed for the holding of the inquiry, where that day falls within the period mentioned in whichever of those paragraphs is applicable to the case.

(5) The appellant and the local planning authority may require the other to send them a copy of any document, or of the relevant part of any document, referred to in the list of documents comprised in that party's statement of case; and any such document, or relevant part, shall be sent as soon as practicable to the party who required it.

(6) The Secretary of State may in writing require any other person who has notified him of an intention or a wish to appear at an inquiry to serve a statement of case, within 4 weeks of being so required, on the appellant, the local planning authority, the Secretary of State and any (or any other) statutory party.

(7) The Secretary of State shall supply any person from whom he requires a statement of case in accordance with paragraph (6) with a copy of the appellant's and the local planning authority's statement of case and shall inform that person of the name and address of every person on whom his statement of case is required to be served.

(8) The Secretary of State may require any person who has served a statement of case in accordance with this rule to provide such further information about the matters contained in the statement as he may specify; and a person so required shall provide the Secretary of State with that information in writing and shall, at the same time, send a copy to any other person on whom the statement of case has been served.

(9) Any person other than the appellant who serves a statement of case on the local planning authority shall serve with it a copy of any document, or of the relevant part of any document, referred to in the list comprised in that statement, unless a copy of the document or part of the document in question is already available for inspection pursuant to paragraph (11).

(10) The Secretary of State shall transmit any statement of case served on him in accordance with this rule to the inspector.

(11) The local planning authority shall afford to any person who so requests a reasonable opportunity to inspect and, where practicable, take copies of any statement of case or other document which, or a copy of which, has been served on them in accordance with this rule, and of their statement of case together with a copy of any document, or of the relevant part of any document, referred to in the list comprised in that statement or otherwise served by them pursuant to this rule; and shall specify in their statement of case the time and place at which the opportunity will be afforded.

Statements of matters and pre-inquiry meetings

7.—(1) An inspector may, not later than 12 weeks after the relevant date, cause to be served on the appellant, the local planning authority and any statutory party a written statement of the matters about which he particularly wishes to be informed for the purposes of his consideration of the appeal.

(2) An inspector may hold a pre-inquiry meeting where he considers it desirable and shall arrange for not less than 2 weeks written notice of it to be given to the appellant, the local planning authority, any statutory party, any other person known to be entitled to appear at the inquiry and any other person whose presence at the meeting appears to him to be desirable.

(3) The inspector shall preside at the pre-inquiry meeting and shall determine the matters to be discussed and the procedure to be followed, and he may require any person present at the meeting who, in his opinion, is behaving in a disruptive manner to leave and may refuse to permit that person to return or to attend any further meeting, or may permit him to return to attend only on such conditions as he may specify.

Inquiry time-table

8.—(1) An inspector may at any time arrange a time-table for the proceedings at, or at part of, an inquiry and may at any time vary the time-table.

(2) An inspector may specify in a time-table arranged pursuant to this rule a date by which any proof of evidence and summary required by rule 14(1) to be sent to him shall be so sent.

Notification of appointment of assessor

9. Where the Secretary of State appoints an assessor, he shall notify every person entitled to appear at the inquiry of the name of the assessor and of the matters on which he is to advise the inspector.

Date and notification of inquiry

10.—(1) The date fixed by the Secretary of State for the holding of an inquiry shall be, unless he considers such a date impracticable, not later than 20 weeks after the relevant date; and where he considers it impracticable to fix a date in accordance with the preceding provisions of this paragraph, the date fixed shall be the earliest date after the end of the period mentioned which he considers to be practicable.

(2) Unless the Secretary of State agrees a lesser period of notice with the appellant and the local planning authority, he shall give not less than 4 weeks written notice of the date, time and place for the holding of an inquiry to every person entitled to appear at the inquiry.

(3) The Secretary of State may vary the date fixed for the holding of an inquiry, whether or not the date as varied is within the period of 20 weeks mentioned in paragraph (1); and paragraph (2) shall apply to the variation of a date as it applied to the date originally fixed.

(4) The Secretary of State may vary the time or place for the holding of an inquiry and shall give such notice of any such variation as appears to him to be reasonable.

(5) The Secretary of State may require the local planning authority to take one or more of the following steps–

    (a) not less than 2 week before the date fixed for the holding of an inquiry, to publish a notice of the inquiry in one or more newspapers circulating in the locality in which the land is situated;

    (b) to serve a notice of the inquiry on such persons or classes of persons as he may specify, within such period as he may specify;

    (c) to post a notice of the inquiry in a conspicuous place near to the land, within such period as he may specify;

(6) Where the land is under the control of the appellant he shall, if so required by the Secretary of State, affix a notice of the inquiry firmly to the land or to some object on or near the land, in such manner as to be readily visible to and legible by members of the public; and he shall not remove the notice, or cause or permit it to be removed, for such period before the inquiry as the Secretary of State may specify.

(7) Every notice of inquiry published, served or posted persuant to paragraph (5), or affixed pursuant to paragraph (6), shall contain–

    (a) a clear statement of the date, time and place of the inquiry and of the powers enabling the inspector to determine the appeal in question;

    (b) a written description of the land sufficient to identify approximately its location; and

    (c) a brief description of the subject matter of the appeal.

Appearances at inquiry

11.—(1) The persons entitled to appear at an inquiry are–

    (a) the appellant;

    (b) the local planning authority;

    (c) any of the following bodies if the land is situated in their area and they are not the local planning authority–

        (i) a county or district council;

        (ii) a National Park Committee within the meaning of paragraph 5 of Schedule 17 to the Local Government Act 1972;

        (iii) a joint planning board constituted under section 2(1) of the Planning Act or a joint planning board or special planning board reconstituted under Part I of Schedule 17 to the Local Government Act 1972;

        (iv) an urban development corporation established under section 135 of the Local Government, Planning and Land Act 1980;

        (v) an enterprise zone authority designated under Schedule 32 to the Local Government, Planning and Land Act 1980;

        (vi) the Broads Authority, within the meaning of the Norfolk and Suffolk Broads Act 1988;

        (vii) a housing action trust specified in an order made under section 67(1) of the Housing Act 1988;

    (d) where the land is in an area designated as a new town, the development corporation for the new town or the Commission for the New Town as its successor;

    (e) a statutory party;

    (f) the council of the parish or community in which the land is situated, if that council made representations to the local planning authority in respect of the application in pursuance of a provision of a development order;

(g) where the application was required to be notified to the Commission under section 14 of the Listed Buildings Act, the Commission;

(h) any other person who has served a statement of case in accordance with rule 6(6).

(2) Nothing in paragraph (1) shall prevent the inspector from permitting any other person to appear at an inquiry, and such permission shall not be unreasonably withheld.

(3) Any person entitled or permitted to appear may do so on his own behalf or be represented by counsel, solicitor or any other person.

Representatives of government departments and other authorities at inquiry

12.—(1) Where–

(a) the Secretary of State or the Commission has given a direction such as is described in rule 4(2)(a) or (b); or

(b) the Secretary of State or any other Minister of the Crown or any government department, or any body falling within rule 11(1)(c), has expressed a view such as is described in rule 4(2)(c) and the local planning authority have included its terms in a statement served in accordance with rule 6(1),

the appellant may, not later than 2 weeks before the date of an inquiry, apply in writing to the Secretary of State for a representative of the Secretary of State or of the other Minister, department or body concerned to be made available at the inquiry.

(2) Where an application is made in accordance with paragraph (1), the Secretary of State shall make a representative available to attend the inquiry or, as the case may be, transmit the application to the other Minister, department or body concerned who shall make a representative available to attend the inquiry.

(3) A person attending an inquiry as a representative in pursuance of this rule shall state the reasons for the direction or expressed view and shall give evidence and be subject to cross-examination to the same extent as any other witness.

(4) Nothing in paragraph (3) shall require a representative of a Minister or a government department to answer any question which in the opinion of the inspector is directed to the merits of government policy.

Inspector may act in place of Secretary of State

13. An inspector may in place of the Secretary of State take such steps as the Secretary of State is required or enabled to take under or by virtue of rule 6(6) to (8), rule 10, rule 12(1) or (2) or rule 20; and where an inspector requires further information pursuant to rule 6(8), that information shall be sent to him.

Proofs of evidence

14.—(1) A person entitled to appear at an inquiry who proposes to give, or to call another person to give, evidence at the inquiry by reading a proof of evidence shall send a copy of the proof to the inspector together with, subject to paragraph (2), a written summary.

(2) No written summary shall be required where the proof of evidence proposed to be read contains no more than 1500 words.

(3) The proof and any summary shall be sent to the inspector not later than–
    (a) 3 weeks before the date fixed for the holding of the inquiry, or
    (b) where a time-table has been arranged pursuant to rule 8 which specifies a date by which the proof and any summary shall be sent to the inspector, that date.

(4) Where the appellant or the local planning authority send a copy of a proof to an inspector in accordance with paragraph (1), with or without a summary, they shall at the same time send a copy of that proof and any summary to the other party, and to any statutory party; and where any other party so sends a copy of such documents he shall at the same time send a copy to the appellant, the local planning authority and any (or any other) statutory party.

(5) Where a written summary is provided in accordance with paragraph (1), only that summary shall be read at the inquiry, unless the inspector permits or requires otherwise.

(6) Any person required by this rule to send a copy of a proof to any other person shall send with it a copy of the whole, or the relevant part, of any document referred to in it, unless a copy of the document or part of the document in question is already available for inspection pursuant to rule 6(11).

(7) The local planning authority shall afford to any person who so requests a reasonable opportunity to inspect and, where practicable, take copies of any document send to or by them in accordance with this rule.

Procedure at inquiry

15.—(1) Except as otherwise provided in these Rules, the inspector shall determine the procedure at an inquiry.

(2) Unless in any particular case the inspector with the consent of the appellant otherwise determines, the appellant shall begin and shall have the right of final reply; and the other persons entitled or permitted to appear shall be heard in such order as the inspector may determine.

(3) A person entitled to appear at an inquiry shall be entitled to call evidence and the appellant, the local planning authority and any statutory party shall be entitled to cross-examine persons giving evidence, but, subject to the foregoing and paragraphs (4) and (5), the calling of evidence and the cross-examination of persons giving evidence shall otherwise be at the inspector's discretion.

(4) The inspector may refuse to permit–
    (a) the giving or production of evidence,
    (b) the cross-examination of persons giving evidence, or
    (c) the presentation of any other matter,
which he considers to be irrelevant or repetitious; but where he refuses to permit the giving of oral evidence, the person wishing to give the evidence may submit to him any evidence or other matter in writing before the close of the inquiry.

(5) Where a person gives evidence at an inquiry by reading a summary of his evidence in accordance with rule 14(5), the proof of evidence referred to in rule 14(1) shall, unless the person required to provide the summary notifies the

inspector that he now wishes to rely on the contents of the summary alone, be treated as tendered in evidence, and the person whose evidence the proof contains shall then be subject to cross-examination on it to the same extent as if it were evidence he had given orally.

(6) The inspector may direct that facilities shall be afforded to any person appearing at an inquiry to take or obtain copies of documentary evidence open to public inspection.

(7) The inspector may require any person appearing or present at an inquiry who, in his opinion, is behaving in a disruptive manner to leave and may refuse to permit that person to return, or may permit him to return only on such conditions as he may specify; but any such person may submit to him any evidence or other matter in writing before the close of the inquiry.

(8) The inspector may allow any person to alter or add to a statement of case served under rule 6 so far as may be necessary for the purposes of the inquiry; but he shall (if necessary by adjourning the inquiry) give every other person entitled to appear who is appearing at the inquiry an adequate opportunity of considering any fresh matter or document.

(9) The inspector may proceed with an inquiry in the absence of any person entitled to appear at it.

(10) The inspector may take into account any written representation or evidence or any other document received by him from any person before an inquiry opens or during the inquiry provided that he discloses it at the inquiry.

(11) The inspector may from time to time adjourn an inquiry and, if the date, time and place of the adjourned inquiry are announced before the adjournment, no further notice shall be required.

Site inspections

16.—(1) The inspector may make an unaccompanied inspection of the land before or during an inquiry without giving notice of his intention to the persons entitled to appear at the inquiry.

(2) The inspector may, during an inquiry or after its close, inspect the land in the company of the appellant, the local planning authority and any statutory party; and he shall make such an inspection if so requested by the appellant or the local planning authority before or during an inquiry.

(3) In all cases where the inspector intends to make an inspection of the kind referred to in paragraph (2) he shall announce during the inquiry the date and time at which he proposes to make it.

(4) The inspector shall not be bound to defer an inspection of the kind referred to in paragraph (2) where any person mentioned in that paragraph is not present at the time appointed.

Procedure after inquiry

17.—(1) Where an assessor has been appointed, he may, after the close of the inquiry, make a report in writing to the inspector in respect of the matters on which he was appointed to advise, and where he does so the inspector shall state in his notification of his decision pursuant to rule 18 that such a report was made.

(2) If, after the close of an inquiry, an inspector proposes to take into considera-tion any new evidence or any new matter of fact (not being a matter of government policy) which was not raised at the inquiry and which he considers to be material to his decision, he shall not come to a decision without first–

   (a) notifying the persons entitled to appear at the inquiry who appeared at it of the matter in question; and

   (b) affording to them an opportunity of making written representations to him with respect to it within 3 weeks of the date of the notification or of asking within that period for the re-opening of the inquiry.

(3) An inspector may, as he thinks fit, cause an inquiry to be re-opened, and he shall do so if asked by the appellant or the local planning authority in the circum-stances and within the period mentioned in paragraph (2); and where an inquiry is re-opened–

   (a) the inspector shall send to the persons entitled to appear at the inquiry who appeared at it a written statement of the matters with respect to which further evidence is invited; and

   (b) paragraphs (2) to (7) of rule 10 shall apply as if the references to an inquiry were references to a re-opened inquiry.

Notification of decision

18.—(1) An inspector shall notify his decision on an appeal, and his reasons for it, in writing to all persons entitled to appear at the inquiry who did appear, and to any other person who, having appeared at the inquiry, has asked to be notified of the decision.

(2) Any person entitled to be notified of the inspector's decision under para-graph (1) may apply to the Secretary of State in writing, within 6 weeks of the date of the decision, for an opportunity of inspecting any documents listed in the noti-fication and any report made by an assessor and the Secretary of State shall afford him that opportunity.

Procedure following quashing of decision

19. Where a decision of an inspector on an appeal in respect of which an inquiry has been held is quashed in proceedings before any court, the Secretary of State–

   (a) shall send to the persons entitled to appear at the inquiry who appeared at it a written statement of the matters with respect to which further rep-resentations are invited for the purposes of the further consideration of the appeal; and

   (b) shall afford to those persons the opportunity of making, within 3 weeks of the date of the written statement, written representations to him in respect of those matters or of asking for the re-opening of the inquiry; and

   (c) may, as he thinks fit, direct that the inquiry be re-opened, as if he does so paragraphs (2) to (7) of rule 10 shall apply as if the references to an inquiry were references to a re-opened inquiry.

Allowing further time

20. The Secretary of State may at any time in any particular case allow further time for the taking of any step which is required or enabled to be taken by virtue of these Rules, and references in these Rules to a day by which, or a period within which, any step is required or enabled to be taken shall be construed accordingly.

Service of notices by post

21. Notices or documents required or authorised to be served or sent under these Rules may be sent by post.

Revocation, savings and transitional

22.—(1) Subject to paragraph (2), the Town and Country Planning Appeals (Determination by Inspectors) (Inquiries Procedure) Rules 1988 are hereby revoked.

(2) Any appeal to which the 1988 Rules applied which has not been determined on the date when these Rules come into force ("the commencement date") shall be continued under these Rules, but–

    (a) rules 14 and 15(5) of the 1988 Rules shall continue to apply, and rules 8(2), 14 and 15(5) of these Rules shall not apply, in a case where at the commencement date–

        (i) an inquiry has been opened but not closed; or

        (ii) a date has been fixed for the holding of an inquiry which is less than 6 weeks after the commencement date; and

    (b) persons who were section 29(3) parties under the 1988 Rules shall be treated as statutory parties.

Mackay of Clashfern, C.

24th August 1992.

EXPLANATORY NOTE

(This note is not part of the Rules)

These Rules regulate the procedure to be followed in connection with local inquiries in England or Wales held by inspectors appointed by the Secretary of State to determine appeals made to him in relation to planning permission, listed building consent and consent for the demolition of unlisted buildings in conservation areas (known as "conservation area consent").

They replace, with amendments, the Town and Country Planning Appeals (Determination by Inspectors) (Inquiries Procedure) Rules 1988, which are revoked, subject to transitional provisions contained in rule 22.

The principal changes made by these Rules are as follows.

The statements of case required by rule 6 must now be served, in certain circumstances, no later than 4 weeks before the date on which the inquiry is due to open (paragraph (4) of that rule).

The appellant and the local planning authority may now require from one another a copy of any document, or relevant extract, which the party so required intends to refer to or put in evidence at the inquiry (rule 6(5)).

Rule 14 now requires that copies of proofs of evidence sent to the inspector must be accompanied by a written summary where the proof contains more than 1500 words, not merely, as formerly, where the inspector expressly required such a summary (paragraphs (1) and (2) of that rule). Where provided, only the summary shall be read at the inquiry, unless the inspector permits or requires otherwise.

There are also minor and drafting amendments, some of which are consequential upon the consolidation, in 1990, of planning legislation, or upon provisions introduced by the Planning and Compensation Act 1991 (c.34).

Appendix IX

Planning Conditions & S. 106 Planning Obligations

Planning Conditions

Whether planning permission is granted by the LPA, or by the Secretary of State, it may be granted outright, or subject to conditions. The validity of such conditions have been the subject of repeated battles in the courts but, in general, the advice in DoE Circular 11/95, para.14, holds good:

Conditions should only be imposed where they are:
(a) necessary;
(b) relevant to planning;
(c) relevant to the development permitted;
(d) enforceable;
(e) precise; and
(f) reasonable in all other respects.

Any given condition has to comply with *all* the tests outlined above. To see precisely what they mean, and don't mean, study Circular 11/95, paras.15–42. Conditions may be imposed on a full permission, an outline permission, and be directly related to reserved matters.

Planning Obligations

As has been indicated above, planning conditions are likely to be negative in character and subject to stiff tests of legitimacy. Planning obligations have been devised in order to allow for a more imaginative approach to development. There are times when a developer wishes to make a contribution over and above that which is strictly necessary e.g. additional infrastructure, the catering for future needs, financial provision by means of a community trust. In these days of financial stringency, LPAs are frequently only too pleased to accept such offers.

The term *planning obligation* has been brought in under the 1991 P&C Act so that it covers not only the s.106 agreements between developers and LPAs, formulated either at the application stage or during an appeal, but also the so called Unilateral Undertakings. These were invented in order to fill the gap caused by the failure to reach an agreement with the LPA. If the matter went to appeal, the developer could make an offer unilaterally over a matter not suited to a condition. If the inspector was minded to allow the appeal, the developer could sign a s.106 planning obligation.

Whatever their origins, s.106 obligations can be entered into by any person with an interest in the land, and it binds their successors in title. The content of such an obligation may include:

a) restricting the development or use of land in a specified fashion;

b) requiring specified operations to be undertaken on, in, under or over the land;

c) requiring the land to be used in a specified way;

d) requiring money to be paid to the LPA on a specified date(s) or periodically.

Such an obligation may itself be unconditional or subject to conditions. Periodic payments may be imposed either indefinitely, or for a given length of time. The obligation takes the form of a deed, which is entered as a local land charge, i.e. recorded in the local land charges registers kept by LPAs (Land Charges Act 1975).

The dangers of s.106 planning obligations are twofold. Firstly, that planning permissions are 'bought' and 'sold': potential developers may be over-eager to develop a site because of its anticipated returns and/or LPAs may be desperate for a means of funding some infrastructure, or other project currently beyond their reach because of financial restrictions. Needless to say there have been a succession of High Court cases which define, at any given time, what is deemed to be fair and reasonable to both parties. What has emerged so far is that: unacceptable planning proposals should not be allowed because of juicy benefits; acceptable proposals should not be turned down because they lack benefits; and any benefits should be fairly and reasonably related to the proposal and constitute a material consideration. Unfortunately the Courts have decided that excess benefits are not unlawful and therefore it has been left to the DoE to issue guidance on what is reasonable (see Circular 1/97).

The second hazard is that widespread use of s.106 planning obligations could endanger the basic principles underlying the development control system. The latter should be a process of regulation: the LPA or Secretary of State adjudicates in public on proposals for development. Planning by agreement is the antithesis of this: it conjures up the image of deals hatched in smoke-filled rooms. To overcome this seedy image, DoE Circular 1/97 counsels that:

> As a minimum, planning obligations and related correspondence should be listed as background papers to the committee report relating to the development proposal concerned ... Authorities would need a very strong case either to exclude the press and public when discussing a

planning obligation or to determine that connected correspondence should be kept from public view. Only in very exceptional cases should LPAs agree to the imposition of a duty of confidentiality in respect of planning obligations.

(para.B.19)

Whilst the occasional use of creative agreements to overcome real planning objections may be no bad thing, the situation has to be watched – literally. Any long term solution would involve facing up to, and dealing with, wider issues. Unfortunately such vision is not 'politically correct'. (see Section VI). Betterment is unfashionable.

DoE Circular 11/95, The Role of Conditions in Planning Permissions
DoE Circular 1/97, Planning Obligations

The Enforcement of Planning Obligations

The LPA may take enforcement action, not only against whoever signed the obligation, but also against whoever owns the site thereafter. If they default on their obligation, then an injunction may be served on them, but they can lodge an appeal in the High Court, and it is not unknown for the latter to take a pragmatic view of the situation e.g. delay making a judgement until the planning application had been determined on appeal.

The LPA has powers to enter the land, undertake the operations and send the bill to the owner, provided they have given them 21 days notice. Anyone obstructing these operations, or worse, is liable to be fined.

Appeals Against s.106 Agreements & Planning Obligations

A planning obligation may not be as 'permanent' as it sometimes appears when one is involved at the planning application stage or at a public inquiry. It can be terminated by agreement between the LPA and the owner, or by means of an appeal. Under the P&C Act 1991, the owner is free to make an application to have it discharged or modified after 5 years. There are now two appeal procedures: one for s.106 agreements signed before 25th October 1991, and another for s.106 obligations entered into after that date.

S.106 Agreements

With regard to the former group, appeals have to be made to the Lands Tribunal under s.84 of the 1925 Law of Property Act. This is restricted to dealing with restrictive covenants rather than positive aspects of obligations: on the other hand what is and what is not 'restrictive' can be a moot point in the eyes of the Courts. Before discharging or modifying the restrictive covenant, the Lands Tribunal must be satisfied that:

a) by reason of changes in the character of the property or the neighbourhood, or other circumstances, the restriction ought to be deemed obsolete; or

b) that the continued existence of the restriction would impede some reasonable use of the land for public or private purposes, or, would, unless modified, so impede the user; or

c) the persons of full age and capacity entitled to the benefit of the restriction have agreed, either expressly or by implication, by acts of omissions, to the restriction being discharged or modified; or

d) that the proposed discharge or modification will not injure the persons entitled to the benefit of a restriction.

With regard to (a) above, the Lands Tribunal must take into account the development plan, and *'any declared or ascertainable pattern for the grant or refusal of planning permission in the relevant areas, as well as the period at which the context in which the restriction was created or imposed and any other material circumstance.'* Thus, the Lands Tribunal is obliged to consider the development plan, and the general planning framework, as well as just scrutinizing the agreement itself.

Planning Obligations

For obligations entered into post October 25th 1991, the procedure is laid down in S.I.1992 No.2832. Given the statutory five year interlude, none of them are eligible for modification or discharge until November 1997 at the earliest. Appeals are lodged with the LPA, using a specially designed form and publicised in much the same fashion as planning applications. The LPA has to make publicly available the relevant part of the s.106 obligation. Butterworth's Planning Law Encyclopaedia wryly observes that this may be a spur to a negotiated settlement in that neither party may wish to attract public attention in the direction of too cosy a s.106 agreement: having had its appetite whetted, the public may ask to see the rest of the document!

The LPA may not determine the application within 21 days of its arrival in order to allow parties a chance to respond. The LPA is required to give a written decision within 8 weeks, or longer by agreement between the parties. There are three possible verdicts: a refusal; to discharge the obligation if it serves no useful purpose; or acceptance of the fact that the purpose would be equally well served if it had effect, subject to modifications set out in the application. The advice on this given in DoE Circular 28/92 is somewhat vague, and is, in any case, non statutory, so in fact the LPA is free to take its own view of what constitutes 'a useful purpose.'

If the applicant does not accept the refusal of the s.106 obligation, then he can appeal to the Secretary of State. This is likely to be a quicker and less expensive procedure than appealing to the Lands Tribunal. As with a planning appeal, it must be within 6 months of the decision. What happens then? Neither the 1991 P&C Act nor the Statutory Instrument actually say.

The reason, apparently, is that the DoE wish the procedure to conform with that for a s.78 appeal, be it by written representations, a hearing or a full inquiry. The Inspectorate expect that planning appeals, and appeals to discharge or modify s.106 obligations on the existing permission, will be heard at the same inquiry. It will be interesting to see whether the approach of the Inspectorate, who are mainly land use professionals, differs from the lawyers presiding over the Lands Tribunal. It would appear that, like the LPA, the Inspectorate are able to take into account non planning factors e.g. social or economic issues when deciding if the s.106 planning obligation still serves a useful purpose.

Any land use planning applications, which involve the discharge or modification of an existing s.106 obligation, will have had to await the witching hour of midnight on 24th October 1996 before they could make an application to the LPA. However planning permission for the new proposal could already have been given by the LPA or on appeal, and this could be helpful in persuading the LPA to agree with the developer over the existing s.106 planning obligation: the LPA might not have the stomach for a fight at a second appeal before the Inspectorate over the s.106. In any case, the latter, nurtured on the presumption in favour of development, incline favourably towards an application where planning permission has already been granted.

It should be noted that Third parties have no legal right to compel any party to a s.106 obligation stick to. Of course they may lobby them, but at least under the post 1991 procedures, they will know that an application has been lodged, and if their lobbying is successful and the application is refused, they may appear at the appeal into the proposed development and have their say over the s.106 on the existing use of the site.

Crown Land

Although the Crown acquired the right to obtain planning permission, prior to disposal, in 1984, it was not until the 1991 P&C Act that it could take advantage of s.106 obligations. In the typically cack-handed way in which the legislation has been framed, s.299 of the 1990 Act, on provisions relating to Crown Land, was amended by inserting a new s.299 A, and where do you find it? In s.12 of the 1991 P&C Act, along with all the other amendments to s.106 1990 TCP Act. Obvious isn't it?

Having found it, what does it say? Basically that the LPA has to enter into the obligation on behalf of the Crown and that there has to be consultation over enforcement action e.g. entering land or serving an injunction.

Appendix X

DEVELOPMENT PLANNING IN THE ENGLISH SHIRES

Once upon a time, in the English shires there were 38 county councils each preparing a structure plan and 294 district councils each preparing a local plan. But that was too straightforward. Following local government reorganisation, there appears to be a bewildering hotchpotch of different arrangements.

As a first step it is helpful to remember that the fact that Barchester City Council has become a unitary authority (UA), does not necessarily mean that it will be preparing a unitary development plan: it may be a UA in all respects except planning because its population is not large enough, for example. Thus, unlike the metropolitan authorities, the vast majority of the new UAs will not produce UDPs.

Basically there are three scenarios:

1.   Where a county has been eradicated, the new UAs, based on the districts will cooperate to produce a structure plan between them, and a local plan each:

4 in Avon, 6 in Berkshire; 2 on North Humberside; 2 on South Humberside; 4 in Cleveland with Darlington.

2.   Where a UA has been extracted from a county which remains in being, albeit diminished in area, the UA works with the county to produce a joint structure plan. Then the UA and each of the districts produce an area wide local plan:

> *Bedfordshire with Luton*
> Buckinghamshire with Milton Keynes
> Cambridgeshire with Peterborough
> Derbyshire with Derby
> Devon with Plymouth and Torbay
> Dorset with Bournemouth & Pool
> East Sussex with a combined Brighton & Hove
> Essex [minus Thurrock] with Southend
> Hampshire with Portsmouth and Southampton
> Kent with a combined Rochester upon Medway, and Gillingham

Lancashire with Blackburn and Blackpool
Leicestershire with Leicester and Rutland
North Yorkshire with a new greater York
Nottinghamshire with Nottingham
Shropshire with the Wrekin
Staffordshire with Stoke on Trent
Wiltshire with Swindon [alias Thamesdown]
The National Park Authorities with their host counties.

3.   There are only five new UAs producing UDPs:
Halton, Warrington, Thurrock, Herefordshire and the Isle of Wight.

Having extracted the UAs, what is left?

4.   There are three rump counties producing their structure plan on their own, and the remaining districts devising their respective local plans:
Cheshire; Durham; and Worcestershire.

5.   Last but not least, there are fourteen counties continuing to produce a structure plan with each district generating its respective local plan:
Cornwall; Cumbria; Gloucestershire; Hertfordshire; Norfolk; Northamptonshire; Northumberland; Oxfordshire; Somerset; Suffolk; Surrey; Warwickshire and West Sussex.

Given the reliance on voluntary cooperation between LPAs with disparate interests, it remains to be seen whether they all live happy ever after. Those in the know have severe reservations.

DoE Circular 4/96: Local Government Change and the Planning System.

Index